Film Alchemy

Film Alchemy

*The Independent Cinema
of Ted V. Mikels*

CHRISTOPHER WAYNE CURRY

Foreword by John W. Curry

McFarland & Company, Inc., Publishers
Jefferson, North Carolina, and London

The present work is a reprint of the illustrated case bound edition of Film Alchemy: The Independent Cinema of Ted V. Mikels, *first published in 2008 by McFarland.*

LIBRARY OF CONGRESS CATALOGUING-IN-PUBLICATION DATA

Curry, Christopher Wayne, 1970–
Film alchemy : the independent cinema of Ted V. Mikels / Christopher Wayne Curry ; foreword by John W. Curry.
p.   cm.
Includes bibliographical references and index.

ISBN 978-0-7864-7507-0
softcover : acid free paper ∞

1. Mikels, Ted V.—Criticism and interpretation.
I. Title.
PN1998.3.M498C87   2013
791.4302'22092—dc22   2007031871

BRITISH LIBRARY CATALOGUING DATA ARE AVAILABLE

© 2008 Christopher Wayne Curry. All rights reserved

No part of this book may be reproduced or transmitted in any form or by any means, electronic or mechanical, including photocopying or recording, or by any information storage and retrieval system, without permission in writing from the publisher.

On the cover: Ted V. Mikels in 2000;
background image © 2013 Shutterstock

Manufactured in the United States of America

*McFarland & Company, Inc., Publishers
Box 611, Jefferson, North Carolina 28640
www.mcfarlandpub.com*

Acknowledgments

(in no particular order)

Rebecca Carlton (Mom), John W. Curry (Dad), Walter O'Reilly, Scott Blacksher, William D. McDonald, Ari Richards, Mark Seiber, Lance Ozanix and Skitzo, Ted Rogers, Ellen Emser, Eric LaRue, Pat Sobolewski, Eric Campos, Alex Zander, Herschell Gordon Lewis, David F. Friedman, Tura Satana, John Waters, Wendy O. Altamura, Bill Rebane, Ray Dennis Steckler, Andrew Sheppard, Eric Powell, Tom Mandrake, Bob McLeod, Kerry Gammill, Geof Isherwood, Norm Breyfogle, Tom Nguyen, Al Rio, Frank Brunner, John Hamilton, Julie Owens, Sarah Stoops, Paul Walters (!), Robby Banes and the crew at The Shed, Bob and Karin Fischer, Terry and Jane Tharp, Serif and Shelly C., Mike Padgett, Jon and Christina, The Doll Squad (Australia), The Astro Zombies (France), Marc Morabito, Pat Leer, Rob Spay, Scott Crawford, Andy Starke at Mondo Macabro, Marie LeClaire at Vintage Movie Classics, Lloyd Kaufman at Troma, Chris Hester at Dark Sky, Creation Books, Jonathan Ross and *The Incredibly Strange Film Show*, and Joe Bob Briggs. Special thanks to Christopher J. Jarmick for permission to use parts of his interviews and articles on Ted V. Mikels that were originally published in *Cult Cuts* magazine in 2002 and *Brutarian* magazine in 2003. Lastly, thanks to the one who listened as I "...ranted to the shadows."

All photos and illustrations are used with the kind permission of Ted V. Mikels. They were culled from the collections of Ted V. Mikels and the author unless otherwise noted.

Table of Contents

Acknowledgments v
Foreword by John W. Curry 1
Preface 5
Introduction. 7

Part One: The Films of Ted V. Mikels 11
   1. *Strike Me Deadly* 11
   2. *Dr. Sex* 16
   3. *One Shocking Moment* 22
   4. *The Black Klansman* 27
   5. *Astro Zombies* 37
   6. *Girl in Gold Boots* 53
   7. *The Corpse Grinders* 61
   8. *Blood Orgy of the She Devils* 72
   9. *The Doll Squad* 80
 10. *Alex Joseph and His Wives* 90
 11. *10 Violent Women* 97
 12. *War Cat* 107
 13. *Mission: Killfast* 114

Part Two: The Videos of Ted V. Mikels 125
    Introduction 125
 14. *Dimension in Fear* 126
 15. *Female Slave's Revenge* 131
 16. *The Corpse Grinders 2* 134
 17. *Mark of the Astro Zombies* 139

18. *The Cauldron: Baptism of Blood* 150
19. *Heart of a Boy* 158

Part Three: Cinematic Timeline, Homage, Memorabilia 163

20. A Comprehensive Ted V. Mikels Cinematic Timeline 163
21. Homage: Reverence and Respect for Mikels 176
22. Collect 'Em All! An Overview of the Memorabilia. 179

Part Four: The Interview 185

Closing. 205
Bibliography 207
Index 209

Foreword

by John W. Curry

Date: June 2000. I was on summer vacation from my job as a high school social sciences teacher. Most previous summers were spent pursuing the near never-ending graduate and post-graduate credits and degrees required perennially in this field; but not this year, not this time. It had been fifteen years since I'd last flown to Las Vegas. Peering from my window seat into the night, the city looked like a sprawling amusement park at Christmastime. This, I knew, was going to be better than Christmas.

Author Christopher W. Curry and I had just recently completed the book *A Taste of Blood: The Films of Herschell Gordon Lewis*. It was Christopher who had put me in touch with the extraordinary independent filmmaker Ted V. Mikels. Within the hour I was to meet with, and begin a near-two-week, twelve-to-fifteen-hour-a-day regimen with, the maverick showman. The film: *The Corpse Grinders 2*.

Christopher had briefed me in some detail as to what I might expect upon meeting Ted. "He's totally down to earth. He's kind, a true gentleman who will make you feel completely at ease and at home. The man just loves to make movies," Christopher insisted. Often such sterling praises say more about the speaker than those who are spoken about.

I was nervous yet incredibly excited at the prospect of meeting the writer, director, and producer of scores of films released over the past forty years. Ted had made films that I had grown to love: *Astro Zombies, The Black Klansman, The Doll Squad*, and, of course, *The Corpse Grinders*. Still, I was very nervous. No one is ever so truly kind and genuine as described by friends, is he?

In the airport baggage claim area I had barely begun the search for my luggage when I turned to see the distinguished, ponytailed, athletic, barrel-chested gentlemen with a far-reaching handlebar mustache. With this mustache came an equally wide and striking smile. "Hello, John Curry! John Curry!" My name was bellowed from that smiling face. Large hands reached to shake mine and to kindly clasp my upper arm. So began my experience with Ted V. Mikels.

It was approaching midnight when Ted cleared an area for my bags in the back of his unpretentious but fully functional station wagon. I think it was a GM product (some sort of an Oldsmobuick). Driving through Las Vegas to his townhouse, we talked about Christopher, Herschell and, of

Director Ted V. Mikels in 2000.

course, some of what I knew about his (Ted's) films. The moviemaker, too, seemed genuinely interested in me, my family, my life.

My host eventually insisted that I be his guest overnight and that I could relocate later should I wish. I accepted the offer, and what followed was an evening of movie talk and discussion of the countless furnishings, props, and movie memorabilia previously housed in the Castle. The Castle that the cult horror king once shared with eight young and beautiful women. From floor to ceiling and wall to wall were shields of armor, as well as life-sized figures clad in armor from head to toe. Movie posters, stills, lobby cards and the like documented this man's life's work.

The next morning we began around ten. Since (I was to learn) we would work until ten and sometimes midnight, this start time was to become the custom. Some days were spent in the TVM Studios building or repairing props (the corpse grinding machine needed grinding "teeth" replaced daily), working in costuming, reviewing previously shot film (dailies) and then editing. Others took us on location to the UNLV campus, and to the magnificent home and planetarium of former Nevada Lt. Governor Lonnie Hammargren. We also scouted a local cemetery, as well as a desert area several miles west of Las Vegas where we shot in sweltering temperatures in excess of 105 degrees. It was hot, really hot.

Ted is the master at procurement of props, locations, actors, and crew members. Time and time again, with incredible patience, Ted brought together everything necessary for a full day's magic making (everything needed that could be gathered with little or no funding, that is). Most days ended with several hours spent determining how and from where tomorrow's necessities would come. Making celluloid magic with virtually no money and an unlimited imagination had become the norm for Ted V. Mikels. He had done this for half a century.

I learned quickly that Ted drew from his volunteer cast and crew the very effort and dedication that many producers and directors couldn't possibly procure, regardless of the monies involved. Ted Mikels' enthusiasm for filmmaking is so contagious that those who share his love of movies give of themselves freely and openly. The demands of long hours and many tedious tasks are no match for the desire to perform up to Ted's visions. With few exceptions (those with large numbers of speaking lines to learn daily), most everyone on the set was expected to pitch in—man the boom, secure this or that light fixture, refill the smoke machine, assist in carpentry, assist in prop production, sit in on editing sessions, and so on. Did any of us get everything right every time? Of course not, but what was consistent at all points was Ted's incredible patience and deep appreciation for every individual who worked on his productions.

I learned of this firsthand one afternoon

Ted V. Mikels (left) in 2002 with the late John W. Curry, a graduate of Western Kentucky University, who coauthored (with his son Christopher Wayne Curry) *A Taste of Blood: The Films of Herchell Gordon Lewis*, and who appeared in Mikels' *The Corpse Grinders 2*.

when I had been asked to take some candid stills between shots. While filming a difficult scene in the Lt. Governor's planetarium (which doubled for the interior of a spacecraft), I inadvertently snapped off a picture. Of course, the camera's click and flash startled the cast, crew and the director. "Cut," Mikels said, then simply smiled at me and added, "Not till we're finished up, John."

Much to my relief, the response of all those on the set reflected the attitude of the master. Work resumed and nothing more was ever said of the incident. Over the next few days I compiled a number of memorable shots. Perhaps of even greater importance were the lessons in patience, humanity and humility—lessons that I would take with me always.

"Ted V. Mikels puts the 'exploit' in exploitation. He's pretty amazing."
—director John Waters (*Pink Flamingos* and *Cecil B. Demented*)

Preface

In the world of low-budget exploitation cinema a few names stand out and above the rest: Ed Wood, Jr., Herschell Gordon Lewis, Al Adamson, Ray Dennis Steckler and Andy Milligan. But that list of names, and a list even longer, could not, and would not, be complete without including the most interesting one of them all—Ted V. Mikels.

It is true that Mikels' actual life is sometimes far more interesting than the quirky tales that he manages to spin into movies. And, in part, it was Mikels' home life that attracted me to the oddball filmmaker. He lived in a castle with secret passageways, was a harem keeper, a fire-eater, a ventriloquist, a body builder, an acrobat and even a master at archery and fencing.

In the mid–80s the British television series *The Incredibly Strange Film Show* introduced a whole new generation of fans, and would-be fans, to Ted V. Mikels, as well as Herschell Gordon Lewis, Ed Wood, Russ Meyer, Doris Wishman and their ilk. This show is also where the world (including myself) learned of Ted V. Mikels' eccentric home life.

Nineteen eighty-six saw RE/Search Publications release a book with a similar theme and title, *Incredibly Strange Films*. This collection of interviews, articles and essays was, for years, the definitive written document on exploitation cinema. Furthermore, within the pages of this amazing compilation of largely unnoticed films and forgotten filmmakers was a 16-page, all-telling interview with director Ted V. Mikels. Even more insight into the man, his life and his cinema was disclosed within this conversation between Mikels and interviewer Boyd Rice.

Over the years a fascination for Mikels, and his patent brand of cinema, began to get the better of me. Owning a copy of *Astro Zombies*, *The Corpse Grinders* and *Blood Orgy of the She Devils* became almost a necessity, almost an obsession. Owning an all-inclusive document of Mikels and his film career also became important, but there was none to be found, and *this* became the catalyst for *Film Alchemy*.

It was the director's eccentric life that first drew in this fan, and the lurid ad campaigns and posters that promoted the films spurred this seeker of cinematic oddities onward. And, quite frankly, Mikels' promotional materials and ads simply cannot be beaten in the realm of exploitation cinema, or any cinema for that matter. Mikels was a good student of P.T. Barnum and his most quotable quote: "There's a sucker born every minute."

However, exploitation films themselves seldom, if ever, lived up to the hype, but

Millennium Ted with his trusty Mitchell camera (2000).

that's part of the fun. The huckstering, the humbuggery and the gimmicks were all part of seeing these types of motion pictures, and Ted V. Mikels' motion pictures in particular. Nurses on duty to administer blood pressure checks, and ambulances at the ready to take scared-nearly-to-death theatergoers to the emergency room, were all part of the experience—the Ted V. Mikels experience. Only the master showman himself, William Castle, could rival Mikels in the ballyhoo department.

Film Alchemy: The Independent Cinema of Ted V. Mikels covers each and every film or video production created by one of the masters of low-budget moviemaking. Mikels' first feature film, *Strike Me Deadly* (1959), is discussed, along with his 18 other movies that followed. *Film Alchemy* even includes a sneak peek at Mikels' latest project, *Demon Bloodlust* (working title; 2007), which, as of this writing, has not yet been completed.

Promotional gimmicks are discussed, where applicable, and behind-the-scenes anecdotes are revealed—some amusing, some shocking and some sad. *Film Alchemy* also includes a full list of cast and crew credits for Ted Mikels' 19 movies, as well as a plot synopsis for each. These plot summaries have been culled directly from the pressbooks or press materials in the interest of appeasing Ted V. Mikels purists who would rather read *his* version of his plotlines than mine. Ultimately, *Film Alchemy* is a direct result of 60-plus hours of telephone interviews with the director himself, 12 months of research, and (perhaps most importantly) the author's love, respect and adoration for Ted V. Mikels—the man and his cinema.

Introduction

Theodore Vincent Mikacevich (pronounced Mee-KAS-se-vitch) is his name. A mouthful of a name for sure, but there is a lot more to this Mikacevich fellow than just an odd moniker. While it was unintentional on the parents' part, abbreviating their family cognomen to Mikels can be seen as a minor asset to young Ted's future career. As time would tell, Ted would eventually want to break into show business, and he didn't need to spend valuable time coaching people on the proper pronunciation of his Croatian handle. Theodore's mother once said that he was born in a hurry and has been in a hurry ever since. So "Ted V. Mikels" it was to forever be.

Ted raced out of the gates at an early age to become an award-winning body builder, a ventriloquist, a musician and a fire-eater. He also came to be an accomplished magician, an acrobat and a Hollywood stunt man. Once upon a time Ted was even a harem keeper, with no fewer than eight women living with him at any given moment. A fascinating man is this Mikels.

Whether through ambition or simply ants in his pants, Ted had to try his hand at filmmaking. Of course, one cannot keep a good Croatian down, and in short order Ted was succeeding in the motion picture business. Couple all of the aforementioned trades and pastimes with a newfound love for the movies, and what kind of man does one get?—quite possibly the most eccentric filmmaker to ever smear his name across a 40-foot silver screen.

Some critics have viewed a few of Ted's endeavors as little more than weekend projects with friends—an observation that couldn't be farther from the truth, as his least problematic efforts took anywhere from five to six months to complete. No shortcuts for this renegade moviemaker. Pre-production, post-production, sound, special effects and scoring are all taken quite seriously, and great consideration, from every conceivable angle, is given to them at every stage.

Still, even if those critics' opinion were true, how many weekend get-togethers have resulted in a marketable 35mm film, let alone a film that plays theaters around the world? Ted and his friends manage to commiserate and party and generally enjoy life through the making of these projects. What's more: the French love Ted's films, and they certainly know a thing or two about culture and style, what with hors d'oeuvres, Godard, Monet and Cocteau. We Westerners could probably stand to listen to our European counterparts at least once in a while.

No, Ted isn't a self-proclaimed cross-dresser like Ed Wood. Ted isn't the creator

A very suave Mikels with his ever-present boar's tusk necklace (1978).

of the gore film. Ted isn't even the man who invented the nudie-cutie. However, Ted V. Mikels is a man who has managed to produce a plethora of ultra-low-budget opuses that have maintained their place (and have been unfairly criticized) alongside big fat bloated Hollywood epics like *Tora! Tora! Tora!*, *Casablanca* and *The Wizard of Oz*. And Mikels' films repeatedly outperformed, in terms of box office, these re-release favorites, at least in the L.A. area.

Is it any wonder that Ted V. Mikels is a legend? Is there any doubt that Ted V. Mikels is an American icon? Well, Ted V. Mikels is presently neither. Mainstream Hollywood and mainstream Hollywood moviegoers seem content to let Ted remain in the "where were they ever?" file. Really, it's at least worthy of debate. He quite possibly deserves a place next to cult icons like Russ Meyer and Ed Wood; and maybe, *just* *maybe*, due to *his* monetary and time constraints (constraints that simply boggle the mind), Ted V. Mikels deserves a place above them both.

Oh, it's not that Ted is completely ignored in the world of filmdom. Ted makes his rounds to the movie conventions and the fright festivals and whatnot. He has spent day after day penning his signature on one-sheets, pressbooks and various ephemera. He is featured in countless magazines and websites. But where's the movie about Ted? At the very least, where's the *E! True Hollywood Story*, and, for that matter, where are the other books?

Tim Burton made a movie about Ed Wood because Wood was an eager (albeit incompetent) filmmaker who loved to wear women's clothing. Someone *will* make a film about Russ Meyer and his obsession with gargantuan female breasts, and rightfully so. But the proof is in this book—Ted V. Mikels' story is the kind of stuff that movies are made of.

Over the years Ted has become a celluloid humanitarian of sorts. He will take under his wing anyone and everyone with a yearning to learn and appreciate the art and craft of making movies. He assesses people's strengths and weaknesses, then places them accordingly within his production. He proceeds to teach while he creates, and, when all is said and done, all involved can lay claim to the completed product.

Furthermore, the long list of credits in Ted's films (especially his later ones) is a consequence of his cohorts' donations of time and effort for even the smallest amount of screen time. This necessary "evil" inevitably creates inconsequential characters, and scenes that on occasion do more to hinder the story than help it. Thus, the plot thickens—and becomes increasingly more and more difficult to follow.

All the more, there is an honesty and a sincerity in a Ted V. Mikels film that helps the production transcend its low-rent trap-

Mikels in his editing bay during the production of *Corpse Grinders II*.

pings to become something wholly unique and almost always entertaining. His stuff isn't formulaic in any sense of the term. It's wildly unpredictable, and one can never know what is about to happen next, if indeed *anything* is going to happen next.

This erratic, and oftentimes confusing, approach to filmmaking is as much a result of small-time funding as it is a reflection of the (in)experience and talent of his cast and crew. The more time Ted spends showing his participants the rudiments of moviemaking, the less time he has to devote to the creative aspects of his productions.

As writer, producer, director, editor, sometimes sound man and lighting coordinator, Ted can be a one-man moviemaking machine. To say that Ted is talented is a gross understatement. The man has written dialogue for screen legends Wendell Corey and John Carradine. Never mind the fact that both stars were in their waning years; they delivered for Ted with all the charm and verve that they ever could or would for Hollywood. When it comes right down to it, Ted V. Mikels is so impassioned and driven by the need to flex his moviemaking muscles, he has become virtually unstoppable.

The main goal of this book, in addition to entertaining and informing, is to encourage movie fans to view Ted's work in a different light. It should come as no surprise to anyone that these films were made very inexpensively. Inexpensively, that is, when it comes to the monies involved.

What is seldom taken into consideration is the blood, sweat, tears, love, hard work and devotion that such a low-budget production entails. Remarkably, Ted has remained independent from the Hollywood machine for nearly 50 years. He's done the things that he's wanted to do, and he's done them *his* way, with only a lack of funds to slow him up.

Are Ted's productions perfect? The celluloid craftsman himself answered this tough question quite amicably for writer Colin Hanson during an interview for *Lighthouse* (no. 2, December 2003):

> I don't feel any of my films are perfect, in fact far from it. I have always said to others that I teach, that making movies consists of

how many compromises you are willing to make. I have had to compromise *severely* on every movie I have ever made. I make the very best movie I can with what I am working with and hope and pray the world audience likes it.

So, with this in mind, please know and understand that the praises, and criticisms, of Ted's films take all of this well into account. Many of Ted's movies boast fantastic performances by the actors and actresses. However, it would hardly be fair to pit Warren Ball's performance of Caleb in *The Corpse Grinders* against Robert De Niro's turn as Travis Bickle in *Taxi Driver*. De Niro was allotted as many takes as he needed to nail a scene; meanwhile, Warren Ball got two, maybe three tries to get it right, and then it was time to move on.

Furthermore, it would be futile to seriously compare the extravagant dolly shots of Dario Argento's *Suspiria* to those in Ted's *Strike Me Deadly*, where a Volkswagen van stood in for an incredibly expensive piece of moviemaking equipment. Time and money are of the essence, and some things just have to be left well enough alone in order to continue the production and bring it in at, or under, budget.

Still, even if the warm and reverent passages contained in this book fail to sway opinions, then perhaps another angle will do the trick. Director Frank Henenlotter (*Basket Case* and *Brain Damage*), longtime Ted V. Mikels fan, tells Andrea Juno in *Incredibly Strange Films*:

Often through bad direction, misdirection, inept direction, a film starts assuming surrealistic overtones, taking a dreadfully clichéd story into new frontiers—you're sitting there shaking your head, totally excited, totally unable to guess where this is going to head next, or what the next loony line out of someone's mouth is going to be. Just as long as it isn't stuff you regularly see. I'll never be satisfied until I see every sleazy film ever made—as long as it's different, as long as it's breaking a taboo, whether deliberately, or by misdirection. There's a thousand reasons to like these films.

In regard to Ted's work, this is not necessarily my opinion. But if this approach, or filmic phenomenon known as "paracinema," allows for a proper reevaluation of Ted's vast filmography, then so be it. Nevertheless, it can hardly be argued that his features aren't at the very least odd and or original.

French exploitation moviemaker Michel Lemoine has his own take on independent cinema. He stated during an interview on the Mondo Macabro DVD release of his 1974 film *Seven Women for Satan*:

> So what if they're just B-films? These guys, with their shoestring budgets, have created incredible films just because they loved cinema. They were mad for it. They didn't care about being rich. They just loved what they did.

No matter how one looks at it, the body of work examined within these pages is entertaining and enjoyable on a multitude of levels, and no perspective should be overlooked. This is Ted V. Mikels' world, and I am thrilled to be a part of it.

PART ONE

The Films of Ted V. Mikels

"Ted V. Mikels loves making movies! It's what he does."—director Ray Dennis Steckler (*The Incredibly Strange Creatures Who Stopped Living and Became Mixed-Up Zombies* and *Rat Pfink a BooBoo*)

1. *Strike Me Deadly*

Synopsis from Pressbook

Jim Grant (Gary Clarke) brings his bride, Lori (Jeannine Riley), to a National Forest Service Station, combining their glorious honeymoon in the wilderness with his summer job as a ranger.

Their bliss is terrifyingly interrupted when Jim witnesses the cold-blooded murder of one hunter by another. The killer spots Jim and begins stalking him through the forest, flinging shot after shot at the desperately running figure. Jim races through the most rugged terrain in a frantic effort to elude the searching eyes of the telescopic lens on the killer's rifle. He narrowly escapes, and, thinking he has outwitted the killer, Jim makes his way back to the Forest Service cabin.

Frantically, Jim tries to explain to Lori what has happened, as he places a call for help. But before the phone call is completed, the killer appears in the doorway, rifle in hand, trapping the young lovers.

Meanwhile, a forest fire has raged to gigantic proportions, heading toward the cabin. The killer forces Jim to answer a phone call from the fire fighters, and to confirm that everything is all right at the cabin. The killer softens slightly at the thought of killing Lori, so young, so pretty and alive. As he ponders, Jim looks at his terrified bride, remembering how happy and carefree she was a few hours ago.

In a flashback we see Lori's sweetness and understanding of Jim's younger brother, Bobby, as the boy leaves the cabin for a hunting trip. Jim then recalls a night he and Lori were in town, dancing and joking with the tenderness of all lovers. The flashback shows a half-forgotten scene from the nightclub in which a crazed man accused another man of stealing his wife. In a fight, the accuser is revealed as the killer.

At the cabin, Jim and Lori are forced around the fire toward the lake, where the killer plans to murder them. Crossing a deep creek, Jim throws him off balance and the couple desperately attempt to escape. The killer overtakes them, trapped on a high cliff with a waterfall below. Lori becomes hysterical, the killer levels his rifle and Jim jumps him in one final effort to save Lori.

A rifle blast and the shock in Jim's eyes give the impression he has been hit, until Bobby is seen across the creek, lowering his hunting rifle. The shaken boy is comforted by Jim and Lori as they leave the scene of their nightmare.

Promotion
(taken from pressbook)

Arrange with your local radio disk jockey to stage a contest among his teenage audience. Let the kids have their own "Oscar" awards, wherein they write their choice for top teenage actor and actress of the year, and why they like their favorites.

The result will be actor and actress named Teen Choice of the Year. Prizes can be given each entry which named the overall winners. The prizes, of course, will be passes to *Strike Me Deadly*, starring popular Gary Clarke and Jeannine Riley. As a fringe benefit of this type contest, the dee-jay will have positive write-in proof of his rating, and the exhibitor will possess an accurate up-to-date poll of the box-office appeal of stars in this age group.

Credits

Cast: Gary Clarke (Jim Grant); Jeannine Riley (Lori Grant); Steve Quinn/Steve Ihnat (the Killer); Michael Johnson (Biff); Brian Clark (Bobby); Gordon Mauser (Chuck); John Hopkins (Dietrick); with H. B. Barnum, Dennis Walton, Phylliss Maitland, Carvel Kirsch, Elaine Glass

Production: *film editor*: Brad C. Berry. *script supervisor*: Elaine G. Lee. *sound*: Frank Smith and G. S. Mouser. *set decorator*: Richard Hollandsworth. *make up*: Ted Mikacevich. *wardrobe*: Judy Rose. *hairstyling*: Gen Mikels. *special effects*: Ray Mercer and Company. *director of photography*: Basil C. Bradbury. *screenplay*: Steve Ihnat/Steve Quinn and Ted V. Mikels. *music*: Nicholas Carras. *associate producer*: Basil C. Bradbury. *written, produced, directed*: Ted Mikels. A Ted V. Mikels Film Production, Inc. *Running Time*: 81 minutes. Black and White. *aspect ratio*: shot at full frame and projected at 1.85:1. *completed*: 1959. *released*: 1963.

The Film

I feel sorry for you. You ugly, ugly sick man.
—Lori from *Strike Me Deadly*

In the beginning, director Ted V. Mikels made every kind of movie that there was to make: documentaries, teaching films, promos and commercials. But once he wrapped his head around the notion of full-length feature films, he, for the most part, has never looked back. Making features became one of Ted's greatest obsessions, and *Strike Me Deadly* was the film that popped his cinematic cherry. After 10 years and a string of independent shorts, Ted struck out with one of his finest films ever, but it came with a price:

> I sold everything I had in order to help finance *Strike Me Deadly*. My bongos, my saxophone and my drums were the first to go. Eventually I even sold my nightclub, the Glenvista. Incidentally, the nightclub used in the film during the fist-fight sequence belonged to my brother-in-law, Carvel Kirsch, and that's him that Steve Ihnat punches out. His club was called Rancho.

Ted has said before that the film's heavy-handed depiction of anger and violence was partially a reaction to his awareness of the disorder around him. People could be violent and impulsive, and *Strike Me Deadly* shows just that. It wasn't all *Father Knows Best* or *Leave It to Beaver*, but quite the opposite; and the film's 20-second promotional radio spot is evidence that the film was marketed towards an audience who were more socially aware and living in the "now":

> If you dig love, don't miss *Strike Me Deadly*. And, man, if you think mystery is the most, you'll flip for *Strike Me Deadly*! A thriller from start to finish ... starring Gary Clarke, *Strike Me Deadly* ... Now at _____ Theater.

Additionally, Hollywood movies and prime-time television have forever been painfully slow at illustrating everyday life in a believable fashion, and 1959 was no different than now. However, Ted worked outside of the Hollywood system and was able to interject truisms that were telling and relevant for the times. The film's believability is also spurred on by Ted's use of real locations rather than something manufactured on a sound stage, and complementing this are three very strong performances by the leads.

The film was lensed in 1959 in and around the lush and lavish mountains of Bend, Oregon, making for some incredibly scenic and photogenic locations. Mikels' black and white photography (a monetary decision) is as remarkable as any for the time, and his direction and pacing leaves little to be desired. In an unfortunate twist, Samuel Z. Arkoff and James Nicholson loved the picture and wanted to buy it for A.I.P., but the board was hesitant to pick up the movie due to it being black and white—the very aspect that lends the film its arresting, tactile quality of light and shade, and, ultimately, good versus evil. Sadly, the film was to live and die by its own look and feel. Still, Ted had done his homework, and *Strike Me Deadly* is a testament to the fledgling filmmaker's capabilities.

Take the chase-across-the-trellis sequence, for instance. Ted handled his 35mm

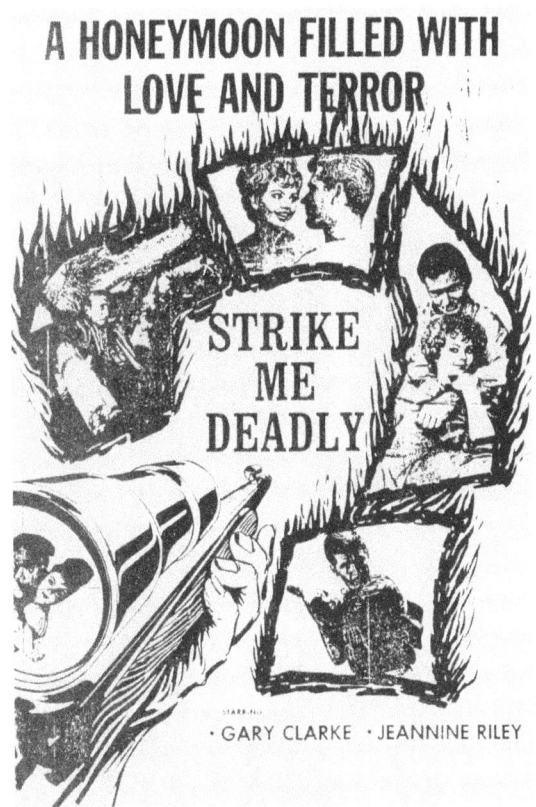

One-sheet for *Strike Me Deadly* (1963).

Mitchell camera with iron-clad authority, resulting in a juxtaposition of visual values that almost gives the picture a film noir look. The director, however, admits that any such approach was an afterthought:

> I knew the shots were going to look good. I had been living in the area, and I'd scouted these locations for some time. I knew exactly what I wanted to shoot and exactly how I wanted it to look. Incidentally, that trellis completely collapsed only two weeks after we were finished shooting there. It's amazing that it didn't collapse while we were there.

Interestingly enough, this backdrop offers an intriguing thematic undercurrent. As Steve Quinn's character maniacally (but no less methodically) stalks his prey (Gary Clarke), the predator runs along the trellis, which hovers above an enormous ravine. His quarry frantically tears through the ribbed

Promotional lobby card depicting the killer (Steve Quinn/Steve Ihnat) squaring off with his timid quarry, Jim and Lori Grant (Gary Clarke and Jeanine Riley), in *Strike Me Deadly*.

structure (almost like a rib cage), fighting for his life as though he were Jonah in the belly of the whale. It's an affecting concept that is again dismissed by the director as happenstance. Nonetheless, it makes for some of the most intriguing visuals in Ted's film career, visuals that are nearly hallucinatory in nature.

In addition to the wonderful images, Ted wrote a believable script that his cast could really sink their teeth into. The newlyweds are convincing and quite likeable, but the real powerhouse of this picture is Steve Quinn (a.k.a. Steve Ihnat). As the killer, Quinn murders another man out of jealousy over his wife. For him things would have ended there, but Gary Clarke's character, Jim Grant, witnesses the slaying, and the murderer now has to eradicate Jim before he can notify the police. The killer sincerely does not want to shoot Jim, nor his wife Lori, but he sees it as his only alternative.

In the final reel of the film, with his rifle leveled at the two, Quinn displays great remorse and confusion. This madman has become a sympathetic character. He's like a frightened animal that is only trying to protect its life. It's in this scene that he says, "A man's gotta do what a man's gotta do ... right?" He really isn't sure any more of what he is doing, or even why. As an animal in the woods would do, he's acting, or rather reacting, on instinct. This sequence ties together with the shots of animals interspersed throughout the film. Some of the creatures are cute and cuddly (like the newlyweds), while others are hissing and baring their fangs (as the aggressive yet nervous killer does). It's a shame such potent symbolism has been written off as mere filler by some critics.

Ted only brought 3 people with him to the *Strike Me Deadly* shoot, with the balance of the cast and crew made up of natives from the surrounding areas. Setting a path from which he would never deviate, Ted went about the task of teaching his crew the rudiments of filmmaking. Such teachings included the workings of the Nagra film sound recorder, proper miking, the stringing of cables, and the creation of small but necessary special effects (like fires and bullet holes).

Initially, the film was called *Cross-hairs*, a more fitting title that ultimately befuddled Hollywood execs, resulting in a moniker change. Another alteration involved the film's flashback sequence. Originally, there was no such bit. Ted wanted to tell a linear story, and so placed the chase scene towards the end; but again someone stepped in and suggested a revision. This time the change came in the form of re-editing the picture to situate a large portion of the action at the beginning of the film (as opposed to Ted's original intent). Whether this actually helped the picture's marketability is unknown; but had it not happened this way the flashback wouldn't have been book-ended by those groovy, swirling, psychedelic pinwheels.

With *Strike Me Deadly* Ted utilized many of his talents as a film creator, most notably his ability to overcome obstacles that would grind many productions to a screeching halt. For instance, the brilliantly executed tracking shots of the protagonist pursued by the antagonist were not realized by using miles of expensive tracks and dollies, but rather a Volkswagen with deflated tires. When Ted wants a particular shot, he gets it by any means necessary! Ted merely let the air out of his tires, flung the side door of his van open, mounted his camera, called "action" and was driven alongside his actors as he filmed the sequences (which look just as impressive as any of their type). No pompous Hollywood production could have, or would have, pulled this off with the same finesse or penny-pinching talents as did Ted Mikels.

At one point it was suggested that Ted use stock footage for the forest fires. Nothing doing. The stock footage in question was in color, so the only thing to do was set the forest ablaze—and that's just what happened. With the aid of forest rangers and the local fire department (all for the nominal fee of zilch), Ted torched a portion of the wooded area and captured the footage that he needed to continue his little independent mini-epic action-thriller. Stock scenes of paratroopers wouldn't suffice, either. Forever the trooper himself, Ted hauled his 16mm Bolex into the sky and shot the footage his own darn self.

Strike Me Deadly marks several firsts for Ted, not the least of which was his ballyhoo approach to promotion. Whether aware of it or not, Ted was most surely influenced by the shenanigans of gimmick kingpin William Castle. Castle had treated his audiences to electric buzzers under the seats, floating skeletons overhead, "death by fright" insurance policies and even a special viewer that revealed or concealed the ghosts on screen (your choice). Of course, Ted was new at this, and his first go-round was quite tame in comparison to his later stunts. For his first picture he encouraged theater owners to hold "Oscar"-type contests for their teenage clientele, with the winners given free tickets to the movie. Such a simple ploy was not nearly as bombastic nor bizarre as his promotional devices would later become, but Ted was on the right track.

Another point worthy of mention is the fact that *Strike Me Deadly* marked the beginning of Ted's love affair with the powerful and dominant female. Jeannine Riley's character, Lori, doesn't just sit idly by, whimpering and begging her husband for help while their captor holds them hostage. On the contrary, she takes matters into her own hands and attempts an attack on the murderer that is only cut short by her concerned husband. It's a small scene, but it packs a wallop. Of course, Ted would go on to exploit this type of characterization to greater effect in the likes of *Blood Orgy of the She Devils* and *10 Violent Women*, but an important seed was planted here. It was a seed that Ted would nurture for some years to come, and his women-in-charge concept would eventually see itself in full bloom in the hugely popular *The Doll Squad*.

Strike Me Deadly took nearly fifteen thousand dollars and 4 years to complete, finally making its theatrical debut in 1963. Unfortunately, it didn't exactly rip the box office asunder. It did, however, prove conclusively that when given the time and resources to make a film, Ted could deliver. *Strike Me Deadly* was a good start, a really good start, and it's no small wonder that his children still feel it is his best ever. But what of his parents?

Ted recalled to interviewer Christopher J. Jarmick of *Cultcuts* magazine in 2002:

> It's sad. They were excited about *Strike Me Deadly* and what I was doing. They had helped me a great deal in getting money together to finish the picture, and even bought a second mortgage I had taken out to help me. It was something like $5,000, which was a lot of money for them, and a lot of money back then. They never saw the finished movie. They also didn't see my brother graduate from the military academy with high honors. I was in the middle of working on the movie and I buried myself in the work. Both my parents lost their lives in a head-on crash with a logging truck, while heading back to Oregon from a visit with myself and family in North Hollywood. I received the news in Hollywood while I was in the process of the master-mix of all audio tracks on *Strike Me Deadly*.

On a brighter note, sometime in 1975 MGM Studios were playing host to around 1,700 Boy Scouts and Eagle Scouts. From all the films they had to choose from, the studio chose *Strike Me Deadly* to entertain the boys on a Saturday evening. Ted was taken aback by their decision to screen his little independent feature, but was no less excited and proud.

To assess Ted's work properly one must view *Strike Me Deadly* with the idea that *this* is the type of picture that Ted V. Mikels most enjoys making. He means this as no disrespect to fans of his horror films, but Ted is an action/adventure kind of guy, with a love for women and campiness. All of these ingredients collided quite nicely in *The Doll Squad*, but we're still 10 or more years from that. The fact of the matter is this: Ted made *Strike Me Deadly* because he wanted to. He had complete and total control over the production, as he was the writer, producer, director, editor and so on. It is a film that comes straight from the heart and soul of a man who adores making movies, possibly more than anyone else ever could.

2. Dr. Sex

Synopsis from Pressbook

Dr. Sex is the story of a mad, marvelous psychiatrist and his wild and extravagant world of beautiful and exotic girls. As he explains to us, he was once a prominent analyst who for reasons beyond his control lost his license to practice. In a meeting between him and his associates, Dr. Diaphanous Lovejoy, a dynamically built beauty, and Dr. Emil Schmutz, an incurable "square," we find that Dr. Sex is writing a book concerning his new experiments in the field of sexology.

The first "chapter" of his book, he explains, will consist of the case of an associate whose erotic impulses are so overwhelming as to make him afraid that he will do something irresponsible. In a flashback sequence we see the "patient" in the apartment of an outrageously beautiful girl. This young lovely disrobes, takes a seductive bath, revels in an erotic telephone conversation on a blood-red bedspread, finally dresses and departs. We discover that the "patient" is a poodle-dog and that the associate has, in turn, developed a problem: he wants to become a dog so that he too can indulge in spectacular delights.

The second chapter is suggested by Dr. Lovejoy. She explains that she was treating a window dresser who suffered from hallucinations, in that he thought the mannequins he dressed, in fact, were living "dolls." She takes us back in time to a sequence where the window dresser explains his "problem," and we see what he sees: a magnificent creature with a terrific body who turns from a mannequin into a girl as he undresses her, has a scene with her, and re-dresses her in a filmy negligee. Dr. Lovejoy then explains that in order to cure him she tried a wild experiment. She has a dress mannequin in her office when the window dresser arrives for a session. She asks him to undress the mannequin and then to undress her, which he does. She points out that the mannequin cannot move around like she can as she walks about in a number of erotic poses while clad in scanty panties and bra. She reveals, however, that the experiment was a failure because, as we see through the eyes of the window dresser, he sees her, Dr. Lovejoy, as a mannequin as well.

Dr. Sex is ecstatic over the bizarre nature of Dr. Lovejoy's case. He says that it will be perfect for inclusion in the book. She then excuses herself to make coffee for all of them while Dr. Schmutz tells of his latest case. It involved a girl who was an exhibitionist. She had the problem of always wanting to expose herself, which she did at the slightest provocation. We see her in a comic sequence with a painter where she is revealed in all her natural beauty, which is more than ample. In fact, the development on this girl is in excess of forty inches. Next we find that she has adapted herself to the rigors of modern society by finding work as a strip-tease artist. This turns out to be one of the sensations of modern burlesque, as we see her in a fantastic display of erotic revelations and contortions. Then we cut back to the office meeting at the home of Dr. Sex, where he says to Dr. Schmutz that the case is worthy of consideration. Sex then tells Schmutz of the case that represents the final chapter in the book: that of the house haunted by nudes. It seems he had a patient who saw and heard strange things in his house, which he later discovered to be nude girls. These beautiful girls were friendly enough but prevented him from having normal relations with people outside the confines of his house. Dr. Sex says that he tried to cure him but failed, and finally advised him to sell the house. Then he, Dr. Sex, bought the house. Suddenly Dr. Sex's true nature is revealed. We find that he too sees these girls, and that Dr. Lovejoy is one of them — and appears resplendently nude to prove it. Schmutz is appalled by what he sees to be a "nut" and leaves to report Dr. Sex to the proper authorities. In the meantime, Dr. Lovejoy and all the girls involve Dr. Sex in a Bacchanalian party. Then as Dr. Schmutz returns to keep an eye on Dr. Sex, he undergoes a strange metamorphosis, turning into a poodle-dog. He then joins the party as the poodle, and we end in a wild triumph of music, drinks and girls, with Dr. Sex jubilantly proclaiming success.

Credits

Cast: Victor Sandor/Victor Izay (Dr. Sex); Julia Calda (Dr. Lovejoy); Max Joseph (Dr. Schmutz); with Ave Lezli, Guido Lavotelli, Mario Barco, Bibo Tao, Marcia Jor-

danus, Lolita Angeles, Giovanni Duvalier, Palva Itano, Nina Lucia, Chan Wingo
Production: *cinematografia*: Gregory Sandor. *sceneggiatura*: Igo Nammus. *assistente al swono*: Serg' Czalov. *truccatoria*: Ellio Fayad. *parruchiere*: Joanelle. *gaffiere*: Villar Nipperetti. *arredatore*: Te'odor Vincente (Ted V. Mikels). *musica*: Icaros Dedocoras (Nicholas Carras). *montatore*: Gregeorio Martino. *scritto ed prodotto*: Juan Rogero (Wayne Rogers), Theo Mikacecci (Ted V. Mikels). *regia*: Theo Mikacecci (Ted V. Mikels). R-S Productions. A Romike Film. *running time*: 63 minutes. Color. *aspect ratio*: shot at full frame and projected at 1.85:1. *completed and released*: 1964.

The Film

Some have called me a great psychoanalyst. Others have called me a quack. —Dr. Sex from *Dr. Sex*

With *Strike Me Deadly* Ted Mikels proved to himself, and anyone interested, that he could truly create a savvy feature-length motion picture utilizing any and all elements at hand. It was a film that he adored making and being a part of; but as fulfilling to the soul as the experience was, it hardly filled his bank account. Wayne Rogers (TV's *M*A*S*H*) was really impressed, though, as Ted remembers:

> Actually, Wayne Rogers came to the very first screening of *Strike Me Deadly* in Hollywood, and really loved it. He was most complimentary, and wanted to be a part of my future endeavors. He got the word about it from a friend of his, I guess. He suggested I move to England where [he said] they really appreciated genius talents, much more so than Hollywood. Soon thereafter, his attorneys presented me with a very tight binding contract that would put him into an effective control position on every film project I would ever get into. It was too binding for me to accept, but we did go on to three involvements: *How Little, How Big*, a children's classroom educational film, one of many I did; *Dr. Sex*; and *Astro Zombies*. He had great contacts; maybe it was a mistake to pass on the offer. We have been friends since, and I used to call on him whenever I needed to communicate with an actor, as he seemed to be acquainted with all the talent in Hollywood.

So in 1963, shortly after the release of his first feature, Ted found himself looking for a marketable project. Action/adventure wasn't panning out, so his next stop became the skin-flick. It was an exploit that didn't necessarily suit his character, but his new friend Wayne Rogers felt that this could be the proverbial cash cow that they were looking for. Somewhat reluctantly, Ted agreed to make the film, and proceeded with production under the working title *The Doctors*. But Rogers had other plans, as the film's director recalls:

> Wayne insisted on calling the film *Dr. Sex*, and I wanted to call it *The Doctors*. Then later he wanted to use Italian names and titles for the credits, as he was of the opinion that foreign product was more valid than Stateside product. In the end I was glad to use the Italian pseudonyms, as I didn't want to be connected to anything that might be considered a porno film. *Dr. Sex* is actually a cute and harmless piece with some pretty girls that get topless. I didn't want then, or now, the word "sex" in the title because it lent an air of seediness to it that I was not completely happy with. The movie itself is fine; it's just the title I'm not crazy about.

It's interesting to note that *Dr. Sex* (alternately called *Strange Loves of Dr. Sex*) is one of the few films of its kind that actually had the word "sex" in the title—as opposed to some provocative double-entendre like *Adam Lost His Apple*, *Eve and the Handyman*, or *Goldilocks and the Three Bares*. Whether comfortable with it or not, *Dr. Sex* became Ted's entry into the lucrative nudie-cutie sweepstakes that had been initiated in 1959 by mammary-mogul Russ Meyer.

Meyer had spent his tenure in the military as a news cameraman, and a very accomplished and talented one at that. Eventually he returned home to find himself taking "cheesecake" photographs. One day the urge to mate the two mediums (the static and the moving pictures) overcame him, and *The Immoral Mr. Teas* was born, along with what was to be forever known as the nudie-cutie.

Now, the nudie-cutie differs greatly from the "stag" films that were available at that time. The stag film was primarily relegated to back alley warehouses, basements and "men's only" gatherings. They were shot using grainy black and white film, and were mostly silent or contained canned library music (orchestral instrumentals and big-band ragtime were the norm). These films were "loops" that ran, at best, a scant 10 minutes. These loops were considered "dirty" and "seedy," possessing no socially redeeming qualities, thus leaving little room for acceptance from the masses.

The other avenue a lonely or curious man could explore was the more accessible "nudist colony" flick. These exercises in the forbidden world of female nudity were oftentimes touted as educational or a public service announcement. The producers would include voice-overs advocating the good and wholesome qualities and effects of nudism. It may have been true, but stuffy America in the 1950s wasn't impressed; and more often than not these pictures found themselves up against the Legion of Decency (the M.P.A.A. of the day), churches, and even self-appointed censors. Nudity, according to the moral majority, was pornographic; but filmmakers knew that it was profitable.

Russ Meyer wanted to see *his* picture in a legit movie theater (or at least a quasi-reputable one), as this was where the real money was. In order to achieve this, some things about this particular breed of film had to change. Meyer certainly knew a thing or two about the male sex drive (being male himself and all), and black and white photography would no longer suffice, nor would those obtrusive brassy orchestral numbers.

One-sheet for *Dr. Sex* (1964).

The skin-flick needed a tune up, and Russ Meyer was just the man to give it one—or maybe he just got there first.

First up, Meyer nixed the seediness, along with the preachy stuff, and inserted a modicum of rib-tickling goofs. This funny-bone humor would (hopefully) help defuse the detractors, and in essence render the film harmless. Again, all were not impressed, nor impassive, and Meyer marched headfirst into a censorship war, where he "fought the good fight," as Meyer's compatriot in the adults-only filmmaking world, David F. Friedman, is so fond of recalling.

By the early 1960s the formula for the nudie-cutie, and its skin-flick trappings, had been tried and tested. It was a successful cinematic cocktail that any independent filmmaker might consider mixing, and Ted took a chance. The movies were easily produced, with only the story angle being of any relative

Dr. Sex (Victor Sandor/Victor Izay) with a gaggle of topless cuties in *Dr. Sex*.

importance (if indeed it was important at all). Storylines, wacky characters and gimmicks were all that separated these films from one another, and Ted was up to the challenge.

In fact, the entire nudie-cutie racket was summed up perfectly by Eddie Muller and Daniel Faris in their wonderful book *Grindhouse*: "...a sheepish voyeur spies on a nude woman; she's an ambulatory masturbation fantasy, straight from *Playboy*'s pages." *Dr. Sex*, costing only $18,000, strayed very little from this template; but Ted was always looking for a unique angle, and he and his partner found one.

Their playful story involves Dr. Sex and his two assistants, Dr. Schmutz and Dr. Lovejoy. The three regale one another with case studies of some of their stranger psychotherapy patients. As the title of the film suggests, all of these victims display and nurture some sort of sexual hang-up. One man thinks himself a horny poodle, while another longs to make love with mannequins. Still another is a female exhibitionist who finds peace as a stripper. Lastly, one fellow is haunted by the ghosts of semi-nude women who seemingly will never deliver the goods. All of this information is shared and collected for a book that the three doctors are co-authoring.

All that really matters for the audience is that many gorgeous gals parade about the screen au naturel. This happens frequently, but Dr. Lovejoy, an attractive female sporting geeky glasses, seems to be the centerpiece of the film. Midway through the picture she painstakingly strips her office wear down to her underthings, and later *we* painstakingly witness her replace her office wear.

Finally, as the last reel rolls around, Dr. Lovejoy appears in all of her exposed beauty. It was a real bell ringer for Ted to save Ms. Lovejoy for the end. It's another example of Ted's "women-in-charge" theory that works so well for cinema. This particular case doesn't

A small tear-sheet ad for *Dr. Sex*.

depict the female as an aggressor on screen, but rather an aggressor *off* screen. As enticing as the other women were, male viewers were craving the forbidden fruit—in this instance, a female bookworm with nerd glasses.

As stated before, Ted was not crazy about making a nudie-cutie, but he needed the work. According to his recollection, the notion of doing a nudie film came from Wayne Rogers. Apparently, Wayne and many of his cohorts were excited at the prospect of interviewing a bevy of beautiful women, and so the happily married Ted was coaxed into taking the job. Incidentally, Ted's lovely wife (at the time) Geneva turns up early on in the film as the woman who is adjusting her stockings.

Another cameo is that of Wayne Rogers himself as a "rain-coater" in the nightclub scene. Wayne is the gent with his collar turned up, smoking a cigarette. Due to budgetary constraints, the film's director also appears in this sequence, with very little (if any) disguise (smoking a pipe and wearing fake glasses). Ted was the "peeping tom" of the film, as well.

> I wanted this scene where I look into a window, but at that moment I had no cast or crew. So, I went in the room and lit it, ran back outside and turned on the camera, ran back into the room and did my part, and then ran back out and turned off the camera. I then took the film, which was short-ends, to the lab for developing. The next day I checked the dailies, and they were okay, so I cut them into the picture the very next day.

> I also shot the outdoor scenes myself, without any crew, for another week or more. It took three months to edit it the old-fashioned way, on 35mm film on the Movieola using a work print before conforming to negative. Then I edited in the sound effects and music.

Unlike the majority of Ted's films, *Dr. Sex* went off without a hitch, though an interesting footnote involves the film's primary locations, or rather *location*. Once the action retires to the confines of an interior, it remains there. The tiny budget did not allow for extensive location changes or the expensive shooting permits to film at such places, so 90 percent of *Dr. Sex* was lensed in one room. This exercise in enforced conservation was not at all alien to the world of independent filmmaking, but rather a necessity.

Exploiteer Doris Wishman became somewhat (in)famous for this type of penny-pinching activity, but Ted took the form even further. Rather than dressing the set walls with curtains, blankets or drapery, as Wishman had, he opted to employ a more solid approach. Several sheets of plywood were painted and decorated, then erected in order to conceal the existing room and its walls, thus creating the illusion of multiple sets. Incidentally, the actual room can be seen during the "haunted honeys" sequence.

As with all of his films, Ted displayed unfathomable amounts of ingenuity and determination. The film took a mere three weeks to shoot, five months to find a theater, and then ultimately left audiences tickled perfectly pink. History has recorded that the nudie-cutie racket ran at a feverish pitch from 1959 through the mid–60s before (ahem) petering-out and making way for soft-core porno. As it was, Ted got in the game right on time, and *Dr. Sex* became (and remains) one of the genre's most entertaining and memorable efforts. Reportedly, the film was banned in Finland.

3. One Shocking Moment

Synopsis from Pressbook

Cliff and Mindy Newhall, a handsome young couple, move to Los Angeles from Grand Rapids after Cliff receives a promotion. As we see them moving into their new apartment, they meet Joanie, a voluptuous blonde who lives across the hall. Joanie shares her apartment with Tanya, a woman with a bizarre and sensual appetite. Tanya owns a small, intimate nightclub where Cliff and Mindy soon become regular customers. But we see that this club is not Tanya's only source of income. We follow her into the night as she accepts money for such weird practices as whipping a wealthy patron in his large, expensive home—we see her unusual relationship to Joanie ... and how this same female, Tanya, attempts to seduce *both* Cliff and Mindy.

In the subplot of the story, Cliff becomes successful in business, but he and Mindy, thanks to Tanya, have slowly become driven wide apart. At the end, in a wild party, Mindy does a strip while Cliff is in the next room attempting to rape Joanie. Tanya interrupts Cliff in his efforts, sends Joanie out of the room, and commands Cliff to make love to her. Cliff suddenly realizes what has been happening to him, leaves Tanya in the bedroom, and he and Mindy start a new and more meaningful relationship in life.

Credits

Cast: Phillip Brady/Gary Kent (Cliff Newhall); Lee Anna (Mindy Newhall); Verné Martine (Tanya); Maureen Gaffney (Joanie); Jerry Fitzpatrick (Rick); Victor Sandor/Victor Izay, Shirl Simmons, Marie Moore, Dominic Levi, Robin Willas, Dick Bing, Zenobia

Production: *director of photography*: Greg Sandor. *art director*: W.B. Moon. *assistant director*: Art Names. *make-up*: Tony Tierney. *sound*: Austin McKinney. *music*: Icaras De Docaras/Nicholas Carras. *supervising film editor*: Theo Mikacevich. *script supervisor*: Igo Monaco. *still photography*: Stan Feldstein. *property master*: Waldo K. Berns. *wardrobe*: Marc Khoury. *second unit camera*: T.V. Mikels. *executive producers*: Jay M. Fineberg and Ron B. Fineberg. *written, produced, directed*: Ted V. Mikels. *running time*: 71 minutes. Black and White. *aspect ratio*: shot at full frame and projected at 1.85:1. *shot*: 1964 *completed and released*: 1965.

The Film

This kid's got some kicks coming before the big hitch. —Joanie from *One Shocking Moment*

Originally shot as *A Suburban Affair*, *One Shocking Moment* represents Ted Mikels' second consecutive flirting with the sexploitation racket. The difference between his previous effort, *Dr. Sex*, and *One Shocking Moment* is that this film fell into the category that would soon become known as the "roughie." Herschell Gordon Lewis kickstarted this subgenre with his 1963 movie *Scum of the Earth*. Herschell's partner in crime, David F. Friedman, later made what is commonly referred to as the definitive roughie, *The Defilers*. Just the same, none of that takes a thing away from Ted's entry into this off-color breed of cinema. But what exactly is a "roughie," and what constitutes its make-up? Authors Eddie Muller and Daniel Faris write in their blissful and brilliant tome *Grindhouse*:

> As the titillation of nudity wore off, filmmakers sought new ways to maintain the audience's interest (and their own). With any depiction of physical intimacy below the waist outlawed by every state censor board, violence became a substitute adrenaline rush. Films like *One Shocking Moment* spawned a whole genre known as "roughies." While it remained against the law to depict a man and woman graphically having consensual sex, there were no rules against showing a man slapping, beating, punching, or whipping a naked woman.

To no great surprise, Ted turned this formula on its ear and had the obligatory violence administered by the females of his film, as opposed to the males. Just more of that Ted V. Mikels women-in-control stuff. Ted's fellow exploiteer, David F. Friedman, furthered this idea when discussing his and Herschell Gordon Lewis' film *Blood Feast*:

> At the time there was no ratings and so we were able to get away scot-free with the blood and gore, but nudity was always a different story. In fact, I've always said about making pictures in America that you'd better not show a guy touch a girl's breast, but you can cut it off with a hack saw.

It's an odd values system here in the States where violence is held in higher regard than lovemaking, but Ted wasn't about to

One-sheet for *One Shocking Moment* (1965).

pass moral judgments. He just wanted to make movies. Brothers Jay and Ron Fineberg scraped up $17,500 and went about Hollywood in search of a producer and director for their film project. They were quickly told that Ted V. Mikels was the one and only person in Tinseltown capable of producing, writing and directing a feature film on such a small budget. Ted's next employment opportunity came knocking, and he was hired.

The Finebergs allowed Ted to write and cast the picture as he saw fit, and so once again viewers get the Ted V. Mikels treatment, warts and all. His self-imposed deadline of five months from beginning to answer print was kept, and the film was shot in only three and a half weeks. In the scope of the genre, *One Shocking Moment* is a pretty good picture, and, as the film's director recalls, it set records at a theater on Santa Monica Boulevard in Hollywood where it was held over for four weeks plus.

He also says that the brothers Finberg only told him that they wanted a movie about suburbanites, and that something confrontational should occur between them and their friends. This was not much to go by, but then Ted always has a wealth of ideas to work with. So the Mikels moviemaking machine started turning its wheels, and characters and situations began to develop.

Ted's script and handling of his cast brings forth a far more realistic depiction of the tale at hand than other films of this type. Pictures like *Olga's House of Shame*, *Touch of Her Flesh* and *She Mob* deal mostly in clownishness. The characters and their actions come across as cartoon-like by comparison. The whippings, bondage, nudity and sex are all in the name of sensationalism; but in *One Shocking Moment* this just isn't the case.

In Ted's film these acts of depravity are neither condoned nor condemned. Again, Ted is not passing judgment, he's just showing it as he believes it could happen. He's telling a story. He only shows these things as they are happening and how they *can* affect a relationship, leaving the viewer to decide for themselves what is acceptable or unacceptable. Ted admits that he'd never even heard of a "roughie," which would help explain why his film differs so much from others in the genre.

Take, for instance, the infamous whipping sequence. Here a man is impatiently awaiting the arrival of someone; he smokes, he drinks and plays solitaire. He appears nervous. The door finally opens and in walks the lesbian Tanya. Tanya slowly disrobes and redresses all in black. She then unfurls a whip and begins flailing the impatient man. He falls to the floor and Tania continues administering her specialty. The ceremony continues, and then, just as quickly as she came in, she leaves.

What's really interesting about this scene is that there is no music, only the ticking of a clock, the cracks of a whip and the moans of the submissive man. It's as it would have been in real life. Composer Nicholas Carras could have easily scored a fantastic piece of cool school jazz for this, or even something dark and sinister to accent the already powerful images, but he did not. It really wasn't his choice, though, as Ted already knew that later he would insert the ticking of a clock to represent what he says was "the passage of time."

Again, Ted has not punched-up this highly suggestive and exploitable turn of events. On the contrary, he has taken the emphasis *off* of the act of whipping. In doing so he forces the viewer to ponder why either one of these characters might be doing this. It's consensual for sure, but the lack of music and the pedestrian editing gives the scene a slice-of-life feel; in fact, the entire film plays out like this. It's like peeking through a window or keyhole. Ted really plays the scene down, and in the end you've only witnessed a moment in time between two consenting adults.

Whipping was not something that Ted had experienced firsthand, but he did remember having a friend tell him about this odd phenomenon. Apparently his acquaintance ran a shop "catering to special needs," and, as Ted recalls, the name of the place was along the lines of "House of Fantasies" or some such bawdy banner. Ted also recounted a tale told to him by a theater's manager wherein following the whipping sequence there was literally seven minutes of silence from the audience afterwards. In other words, they were stunned. "This scene was so effective and so popular around town that many other distributors inserted whipping into their films," recounted Ted, "whether they called for it or not."

In anticipation of censorship problems in some areas of the country, there were two cuts of the film—one "warm" and one "hot"—but the flogging was always there. Still, to assign the film wholly to the "roughie" genre without further analyzing it would be insulting and unfair to the creator of the picture. On the surface the debauchery shines through, but just beneath the sadism is a telling story of true human drama.

As the film moves along there is increasingly more humping and bumping going on in the bedrooms, whether it's male on female or female on female. It also doesn't seem to matter whether or not anyone is married or cheating on their spouse. There's also a lot of drinking going on at the couples' apartments, and especially at Tanya's bar.

These circumstances are shown in the interest of drama and not necessarily for titillation (though it may be difficult for some not to enjoy a frequently topless Maureen Gaffney as Tanya's bisexual girlfriend Joanie). Incidentally, Joanie's character was patterned after Ted's real-life lesbian friend Joanie. Joanie would later play the abusive prison warden in his 1979 film *10 Violent Women*. Also of note is a bit involving the bar that the couples frequent. Ted remembers, "In order to keep the clientele from interfering, we had to 'buy the house' for the nightclub scenes. This was the only way we could have 'quiet on the set.'"

Still, with all of this racy behavior going on, the Finebergs wanted more, and so they spliced in one sequence involving a couple in the bedroom. It's supposed to be Cliff and his wife Mindy, but clearly it is not. It's an entirely different couple altogether. Without knowing it had been a later addition, this sequence would be completely confusing. This is the portion of the film that Ted was most unhappy with; but he was hired to do a job, and once it was completed all rights went to the Finebergs and they could do with the film whatever they saw fit. Honestly, this fairly inconsequential piece does absolutely nothing for or against the film.

One aspect of the movie that some may (and should) find disturbing is Cliff's inappropriate behavior towards women he finds attractive—while in the presence of his wife. Boys will be boys, that's for sure, but in that day and age it seems to be the accepted and proper method of operation. It's important to recognize that *One Shocking Moment* was made before the women's liberation movement, and no matter how it's looked at, a man's wife was his property. So Cliff and Mindy act accordingly; but with the predilections of today it is awkward and embarrassing to witness such a rude and inconsiderate display. But yet again, Ted is not passing judgment, he is only telling a story.

In the beginning, Mindy finds Cliff's rousing flirtation cute and charming. Her ability to overlook her husband's conduct is representative of the last vestiges of naivety that would later give way to the progressive-thinking independent woman. In fact, Mindy herself transforms and blossoms into an open and broad-minded woman as the film plays itself out. Mindy's sexual experimentations with Tanya reveal a whole new world to her, and through this experiment she finds her independence.

Whether or not Mindy was sincerely curious about lesbianism is never conclusively revealed in the film. In all probability she was only attempting to fill an emotional void that Cliff had left her with. Another deduction is that she was merely leveling the playing field that her philandering husband had laid out for them. In either case the final effects are positive ones on the relationship, but not before Cliff has one more romp with Joanie. Tanya has had quite enough of the "Cliff and Joanie" show and summarily shuts it down by stabbing her spiked heel into Cliff's hand. (In actuality, it was *Ted's* hand, as actor Gary Kent had no interest in the possibility of damage to *his* appendage. Apparently Ted's chance of injury was a risk that Kent was willing to take.)

Without haste, Cliff drunkenly stumbles from the bedroom to find his once innocent wife doing a strip tease for the other guests. Like it or not, Cliff and Mindy have

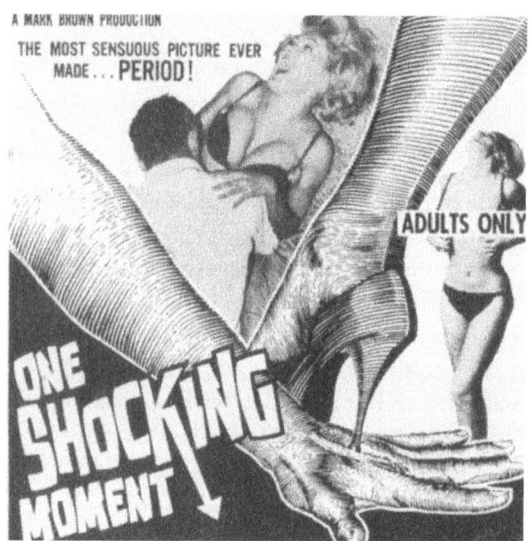

The iconic image of the spiked-heel-in-the-hand that was used to help promote *One Shocking Moment*.

become a part of the L.A. sin-set. Then and only then does he recognize all of the debauchery, reflected in the eyes of the person he loves, for what it is, and so sees the errors of his ways.

Finally, Cliff comes back to reality and accepts that he has helped create this person before him. He is not at all pleased with what he sees, but realizes that he is to blame. Mindy believes that Cliff is the one and only man for her, which lends even more credence to her experimentation with lesbianism. She could have gotten back at him by cheating with any number of men, but that was a line that she was not willing to cross. She loved Cliff, no matter what.

At the film's conclusion the tables have turned. Cliff is remorseful and sensitive to Mindy's needs. He understands and respects the sanctity of marriage and the all important idea of fidelity. Cliff and Mindy have started anew. They have evolved as people and as a couple. It's very likely that the rest of the promiscuous crew will carry on with their shenanigans as before. It's debatable as to how it will affect them, but then that would be another movie altogether.

By design or by accident, *One Shocking Moment* was, and still is, a topical film. Not only does it capture a believable Los Angeles in 1965, but it also lays out a time in American history when women were largely considered to be second class citizens. Their job was to be barefoot and pregnant, and it would be years before the bra-burning would begin. This is a fascinating feature of this form of independent cinema; it's as though the films are some sort of time capsule. Not only are real-life locations, fashion and decor captured within the frames of these movies, but also a mind-set, with all of its good and bad nuances.

Some critics have insinuated that the ending of the film has provided the necessary "socially redeeming value" that was so needed in order to allow a skin-flick to get past the censors. It is, indeed, true that off-color or "blue" movies of the day had to come across more as a public service announcement than anything remotely erotic or sexually stimulating. But this was not at all the case with *One Shocking Moment*, as Ted would never concede to such cinematic contrivances.

A perfect example of this notion comes in the form of the nudist colony picture. These things were simply a way for randy men to see bouncing boobies, but the censor boards wouldn't allow a film to exist as such. So a narration was employed to tell of the "wholesomeness" of nudism, and how it is "natural" to want to go without clothing. The guys and gals of the nudist colony would play volleyball, swim, eat, converse and trampoline entirely naked. The narrator would carry on about how upstanding citizens of the community (doctors, teachers, lawyers, et al) could potentially be nudists, and that skeptics should discard their inhibitions and if not join them then at least accept them.

This seemed to appease the detractors to a certain degree, and hundreds of nudist colony movies were made. The nudie-cutie and the roughie were both different from the nudist colony picture in that they rarely, if ever, had a message to deliver. The fact that *One Shocking Moment* has a socially relevant message is entirely the work and desire of the film's director, and nothing more.

Lastly, take into consideration the film's closing narration:

> This is not the end of the story. Merely the end of the beginning for Cliff and Mindy. They have found a new and, perhaps, more meaningful course of life. Only because they were able to overcome *those* temptations which threatened to divide them. Yet temptations of evil go on. They manifest themselves daily. We are really fortunate. We'll be able to recognize and thereby overcome them, or maybe we would rather not.

Ted never points out what the actual "evil temptation" is, but rather that Cliff and Mindy have decided for themselves what their marriage can and cannot handle. It would be all too easy to hang wife swapping,

A smaller ad focusing almost entirely on the fetching spiked-heel-in-the-hand image.

heavy drinking and S & M with the "evil" banner, whether the behavior was consensual or not. However, Ted wisely allowed his characters to behave in an adult-like manner and pull their lives together as *they* saw fit, not how society might see fit. It's a sentiment that Ted has spent his entire life practicing and perfecting.

4. *The Black Klansman*

Synopsis from Pressbook

In the dressing room of a Los Angeles nightclub, Jerry Ellsworth (Richard Gilden) and his white mistress Andrea (Rima Kutner) are listening to riot news on TV. Later, in Jerry's apartment, he receives a call from Turnerville, Alabama, that his 6-year-old daughter has been killed by the Klan in a church bombing. He decides to change his appearance and identity and goes back to Turnerville to find the killer. He has been told that the Klan head is Rook (Harry Lovejoy), and so goes to his office and proposes that Rook come to Los Angeles and help him form a new Klan. Rook agrees and invites Jerry to a Klan rally the next night.

Farley, whose brother has been killed by the Klan, decides to bring in Harlem gangster Raymond Estes (Max Julien) to fight force with force. Raymond, in a stolen car, breaks up the Klan rally.

Meanwhile, Andrea and Lonnie (Jimmy Mack) follow Jerry to Turnerville, only to find that Jerry is passing for a white man. Sheriff Wallace finds Andrea and Lonnie in a room together, knocks out Lonnie and takes pictures of the two in bed. They take the pictures to an initiation where Jerry has just been inducted into the Klan. All members of the Klan gather up Andrea, Lonnie, and Raymond, and take them to a lynching tree. Jerry helps Andrea and Lonnie escape, then reveals himself to Rook as a negro and prepares to shoot Rook. He changes his mind, but Rook attempts to run him down, meanwhile lynching Raymond, but finally being shot by Jerry.

Jerry then dismisses Andrea and Lonnie, and decides to remain in Turnerville to help his people learn to get along peacefully with the white people in the community.

Credits

Cast: Richard Gilden (Jerry Ellsworth); Rima Kutner (Andrea); Harry Lovejoy (Rook); Max Julien (Raymond); Jackie Deslonde (Farley); Jimmy Mack (Lonnie); Maureen Gaffney (Carole Ann); W.M. McLennan (Wallace); Gino De Agustino (Sawyer); Tex Armstrong (Jenkins); Byrd Holland (Buckley); Whitman Mayo (Alex); Frances Williams (Ellie Madison); Ray Dennis (Sloane); William Collin (Deputy); Kirk Kirkse (Delbert); Jimmy Robinson (Barnaby); Anita Hurrel (Mrs. Ellsworth); Gary Kent (Wilkins).

Production: *screenplay*: John T. Wilson and Arthur A. Names. *music*: Jaime Mendoza-Nava. *song* "The Black Klansman": Tony Harris. *director of photography*: Robert Caramico. *assistant director*: A. Names. *film editor*: Theo Mikacevich. *lighting*: Bob Maxwell. *sound*: Austin McKinney. *art direction*: Wally Moon. *make-up*: Byrd Holland. *wardrobe*: Vana Carroll. *script girl*: Joyce King. *key grip*: Foster Denker. *executive producer*: Joe Solomon. *produced, directed*: Ted V. Mikels. *running time*: 88 minutes. Black and White. *aspect ratio*: shot at full frame and projected at 1.85:1. *completed and released*: 1966.

The Film

I've never hated anyone in my life the way that I hate you... —Jerry from *The Black Klansman*

There's little doubt that if there is only one film in the Ted V. Mikels cannon that attacks or addresses a serious social ill, then it would be *The Black Klansman*. This movie is quite a departure from Ted's previous works. Seamlessly and almost without hesitation, the indie filmmaker moved from action/adventure to nudie cutie to roughie and then on to a serious human drama with heavy socio-political overtones. Ted V. Mikels would apparently try his hand at any genre or form of filmmaking. As it is, *The Black Klansman* was a far, far cry from the seedy depravation of *One Shocking Moment*, which he'd shot only one year earlier. His blacks-versus-whites story ultimately became one of the most historically important films of his career.

In discussing limited-budget films in their book *Sleazoid Express*, Bill Landis and Michelle Clifford wrote that "a special kind of alchemy happens when unintended effects become aesthetically transcendent." They went on to say that "...a scene can turn out more ... powerfully shocking than if it were made by the best cast and crew money can buy." Ted V. Mikels' timeless piece of filmmaking in 1966, *The Black Klansman*, which depicts the story of a mulatto father who travels from Los Angeles to his native home in Alabama to find the killers of his little daughter among the Ku Klux Klan, was just such an endeavor. Shot in black and white, and as gritty as the newspaper headlines of the day, Mikels' film is as dead-on timely and relevant as the gripping and disturbing narrative provided in the pages of John Howard Griffin's *Black Like Me*.

One hundred years after the American Civil War was fought and won by the Union to end the horridly peculiar institution of slavery, many Americans in Dixieland still dragged their collective feet in recognizing the constitutionally guaranteed, unalienable rights of all Americans. Admittedly, the racial equality gains following World War II (and, in particular, those of the 1950s) were noteworthy, but the Southern blacks still suffered indignities and atrocities that Americans across the great span of our country could not imagine. Were it not for the proliferation of televisions in the homes of

One-sheet for *The Black Klansman* (1966).

millions of Americans and the courageous filmmaking of such true patriots of freedom as Ted V. Mikels, the word might never have spread.

Arguably, the movie could have taken place anywhere in North America, as civil unrest was common, even flourishing, throughout the continent. Ted justly aimed his trusty Mitchell camera at Dixieland. The South and its racist stances and platforms were exposed, along with its twisted and deformed manners of thought and social graces. Ted and crew weren't playing around; *The Black Klansman* meant business. It pulled no punches, and even today it packs one helluva wallop. The South was going to bleed.

Movies such as *Mississippi Burning* and *Roots* look *back* at a time and place in American history, particularly black American history, when things were pretty ugly. America was at war from within. However, it is much easier to view those films with the idea that this type of reprehensible behavior is in the past. The realization that these works were made after the fact helps to create a buffer zone of the senses for the viewer. The watcher knows that these and/or similar events did indeed occur, but this was all in another time and quite possibly another place. The same can be said of *Platoon* and *Full Metal Jacket*. Seeing the horrors of the Vietnam War and how mishandled and misguided it was is considerably easier to cope with 30 some odd years later. *The Black Klansman* was different.

The civil rights bill that addressed and attempted to stamp out segregation had been signed by President Lyndon B. Johnson on July 2, 1964. The United States Supreme Court ruled in Brown v. Board of Education that segregated public education was inherently unconstitutional, and that all public schools were to integrate with "all deliberate speed." In the former Confederate States of America, "all deliberate speed" proved a synonym for a decade or more.

In *The Black Klansman*, a wiser and more mature Farley tried to warn his young naïve brother, who sought to exercise his newly guaranteed rights in 1965, that *those* laws come from Washington, and that Alabama was a long way from D.C. The hate-filled Klan members might not have been able to find the nation's capital on a map, but they, too, knew it was far, far away. Later that evening, little brother would be far, far away and gone from the world thanks to the gun-toting cowards who shot him down just outside of town.

In real life, churches were firebombed, children murdered and whole impoverished neighborhoods of Americans whose only "crime" was being of another color shrank from fear and intimidation. All the while local authorities feigned an inability to act since no witnesses could be found. Ted V. Mikels' *The Black Klansman* raises a glimmer of hope when the local mayor advises the Klan-controlled sheriff that "You know we're probably wrong to treat these people this way" foreshadowing the change taking place in the basically good heart of the mayor. Slow to come around was the mayor, and slow to see the light were the American people, but the changes necessary to bring some semblance of civil equality to the South *were* coming.

Seven months after the civil rights bill was signed, civil rights advocate Malcolm X was shot and killed. Later, on April 4, 1968, the pacifist of the movement, Martin Luther King, Jr., would be killed. It was a grim time for the black community, and it was hostile for all, no matter on what side of the fence one stood. *The Black Klansman* was shot in 1966 during the height and heart of this very necessary and honored movement. *The Black Klansman* was real. *The Black Klansman* was now. To perceive it any other way would be both unrealistic and unfair.

Yet much has been written about *The Black Klansman* being exploitation or, even worse, blaxploitation. To seat this film with either one of those descriptions is doing it and its creators a great disservice. Ted V. Mikels has been guilty of masterminding some of the all-time great exploitation films, but this was not one of them. In fact, comparing *The Black Klansman* to the likes of *Superfly*, *Shaft* or *Foxy Brown* is ridiculous, or at least futile. These films and their types sent up black American culture and its nuances, good and/or bad. They also dealt

A small tear-sheet ad from a newspaper promoting *The Black Klansman*.

primarily in caricatures as opposed to realistic and believable characterizations.

Actually, only one film comes to mind that could be sized up against Ted's, and that's Melvin Van Peebles' tour de force, *Sweet Sweetback's Baad Asssss Song*. The tone of both films is similar in the sense that they present an air of fear, dread, sadness and desperation. In Van Peebles' movie the title character, Sweetback, is feverishly fighting against the establishment (the white establishment) and the tortures of inner city life. As stated before, Ted chose to shed some light on the plight of the Southern blacks. Both cultures were/are ravaged beyond reasonable comprehension by racism and oppressions of all sorts.

Sweet Sweetback's Baad Asssss Song is so honest and true in its portrayal of blacks in the projects that for white audiences the film is almost frightening. What may be commonplace for an inner city black man will more than likely be alien to a white man, especially one born and raised in the deep south. By contrast, *The Black Klansman* outraged blacks in some cities to the point of inciting riots and destroying the theaters. Ted's film is just as realistic as Van Peebles', but in a different manner; though both are incredibly sympathetic to the blacks and their circumstances.

Sweet Sweetback's Baaad Asssss Song emits a voodoo-like quality. It's as though Van Peebles intended for his film to put a hex on the white community, and in some areas it seemed to do just that. Ted's film, on the other hand, is laden with white Southerners and their severely warped Christian sensibilities. The backwoods folks justify their evil behavior by hiding behind misinterpreted, misused and largely inapplicable Bible verses. This could easily come across as a form of hexing from the opposite side of the fence. A case could be made that Ted's film and Van Peebles' film are mirror images of one another. The difference is that when the urbanite looks into the mirror he sees one side of this abysmal condition, while the outlander sees another. On the surface they are dissimilar, but the core is very much the same.

The key difference between the two films is that the metropolitan blacks are fighting against "Whitey," while their Dixieland brethren struggle to stay as far away from *their* "Whitey" as humanly possible. Not only is it a geographical issue, but a simple matter of strength in numbers. The rural

South just didn't have as many blacks as the cities did, and the KKK weren't making any effort whatsoever to curb their bloodlust. In those days the Southern black was fairly docile. In *The Black Klansman* it took the introduction of Raymond, an aggressive black activist from the city, to change their tune and make them realize the necessity of standing up for their rights and fighting back.

Another argument against tagging *The Black Klansman* as blaxploitation is its handling of interracial relationships. If Ted had been going for that exploitation dollar, then these scenes would have been played to the hilt; but they are not. In fact, they are executed in such a way as to become almost unnoticeable. Again, Ted aims to keep things realistic, and so the scenes of black men in bed with white women are merely part of the story, not some cheap thrill. Such low-key handling is just further affirmation of Ted's intent to show blacks in a positive light, and perhaps to change our culture's negative perception.

There is absolutely nothing wrong with interracial relationships, legally or morally, then or now. In *The Black Klansman* these couplings are an incidental aspect of the film, and not at all the driving force of the story. Sure it catalyzes the anger and resentment of the small-minded and intolerant, but revenge is the real story here. Jerry's young daughter Mary has been murdered, and the race, color or creed of the man who did this mattered not to him. Avenging her death was all that concerned Jerry, and he was going to make good on his promise by using any means necessary.

Jerry was a light-skinned black man who was able to pass for white and infiltrate the Klan. His seduction of Carole Ann was merely the cherry on top. Carole Ann was the daughter of Rook, the leader of the Turnerville, Alabama, chapter of the KKK. Rook nearly pushes the two into a relationship and then is completely devastated to find out that his daughter's latest suitor is a black man. Now *that* is some cold and calculated justice. Jerry knew exactly what he was doing.

Another defused though potentially exploitative element involves Ted's application of firepower in the film. In the black-oriented pictures of the 1970s and 80s weaponry was a symbol of power. The black man and his family has been stifled in so many ways for so many years that their literal sense of control has been relegated to symbolism in the world of cinema. Pam Grier has pulled revolvers from her afro, while Tamara Dobson ripped her Corvette's

An altered tear-sheet ad. Notice that the emphasis has been taken off the word "black." This ad was perhaps used in territories where the original art may have been too inflammatory for its locals.

door panel away to reveal an arsenal of arms and ammunition that would have Chuck Heston (soylent) green with envy. Fred "the Hammer" Williamson wielded *his* on-screen hardware with a stone cold, unfettered fury and determination, and his bruthas Richard Roundtree, Ron O'Neal and Jim Brown did the same.

What Ted did with *The Black Klansman* was to show the use of firearms in a more realistic sense. As stated before, this is not a film about a black man trying to control "the Man." It's quite the contrary, so when Jerry finally pulls a pistol on Rook at the Klan rally it's very human and it's very desperate. Jerry doesn't really want to shoot him, although he knows that he should and that Rook completely deserves it. However, Jerry realizes that Rook is a man just like himself, and despite Rook's unmerciful actions towards his daughter he will show pity for the murdering Klansman. Rook later dies in an automobile accident, leaving Jerry's conscience clear. Jerry is clearly the hero of the picture, and it may have been his reluctance to kill Rook that outraged blacks in the cities when they saw the film.

Ted had never felt that blacks were second class citizens, and couldn't understand the strife between them and the whites. He also felt the same about the bigotry directed towards the native American Indian. This was a viewpoint he made very clear to the film's producer and distributor, Joe Solomon. Solomon had dollar signs in his eyes, and he knew that a film capitalizing upon the Civil Rights Movement would bring in some bucks. Ultimately, he was right, but Ted simply refused to make the film unless he could do it his way. He would not make a film that glorified racism.

The first thing Ted did was make out a budget. The magic number was $55,000. Next, he solicited the writing talents of John T. Wilson and Arthur A. Names to construct the script. These gentlemen were historians, and they penned the screenplay as though they'd had firsthand experience with the subject matter. The story supposedly took place in Alabama, but it was actually shot outside L.A. in a town called Bakersfield. From here Ted culled the majority of his talent for the picture. For such a small budget, he had plenty of competent people to help with the production, whether in front of or behind the camera, four of whom went on to greater fame. Max Julien made a name for himself in *The Mack*, and Whitman Mayo would later portray Fred Sanford's best friend Grady on the long-running television series *Sanford and Son*. LaWanda Page, who only had a bit part in *The Black Klansman*, would also move on to *Sanford and Son* (as the character Aunt Esther). But the following is one of Ted's very favorite stories to tell:

> I was in a nightclub in North Hollywood. When I walked in [with a date] I heard this guy yelling. It was Jimmy Mack, whom I had cast in *The Black Klansman*. He jumped up on a table and started yelling out loud. Then the house lights went on, and he said, "Everybody, Ted V. Mikels, the greatest movie director in the world, just walked in. He gave me a start in my career, and I want to celebrate him being here by buying the entire house a drink!" He did exactly that, and the house lights stayed on for the occasion. His name was James McEachin, and he also went by the name of Jimmy Mack.

The film was shot and completed within five months. As Ted recalls, the production of *The Black Klansman* went smoothly—except for one amusing incident and a couple that were not so amusing:

> One of the funniest things happened on that picture. We needed a lot of extras for the Klan rally, and in order to remain in good standing with the black community we had *them* wear the white robes and hoods. Then the local police heard a report about a Klan meeting. They came to investigate and I started to laugh and had all the extras remove their hoods, and of course they were all Black! It was a lot of fun, and the police had a good laugh and they left. Now, that was the funny part. Three days into the

The unsettling yet powerful image of a Ku Klux Klan meeting in *The Black Klansman*.

shooting our camera van was robbed and we lost all of our equipment, film and all. I called Hollywood and within hours we had every piece of equipment we needed to continue shooting. Days later the police located the stolen equipment, and all that was ruined was one magazine of exposed film. Then five days into shooting the N.A.B.E.T. union came down from Hollywood and ordered my entire crew off the set. I told them that I loved them and would love for them to stay, but if they had to go I would understand. They all stayed, and they were all fined. I insisted that the union fine me as well. It was around 150 or 200 dollars.

Of some interest is that many newspapers and theaters would not advertise the film under its extremely provocative title. Joe Solomon changed the name to the supposedly less inflammatory *I Crossed the Color Line*. He also switched the graphics to replace the powerful image of a Klansman with a sultry shot of Rima Kutner as Andrea, the white girlfriend of the film's black protagonist, Jerry. While it is not known for sure what region(s) this campaign was specifically created for, it was in all probability intended for the South and their drive-in theaters. At other times the film was simply known as *Brutes*.

Another interesting detail written about by John Howard Griffin was that the male Southerner was quite enamored of the idea of making love to a black woman. He went on to say that if a black man even so much as made eye contact with a white woman, he might very likely find himself looking down the business end of a shotgun or through a noose. The poster art depicting a very white Andrea, with the tag-line "I Crossed the Color Line," would have created quite a stir, and for certain would have been a fireball of controversy in the South.

While *The Black Klansman* deserves more credit than it has ever received, Ted has definite opinions on the film and how it fits into his filmmaking cannon:

> I wouldn't have made this movie on my own. I have never found myself politically motivated to inform the world of my opinions. I never wanted to do controversial things in hopes that it would draw a viewing audience of either those opposing or supporting. I'd rather focus my energies on making movies that entertain people. I don't really feel that my role as a filmmaker is to be confrontational. Still, I think the movie is powerful and I'm very proud to have made it.

Publicity ads for *The Black Klansman* heralded the movie as a major breakthrough in revealing the secret workings of the Ku Klux Klan. Not since 1915, in D.W. Griffith's *Birth of a Nation*, "...has there been a film about the vicious, secret Ku Klux Klan. All major studios in Hollywood have had various stories on the Klan, but because of pressure from various elements, particularly in the South, none have touched the explosive theme." The all-too-real scene in which two black women grieve over the loss of their dead loved one outside the Klan-torched church rivals many a cinematic moment in history. Credit Ted V. Mikels' courage in bringing to the screen an authentic look at one of the most shameful periods in American history, and also in helping to bring about the changes our country had to make.

The Black Klansman closes as President Kennedy's words scroll:

Producer Joe Solomon's stab at exploiting the interracial relationships depicted in *The Black Klansman* by changing the film's title and promotional images.

If an American, because his skin is dark, cannot eat lunch in a restaurant open to the public, if he cannot send his children to the best public school available, if, in short, he cannot enjoy the full and free life which all of us want, then who among us would be content to have the color of his skin changed and stand in his place?

Whatever Ted's opinion of the subject matter, the fact remains that *The Black Klansman* deserves a day in court by all fans of his work. A lost gem in the realm of civil rights cinema and socio-political awareness, the film is an important piece and, historically speaking, is entitled to some long-overdue attention and accolades.

A tear-sheet ad ballyhooing the fact that some of the film's stars and creators would be in attendance ... *plus*(!) a free record giveaway.

5. Astro Zombies

Synopsis from Pressbook

Mutilation murders occur with increasing savagery in a city. The nature of these murders—vital organs ripped from the victims' bodies—leads the C.I.A., headed by Holman (Wendell Corey), to the conclusion that the former chief of the Astro Space Laboratory, Dr. DeMarco (John Carradine), has succeeded in creating an Astro-Man, a zombie with a defective brain! DeMarco, missing since his dismissal from the Space Center, has secreted himself in an old mansion on the outskirts of the city; there he continues his experiments on human bodies with the aid of a deformed assistant. Foreign agents from hostile governments are also trying to locate DeMarco to force him to put his knowledge in their hands. The exotic and voluptuous Satanna, working with two vicious killers, reduces the competition by torture and threat, brutally massacring some of Holman's men. The subsequent mutilation of a beautiful technician at the Space Lab leads Holman to set a trap for the zombie by planting another girl as bait. The suspense tightens when the zombie attacks the girl after Holman's men are gone. After a desperate fight the zombie is tracked down, back to DeMarco's mansion. Meanwhile, the spies are embroiled in ever deepening intrigue but manage to find DeMarco's lab with a frequency rectifier. An explosive finale is inevitable. Holman's men surround the mansion, trapping Satanna inside with DeMarco and the zombies. A bloody gun battle follows, with the zombies butchering indiscriminately. DeMarco is shot down by Satanna, but not before he throws the master switch that deactivates the zombies forever, burying his secret under a mass of electronic rubble.

Credits

Cast: Wendell Corey (Holman); John Carradine (Dr. DeMarco); Tom Pace (Eric Porter); Joan Patrick (Janine Norwalk); Tura Satana (Satanna); Raphael Campos (Juan); Joseph Hoover (Chuck Edwards); Victor Izay (Dr. Petrovich); Wally Moon (Mike Webber); William Bagdad (Franchot); Vincent Barbi (Tiros); Egon Sirany (Foreign Agent); John Hopkins (Thompson); Lynnette Lantz (Ginger); Janis Saul (Lynn); Vic Lance (Chauffeur); Rod Wilmoth (Astro Zombie); Waly Berns, Jean Pirie, Barbara Richards

Production: *screenplay*: Ted V. Mikels and Wayne M. Rogers. *director of photography*: Robert Maxwell. *assistant director*: Art Names. *special effects*: Gary Heacock. *music*: Nico Karaski (Nicholas Carras). *sound recordist*: Frank L. Smith. *gaffer*: Phil Miller. *wardrobe*: Nora Maxwell. *make-up*: Tony Tierney. *script supervisor*: Dody Warren. *assistant cameraman*: Eric Maxwell. *still cameraman*: Sandy Fields. *key grip*: Don Jones. *editor*: Theo Mikacevich. *Satana's wardrobe by*: Rube Panis. *executive producers*: Kenneth Altose and Wayne Rogers. *produced and directed by*: Ted V. Mikels. *running time*: 91 minutes. Color. *aspect ratio*: shot at full frame and projected at 1.85:1. *shot and released*: 1967.

The Film

Beware the astro zombies! They mutilate! They torture! They kill!—Astro Zombies theatrical trailer

As has been made obvious by this point in the chronology of Ted V. Mikels' movie career, the virtues and standards of Hollywood filmmaking cannot, and should not, be applied to him. Ted works entirely outside of the system, and almost every one of his movies flies directly in the face of Hollywood convention. Ed Grant of *Time* magazine seconded this on November 10, 2000, by stating that "in an era when Hollywood entertainment is remarkably predictable, Mikels' work still comes as a cold slap in the face." If Ted's first four films didn't succeed in delivering the "cold slap in the face" that Grant spoke of, then *Astro Zombies* was going to make up for it with a one-two punch.

Knowing that *Strike Me Deadly* was the type of movie that Ted really wanted to do, it's hard to imagine why he would create the ultra-odd and almost surreal *Astro Zombies*. This 1967 baby was about as far away from his action/adventure story as any he would ever make. Horror, science fiction, human transplants, spies and espionage were the order of the day. It was a *mutant* baby. Regardless of his opinions of this—or any other project, for that matter—when Ted signs on he gives 110 percent all the way to the end. *Astro Zombies* was his third and final venture with Wayne Rogers, who co-wrote and produced the picture with Ted.

Good or bad, *Astro Zombies* was, and most likely will forever remain, the film most commonly associated with Ted V. Mikels. Host of the British television series *The Incredibly Strange Film Show* Jonathan Ross apparently believes this as well, and had this to say during the episode dedicated entirely to our man of the hour:

> First and foremost, he made films, every kind of film. From musicals to message movies, from action and adventure to horror and science fiction. Even if he'd never made another movie, *Astro Zombies* would assure him a place in the history of low-budget cinema.

Ted finds it hard to argue with that statement—much to his chagrin, as he feels that many of his other films are more technically adept and, quite frankly, more to his liking in terms of subject matter. Yet, despite all of the hoopla surrounding *Astro Zombies*, Ted is still surprised by its staying power, particularly given its flaws (but who could blame him for a bit of short-changing, as he only had $37,000 to work with, with $3000 of that going to John Carradine alone?).

Author Welch Everman had this to offer about *Astro Zombies* in his enjoyable book *Cult Horror Films*:

> *Astro Zombies* has all the elements of a 1950s horror film. Unfortunately, it came along about ten years too late.... If *Astro Zombies* doesn't hold up very well for viewers today, that's probably because it didn't hold up even for viewers in 1968, who were already too sophisticated to accept the film's mindless clichés.

One-sheet for *Astro Zombies* (1967). This was the image that Ted V. Mikels used to promote the film while distributing it under his newly-founded company Genini.

Had Everman researched the subject a bit before scorning *Astro Zombies*, he may have found the revealing 1986 interview with Ted in RE/Search's *Incredibly Strange Films*. On page 69, Ted stated the following to Boyd Rice:

> I concocted the title *Astro Zombies* 20 or 25 years ago, long before there was ever any such thing as heart transplants.... As with *Astro Zombies*, I'm usually accused of being a few years ahead of whatever's going on. I'm always three or four years ahead, but many times I don't find the money until it's too late.

Ted offered this as an addendum to the quandary:

> I knew that by 1967 organ transplants were fairly common, but I finally had the finances to make *Astro Zombies*, so I went ahead with it, only instead of doing a serious study of such things I decided to play up the camp value of it.

In addition to campiness, *Astro Zombies* also boasts Ted's most colorful cast to date: the mysterious and sexy Tura Satana alongside Hollywood workhorse and resident mad genius John Carradine, topped off by screen legend Wendell Corey. Who could ask for more? Okay, here's more. There's Vince Barbi, the man who is said to have been killed more times on screen than any other actor in history, and Raphael Campos, who turns in a delightful caricature performance of a switchblade-wise Latino. In a brawl, Campos' character, Juan, even goes so far as to put his handgun down in favor of his most prized weapon. It's confounding that some critics and viewers have actually taken Ted and this screwy movie seriously.

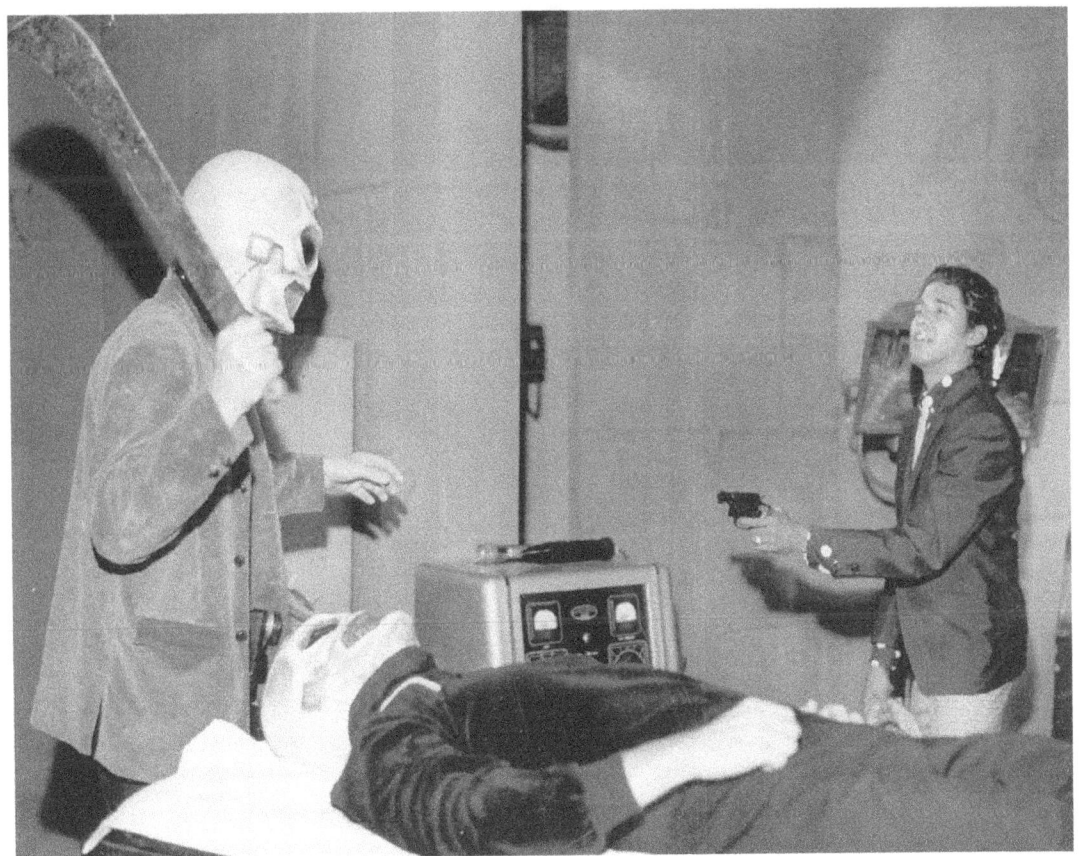

Two terrifying Astro Zombies are confronted by Juan (Raphael Campos).

The cast could have been even more colorful had Ted not made the unlikely decision to cut television regular Peter Falk. Falk was Wayne Rogers' friend, and Rogers asked Ted to include him in the movie. Ted wrote a piece for him, but when it came time to edit the film, Peter Falk, a face and name known nationwide in nearly every single household in America, was cut. It would certainly be interesting to know how the future star of *Colombo* felt about that. Was he disillusioned or relieved? Even more, what the heck was Ted thinking? Here was a man with marquee value who had been on T.V. for well over a decade doing a "freebie," and Ted deems the scene unusable in the context of the story. Ted cut Colombo! The mind reels, but the fact is that Ted *cutting* Falk is far more interesting to ponder than if he'd left the short bit intact. It's just one more example of Ted's unyielding desire to create the best product he can with what he has to work with. You gotta hand it to him, the man's got guts.

Regarding another name performer who *did* make the "cut"—the great John Carradine—Ted reminisced:

> John Carradine was an absolute joy to have on the set. He took direction very well, and any and all suggestions I made were taken into serious account. I mean, I'm just some dumbshit kid making a low-budget picture, and here John Carradine is taking my direction and advice. I'll tell you something else about John. He's not only professional in

Producers Kenny Altose and Wayne Rogers, with Ted V. Mikels, Peter Falk and Tura Satana (seated on Falk's lap), resting in between takes on *Astro Zombies.*

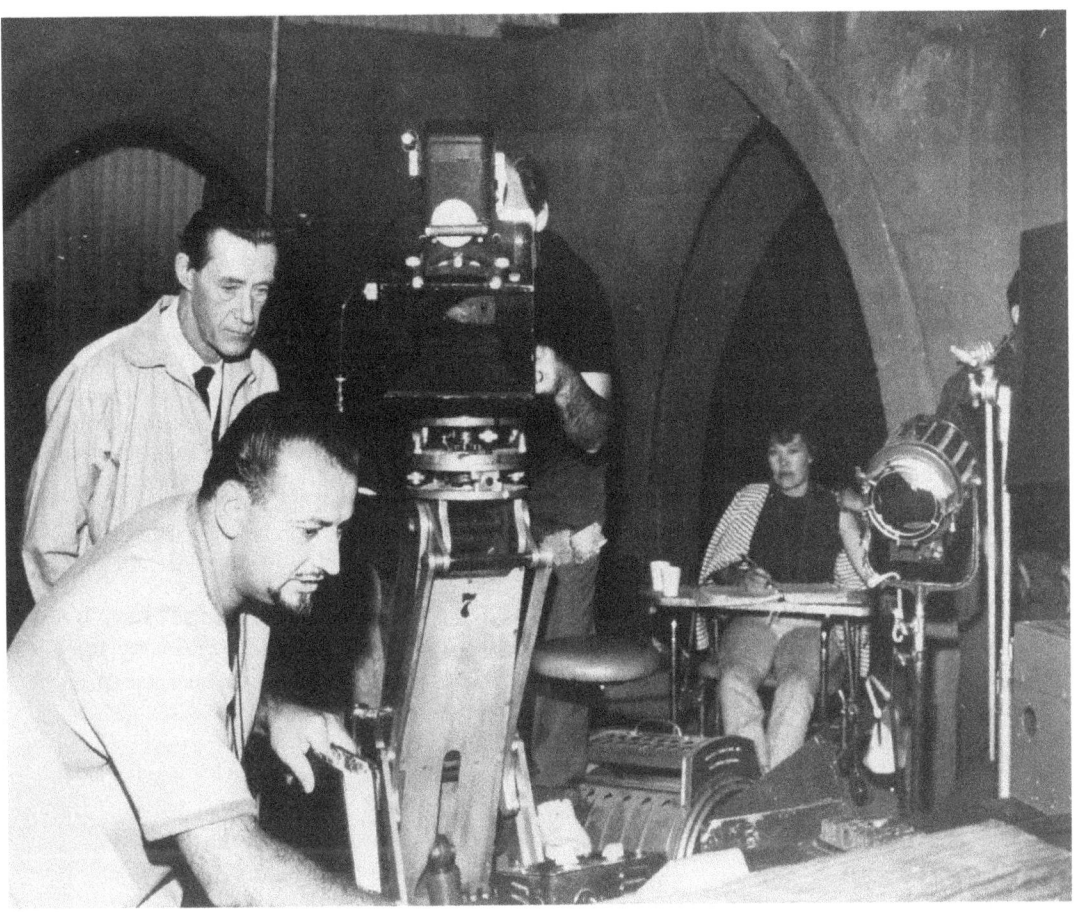

The inimitable John Carradine with the equally inimitable Ted V. Mikels working on the set of *Astro Zombies*. In the background sits script supervisor Dodie Warren.

every way, but he is incredibly wise as well. While we were getting the sets ready to shoot his scenes, John would be off to the side reading his script or a magazine or a newspaper. Now, the crew would be wrapping everything up that was needed for the shot and John would look over the top of his glasses, assess the situation and then put his head back down to continue reading. And, I'm not joking, every time this occurred, sure enough the set would *not* be ready. A light would need to be refocused, the mike reset, just anything, but John Carradine knew. Then when John finally assessed that the situation was correct, he'd get up, and then we, of course, knew that everything was correct for the shot. We all went through this routine for four days of shooting. It was a very funny thing to witness and be a part of. I used to call John a "wise old turtle."

And how was Carradine off-screen?

Very warm and very intelligent. I remember one incident when we were in Des Moines, Iowa, finishing up *The Hostage*, which was around the same time as *Astro Zombies*. We're sitting in this bar having a few drinks and John looks at me and says, "What the hell are you and I doing in Des Moines, Iowa, anyway? We're the only two people on this set who are professionals." That was funny, and then later something not so funny happened. After a few more drinks, John began reciting Shakespeare aloud; and someone at the bar apparently wasn't interested in hearing it, so he socked John square in the eye and put him the hospital overnight.

Astro Zombies' denizen dragon-lady, Tura Satana, relayed an amusing anecdote about Carradine to this writer for *MK Magazine* (vol. 1, no. 1) in 2002:

> It's funny because for that movie I had to do full body make-up every day, and I had to be on the set at four or five o'clock in the morning, and every day there would be John Carradine sitting and waiting. I'd say, "John, what the hell are you doing here? You're not expected on the set for another five hours." And he'd say, "Well, I just didn't want to miss the view."

Ted remembers these episodes very well, and adds that on Ms. Satana's first day of shooting he hardly recognized his star without her trademark make-up, hairdo and attire. Speaking of attire, Ted had many of Ms. Satana's *Astro Zombies* gowns specially made for her, and she wore them well. Ted had found himself quite taken by the half-Japanese–half-Cherokee beauty in 1958, after catching her exotic dance routine in a Las Vegas nightclub called the Silver Slipper. So it was hardly by accident that she landed the role of the villainess foreign spy Satanna. In 1967, while making *Astro Zombies*, Ms. Satana and Ted became very close. This was before Ted's days with the infamous Castle Ladies; but when the time came, Ms. Satana was not asked to join in the fun. As she recalled:

> I couldn't be a "Castle Lady." I am not going to share my man with other women, so that was the end of that. I would have *never* made a good wife for a sheik. That's pretty much what ended our relationship. I would come back from my travels and there would be all of these other women and I asked, "What's this all about?" And he said, "These are going to be my Castle Ladies." To which I said, "Goodbye."

Surely Ms. Satana might have taken this as a backhanded compliment, since it was apparently going to take up to eight women to replace her!

Tura Satana on the set of *Astro Zombies*.

Softening things up a might, and getting back to Welch Everman's disapproval of the film's high "camp" value, it is precisely *this* angle that is *Astro Zombies*' greatest strength. Neither the movie nor its creators take any of this one bit seriously, and *Astro Zombies* is all the better for it. It's as though Ted knew his detractors would be lying in wait. The wit is dry as bone, but everyone has the proverbial two-fingered rabbit-ears behind their heads. The cast is doing everything but winking directly into the camera.

The story is positively fantastic (in both the "strange" and "wonderful" meanings of the word), and the script, along with the acting, is no less so. Several of the cast were Hollywood pros, and these pros manage to deliver some pretty inane dialogue with poker-faced expressions that appear to have been carved from stone. It should be pointed out that this type of delivery was, and is, integral to the success of the film as a whole.

Carradine, as Dr. DeMarco, an ex–Astro Space Laboratory scientist gone bad, is especially brilliant spouting sci-fi psychobabble like, "We must first get the patient into the thermal freeze vault before cellular deterioration takes place," or, "These are the receivers that will relay the knowledge from the memory retention cell into the brain of the transplant. You see, these are tuned to a predestinated frequency cycle beamed from the transmitter." He never had better lines to recite, not even for Al Adamson.

And Dr. DeMarco's pseudo-gothic laboratory is a sight to behold. Hoses, clamps, wires, tubing, and consoles with flashing lights make up the bulk of it. Many of these consoles bear keys, switches or buttons that cause some sci-fi–looking device to bleep, wiz and whirl. It's a veritable nightmare of

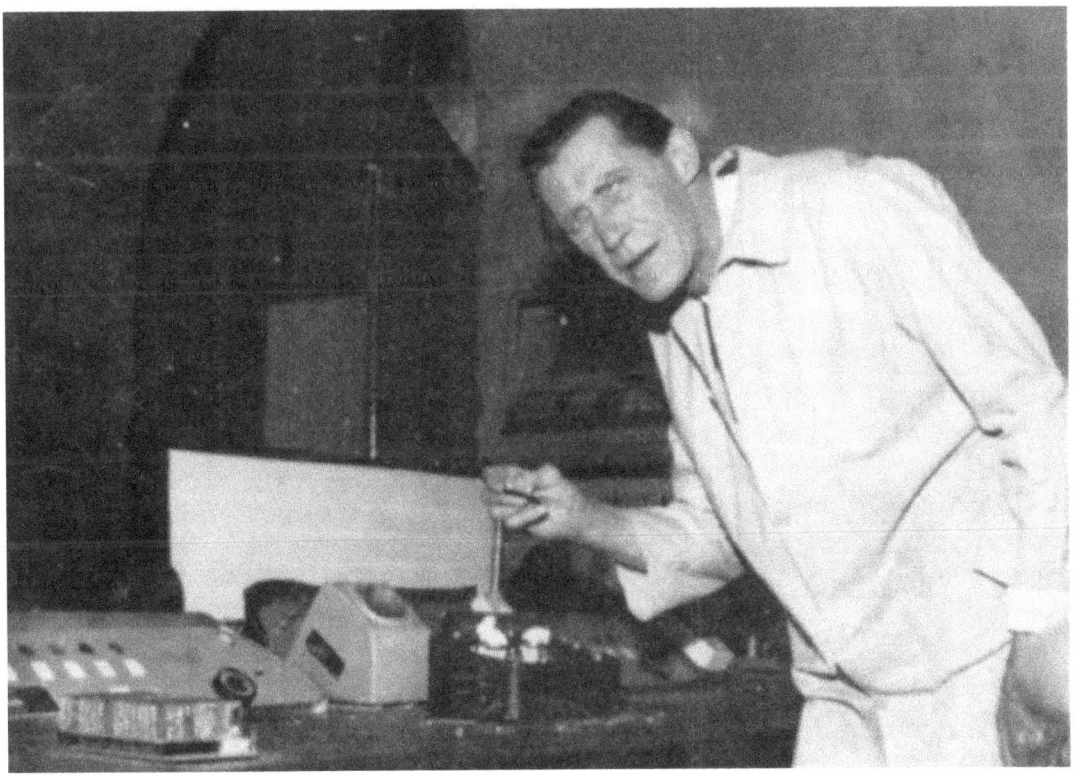

Dr. DeMarco (John Carradine) at the helm of his fully (un)functional laboratory in *Astro Zombies*.

archaic, and largely useless, electronic gizmos, but the cast and crew made the best of it. Incidentally, Ted decorated DeMarco's dungeon, which resided on a Hollywood sound stage, with gadgets found mostly at the local Army/Navy surplus store. As the man himself recalled:

> I bought anything that looked curious or futuristic. These things were way too outdated for the military, so they let this stuff go really cheaply, which was good for us and our tiny budget. Basically if it had buttons and flashing lights then we'd use it. I honestly don't know what most of that stuff was nor what its originally intended use was.

The wackiness continues ... DeMarco's brainchildren, the astro zombies (or, as they are more commonly referred to, the "astro men"), are simply mind-numbing in appearance and design. Nothing about these monstrosities makes a whole lot of sense. Wendell Corey's character, Holman, head of the C.I.A., describes them as best he knows how: "...a man with a synthetic, electrically driven heart, a stainless steel mesh stomach, a plastic pancreas, a cellulite liver."

What Holman has failed to include in his almost poetic description is that DeMarco's handiwork comes equipped with a skinned, mutated skull-head. There are wires and electrodes here and there, and the eye sockets appear to be darkened sunglass lenses (and probably were). But this makes for good cinema, because as killers on the

An *Astro Zombies* behind-the-scenes photo: actor Wendell Cory, Ted V. Mikels and cameraman Robert Maxwell.

5. Astro Zombies 45

A maniacal machete wielding "astro man" (Rod Wilmoth) in a dinner jacket.

prowl they are all-too-conspicuous. Why did DeMarco choose to peel the flesh from their faces rather than leave them as is, or at least alter them with plastic surgery? (Remember, we're dealing with caricatures here, and most cinematic mad scientists know all the tricks of the trade.) Such blatant outrageousness only underscores the notion that Ted had no interest in realism this time around.

Even odder is the fact that they continue to wear the clothing that adorned their bodies before being transformed into quasi-supermen. Consequently, the screen reveals a man in a dinner jacket and dress pants stabbing and slashing his way across town looking through the eyes/viewfinders of a modified skull. It's weird.

More chuckle-inducing fun comes in the form of the space-age, half-robotic creatures' choice of weaponry. Why do they *not* possess high-tech accoutrements like eyes that fire laser beams, or at least some modern pistols? Surely, the highly intelligent DeMarco had the ability to arm his creations with such wonders; but no, they use rusted gardening tools and dulled machetes. Of course, it makes the murders more violent and inherently messier (as lasers would only cauterize a wound).

Another strike against DeMarco's supposed brilliance is the fact that he chose to make his astro men solar powered. Surely, even a hack planning world domination via astro zombies would understand the significance of their being able to travel by night. With this idea, Ted was really living in a "camp" ground. The zombies have solar cells on their foreheads, and a back-up battery pack for return to the laboratory for recharging, but when things go wrong they really go wrong. According to DeMarco, everything is groovy, but an astro zombie drops his battery pack during a nighttime scuffle and seizes a flashlight from his assailant. Watch, slack-jawed, as this digital demon makes his way back to his deranged daddy by holding the beam of the flashlight to his solar cells! But wait, there's more...

DeMarco's partner in crime, Franchot, is a humpbacked mute in the spirit of Universal Studio's Fritz from James Whale's 1931 *Frankenstein*. Franchot, in all of his oddness, is portrayed in a true send-up manner by soon-to-be Ted V. Mikels regular William Bagdad. Franchot seemingly dwells only within the confines of DeMarco's lab, and as the film progresses his imagination and determination begin to run amuck.

DeMarco has taught the little bugger his experimental secrets and how to run all of the mechanical accoutrements. Franchot is adept at operating "the blood exchanger" and the "thermonuclear freeze vault," but he is lonely. Dr. DeMarco will evidently never be enough for him. Poor Franchot desires a mate, so he captures a bikini-clad cutie and goes about the process of transforming her into an astro zombie—and presumably his love slave. Franchot is demented, just like his master, but he drives even further down the madman motorway by making use of this powerful knowledge strictly for self-serving purposes—sex! It's all implied (mostly), but the burning question is: would she have a skull-like head, too; and if so, would Franchot still find her attractive?

Pointing out every single kooky detail of *Astro Zombies* is impractical, as the list goes on and on. But Franchot's deviance pushes the boundaries even for a Ted V.

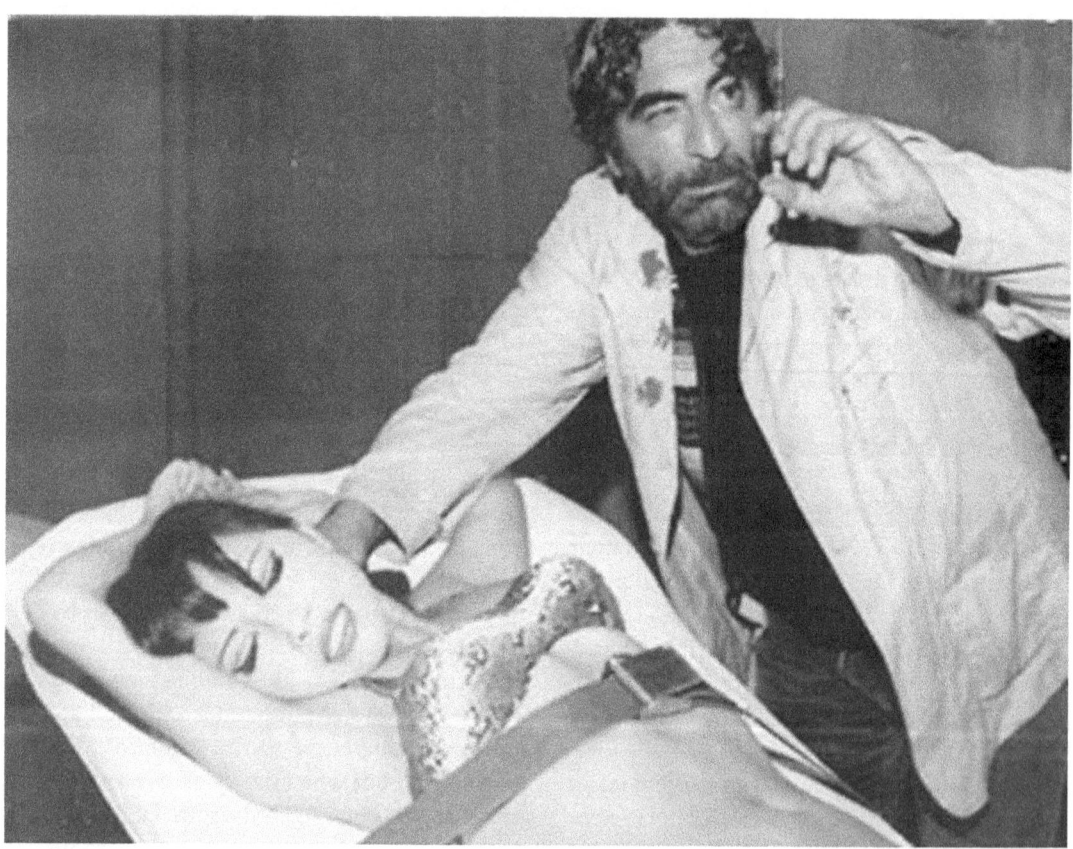

Francot (William Bagdad), Dr. DeMarco's sexually deviant assistant, is about to anesthetize a bikini-clad cutie in *Astro Zombies*.

Mikels production. Years later, when the film was purchased for television, a topless female dance sequence was cut. The dancer was concealed from head to toe in swirling psychedelic body paint, and no offensive (to some) female attributes could be detected. However, Franchot and his displaced sexual yearnings were just fine and dandy with the television censors. Now that's weird, too.

As if promoting this whirlwind of zaniness was going to be a problem, Ted and co. worked overtime on the advertising for *Astro Zombies*. The poster and ad campaign are, to no great surprise, perfectly representative of the delirium within the film. A particular stand-out is Ted's original artwork, with its freakish astro zombie skull clutching the disembodied head of a female victim. Of course, no such extremities were ever lopped off in the film, but these posters were an all-important part of the exploitation movie business in general. In truth, they were key in persuading potential viewers to see the film, and Ted was a master at getting the proper look on a poster or ad that would reflect his movie, or at least how he perceived it.

In reality more times than not the printed ads would promise a great deal more than the meager funding of these films could ever hope to deliver. This is not at all exclusive to the films of Ted V. Mikels, either. Some low-budget filmmakers have gone so far as to actually create a poster and advertising slant before filming even begins! For *Astro Zombies*, to make sure the patrons came in droves, small plastic google-eyed skull necklaces were handed out to every ticket buyer to wear. Ted and company distributed them by the thousands. The film was a success, though not as successful as it could have been.

The astro zombie masks themselves certainly deserve a mention, too, and should really be iconic symbols of low-budget science fiction and horror cinema. With their blacked-out eyes, and foreheads replete with solar powercell diodes, these imaginative guises can hardly be beaten in the world of exploitation cinema.

Just like Frankenstein's Monster, these creatures sprang from the mind and hands of an insane scientist. Universal Studio's Dr. Frankenstein chose to insert a set of electricity-conducting bolts into the sides of his creation's neck. In paying homage to these films, and in an attempt to keep things offbeat, Ted had Dr. DeMarco attach similar appliances to *his* creations, but these were jam-packed with circuits and wires and other electrical devices. What purpose these really serve remains a mystery as there appears to be no practical use for them—they're just cosmetic.

Still, with all of this wacky goodness, it's a shame that Ted wasn't able to fully explore the depths and subtexts of his astro zombie creation. When the script and outline were originally written, almost a decade before its release, a centrifuge was to be spinning directly in front of the camera during the opening sequence of the film. The centrifuge is a massive apparatus used by NASA to help train their astronauts to deal with the feeling of weightlessness.

In the planned opening, the machine would be whipping around and around and eventually come to a stop. A hand would then reach into the machine and pull the head off of the man inside to expose him/it as an android. This would have been an inventive way to start a feature, but Ted didn't feel that his 1967 version of *Astro Zombies* necessarily reflected the same kind of intensity and sincerity that the original script contained. The idea was scrapped. So, in true Ted V. Mikels fashion, he played up the silliness of the film and had battery operated toy robots take the place of a highly complex (for the time) piece of equipment, thus turning hardcore sci-fi fans on their ears.

When examined in this context, the opening sequence, which is confusing to most, begins to take on a much more impor-

tant role in setting the viewer up for what is to follow. To accept this film, and its narrative, in an earnest fashion is difficult, to say the least, and Ted wanted to let the audience in on the joke right from the get-go—*Astro Zombies* was going to be fun.

Artist and writer Scott Blacksher felt that the astro zombies as entities deserved more dissection as well. He offered the following in an essay about the astro zombies on the *Art of the Astro Zombies* website (www.motazart.com); to him the actual astro zombies are representative of:

> ...large groups of people who stop thinking for themselves and mindlessly follow instructions simply because they trust authority completely without question. The formation of a "hive mind" by going along with others in order to fit in. Anyone outside the hive is considered the enemy, whether or not they pose a specific threat. If they are different then they must either conform or be eliminated.
>
> That is who the Astro Zombies are. They represent the callous and corrupt nature of humans who embrace a single norm or a single approach. Astro Zombies are fanatics. Astro Zombies are fascists. And Astro Zombies are constantly winning because a united front breeds corruption when gone unchecked by the apathetic majority. There are no simple answers ... only simple minds.

Ted finds this appraisal of his film's characters a bit deep, but very much appreciates that Blacksher has looked at the movie in such a philosophical manner. While Blacksher's interpretation of the astro zombie is different from the director's, the actual service of the creation was quite deep in another direction. Originally, the astro zombies were to be electronic receptors for the transference of the great minds of astro physicists. The idea was that these quasi-men would be astronauts with the brain power of a genius in the field of space travel, thus eradicating the risk to human life. It's hinted at in the film but never fully realized.

As proud, or as perplexed, as Ted could be over the continuous worldwide and wide-eyed reception of *Astro Zombies*, that film, and the masks in particular, are a bit of a sore spot for him. With all the patience this man has for teaching his crew the fundamentals of moviemaking, there was one instance where he snapped, and those beloved astro zombies were partially to blame.

> The closest I ever got to being really upset was in 1967 when we were doing the *Astro Zombies*. Here's what happened: the young man who was making the astro zombie heads knew that we needed three of them, and he showed up to the set with only one. I didn't know how much time was involved in curing the foam rubber for these heads, and I remember getting upset and saying out loud, "I thought you said we would have more than one astro zombie, and we don't and that ruins the shot!" I did eventually wind up with a second astro zombie head, but that was probably the only time that I raised my voice on the set. I've been very sorry over this incident ever since.

Perhaps Ted's impatience with the astro zombie head sculptor was a gut reaction to, or a bit of foresight about, what was going to happen to him next. As mentioned before, the film was successful and was garnering more and more capital as the days and nights went on. As with many of his features, *Astro Zombies* broke attendance records in numerous theaters; but for the film's investors it just wasn't enough. Sadly, the first film that Ted directed and produced for his newly formed distribution company Geneni was to be callously taken away from him. (Note: "Geneni" is a compound title standing for "Geneva and I," or rather "Gen and I.") As Ted tells it (in an interview conducted on February 18, 2006):

> When I first started *Strike Me Deadly* in the mid–50s, that's when the thought of *Astro*

Opposite: An *Astro Zombies* tear-sheet ad. Notice the emphasis on the "Free Weird Zombie Skull." Promotional gimmicks were always an important part of the fun in seeing an exploitation/drive-in film.

Zombies came to me. As time went on I finished *Strike Me Deadly*, that's how I met Wayne. He came to the initial screening, when I still called it *Crosshairs*, and thought that there was some sort of genius behind the man who made that movie. He wanted to meet and talk and so on. And then that's when I made my move, family and all, after editing in Hollywood for almost a year on *Strike Me Deadly*. I was still trying to find more money to finish mixing the audio and do cut-ins of the forest fires and that sort of thing. In 1961 Wayne got involved with me on a family educational film called *How Little, How Big*, and he gave me a few dollars, I think it was $1200, and I matched it and I shot it. Of course, it was sold to another company, and they gave me tiny money. Wayne made a few dollars on it and I got about four pennies an hour for my time, and that's very accurate. I got four cents an hour for that picture. During that time I was preparing to move my family to Hollywood, and right after I got there is when Wayne said, "Well, let's do this little thing. We can all use phony names and we'll call it *Dr. Sex*." We sat and wrote that out. I did all the typing in my office, and he had some investors—you know, businessmen who had various little businesses in Hollywood. I don't know what kind of money they came up with because Wayne and his partner Kenny Altose handled all that, and Wayne was a business major in college and he was very good, and he also had a running part in the television series *Wagon's West*. Anyhow, we shot *Dr. Sex* in the home of either Wayne or Kenny's friend, and we had a good time; but then after that nothing happened, and this was in 1963 or '64. I kept in touch with Kenny and Wayne, and they were after me for something to finance. I told them that I had this story called *Astro Zombies*, and they liked the idea of it. And as you know, I had written it many years before, and Wayne said, "Let's make it, but let's make it camp." So that's how that came about. So they went around raising dollars, $5000 from this businessman, $5000 from that one. Peter Falk was one

An unusual image used to promote *Astro Zombies*.

of the investors, believe it or not. I was told that he contributed $5000, though I have no way of really knowing, as I didn't handle the money and they did. So eventually they raised a total of $37,000. I should also mention that Wayne and Kenny used a come-on with these businessmen. They told them that if they invested they'd get to interview pretty girls. This was the exact same routine that we went through with *Dr. Sex*. I took no part in it, but what do I care? As long as we find a way to make a movie, and I find a way to feed my family and find a way to keep on going, then I'm happy. Anyway, I typed this thing up at my little studio office. Whenever Wayne would come over we'd laugh and joke as we were working on it. By the way, I have no ill feelings towards Wayne at all, and I'll tell you why in a minute. So we wrote the screenplay, then we started looking for casting. Then we had to look at the budget; we had $37,000, and, unfortunately, I didn't budget myself in that [laughs]. You see, I was anticipating a large return on that picture. They did give me a note, however, for $7,500, but I never got it. Anyway, we did the movie, and I will say that Kenny and Wayne gave me the first shot at releasing it with my new company, which at the time was not really a full-fledged company. So, for a few months it had some showings and it did fine. This was the first picture that I had directed and released through my company Geneni. The first picture that we actually distributed was *Undertaker and His Pals*, which I didn't shoot, but I did re-edit it and marketed it. I think we may have also released *Up Your Teddy Bear* as well. Well, I know we released it, but I can't remember if it was before *Astro Zombies*; but *Undertaker and His Pals* was definitely first. So, even though the picture was successful we weren't getting our money fast enough for Kenny and Wayne, who were having to answer to all those investors. Kenny had come up with a big chunk of it—I think as much as $20,000 of it—and the rest came from those other people. So months went on and we couldn't get a big enough return. Then one or two sub-distributors were withholding funds from *Astro Zombies* that were owed to them from showing *Undertaker and His Pals* and *Up Your Teddy Bear*, even though they'd signed agreements to not mix-match funds. We had sub-distributors all across the country. They were called Foreign Distribution Exchanges and there were 22 across the country. The sub-distributors are the ones that go into the theaters booking these movies. They try and convince the theater owners that they should play such and such picture. They're the ones that are always scavenging around for funds. The theaters paid their debts to the sub-distributors. But if one of my subs over-advertised another one of my pictures, as they were in charge of advertising, and they needed $800 to recoup, then they'd just take it from an advance on another picture I'd given them. They did this even though they'd signed a contract stating that they would do no mixing and matching of funds. Wayne and Kenny didn't like that, and they said that I wasn't able to control my sub-distributors. I told them that I couldn't do anything more and that I had a contract with these people stating that they were not allowed to do such things. So then Wayne wrote me a letter stating that they had to go another distribution route, because you're not able to control your sub-distributors on this money thing. Well, actually it was only $1,700 that had been taken from the sub-distributors on *Astro Zombies* against the other pictures, for shipping and advertising or whatever. Anyhow, I told them to go ahead with it, but I couldn't give them the $1,700 because I never had it to begin with. They weren't worried about it, but Wayne said that Kenny *had* to get his money out of it, and so we're selling the picture to Jack H. Harris. He asked me to deliver all prints and materials to Jack's office, and that's how that all came about. But this is why I have no hard feelings towards Wayne—I know that he was under pressure from Kenny because he took the dollars from his business, which was a clothing business. In order for them to quickly recoup their dollars they really needed a distribution company that had the manpower to see that all receipts and funds were in order, and I couldn't do that, and so I really couldn't argue with their decision. So that's how it was taken from me. But in all the paperwork that was issued to me from the attorneys, there was a letter stating that there was note for $7,500 written to Ted V. Mikels for his work on the movie. Now, there was no note enclosed, *but* I didn't even know that until about two years ago when I was going through a ton of my paperwork!

So there's the scoop on how Ted's most financially successful feature was seized from him, and how a man who had absolutely nothing to do with its production wound up with all the monies. By Ted's own admission, "Jack Harris was a much better businessman than I." Ted is too kind, and if this wasn't convincing enough, just wait for *The Doll Squad* story.

Oddly, when *Astro Zombies* was sold to the video market in the early 80s, the print used was the version with the topless dance sequence excised. Particularly intriguing is the fact that Ted was the bongo player for this famous routine. The powers-that-be didn't even attempt to locate an uncut copy of the film, and therefore years would pass before anyone was able to see the version that theatergoers saw in the 60s and 70s. This truncated print not only was darkened to tone down the gore factor for television audiences, but it also denied viewers a cameo

Right: **A tear-sheet ad for a Genini double feature:** *Astro Zombies* **and** *The Undertaker and His Pals.* **Below:** **Ted V. Mikels, on the bongos, eyeing a lass in full body paint in** *Astro Zombies.*

of the film's director—and his prowess on the bongos. *Astro Zombies* hit the shelves under two alternate titles, *Space Zombies* and the confusing *Space Vampires*.

One final behind-the-scenes story involves the sequence where the police show up. In reality, it was the *real* police! While the crew were filming the scene in which Franchot pulls a gory body from a burning car, nearby neighbors mistook the set-up for an authentic accident and phoned the authorities. Ted saw the squad cars approaching and instructed his cameraman to photograph them as they approached, and also when they vacated the premises. The officers were none the wiser, and Ted and company got a police appearance freebie. What started out as a "shoot first, ask questions later" incident wound up being more in line with "don't ask, don't tell." Ted's an opportunist for sure.

Ted broke the mold on this picture. It's doubtful that any other American movie from that era encompasses so many tweaked and skewed visions of what characters are expected to do or how a narrative is supposed to flow. *Astro Zombies* could certainly be seen as a how-not-to-make-a-movie lesson, but why conform? Ted doesn't. Why make a paint-by-numbers movie? If one *has* to make something stereotypical, then turn that sucker upside down and shake the crap out of it. By low-budget filmmaking standards, *Astro Zombies* is a real barnstormer, a real howler. It's an honest-to-goodness original, and it's this author's favorite.

6. *Girl in Gold Boots*

Synopsis from Pressbook

Buz Nichols, a volatile, tough young hood, is driving cross country to see his sister Joanie, lead dancer in a swinging Hollywood Go-Go nightclub. He meets Michele Casey, who has ambitions of becoming a dancer at a roadside café which her drunken father owns. She accepts Buz's offer of a ride and an introduction to his sister in exchange for relief driving. They have an encounter with two members of a motorcycle gang, escape, and pick up a hitchhiker, Critter Jones, a happy-go-lucky, guitar-playing wanderer, and his broken-down motorcycle. The trio, cycle in tow, proceed on their journey.

A delicate love triangle takes form, with definite appeal on the part of the young men towards Michele, and she for both of them. Their first view of the ocean results in a frolic in the surf, a wild ride on a beach dune-buggy, and open conflict between the two men over the girl.

In Hollywood, Buz introduces the others to his sister, and Joanie promises Michele an audition for a job with Leo McCabe, owner of the nightclub. He is impressed and attracted by Michele's dancing ability and beauty. She starts work immediately, and Critter, feeling responsible for Michele in these new surroundings, accepts a job as janitor. McCabe actually deals in drugs, and Buz is promptly initiated into this end of the business.

Harry Blatz, an elderly hoodlum, contacts McCabe with information that the county jail is holding a hundred thousand dollars worth of drugs in a cell, pending an investigation. Blatz, a genius with skeleton keys and habitual guest of the jail, can easily get in and obtain the drugs. What is needed is an accomplice to make the getaway, and Buz takes on this job.

Meanwhile, Michele has become an overnight success, and now McCabe, tiring of a neurotic and now addicted Joanie, makes a play for her. Michele, however, has fallen in love with Critter, who has, by now, found out about McCabe's drug activities. They quarrel when Critter tries to persuade her to leave, telling her about McCabe's drug dealings and the fact that he, himself, is a draft dodger.

Buz and Harry Blatz succeed in their robbery at the county jail. Buz kills the old man and later boasts of this to McCabe and Marty, bouncer at the club. This conversation is overheard by both Critter and Michele. Not wanting to become involved, Critter insists on the girl leaving with him. McCabe, Buz and Marty bar their way, and in the ensuing bloody battle, Critter manages to overcome all three and calls the police.

Turning their backs on Hollywood, Critter and his new bride resort to hitchhiking in an effort to report back to his induction center in time. Critter sings happily to Michele as they are driven off into the distance, with the inevitable ever-present broken-down motorcycle in tow.

Credits

Cast: Jody Daniel (Critter Jones); Leslie McRae (Michele Casey); Tom Pace (Buz Nichols); Mark Herron (Leo McCabe); Bara Byrnes (Joanie); Harry Lovejoy (Harry Blatz); William Bagdad (Marty); James Victor (Joey); Rod Wilmoth (Officer); Victor Izay (Mr. Casey); Shelia Roberts (Store Clerk); Mike Garrison (Gas Station Attendant); Duke Graham (Motorcyclist); Jerry Ambler (Motorcyclist); Michael Derrick (Car Attendant); Anne McAnn (Waitress); Genji/Geneva Mikels (Cocktail Waitress); the "Gold Boot" Girl Dancers (themselves); Chris Howard (himself); the Third World (themselves); Preston Epps, that "Bongo Rock" Man (himself)

Production: *screenplay*: Leighton J. Peatman, Arthur A. Names, John T. Wilson. *associate producer*: Joe Andary. *director of photography*: Bob Maxwell. *production manager*: Rod Wilmoth. *editor*: Leo Shreve. *music score*: Nicholas Carras. *assistant cameramen*: Jack May, James M. Farquharson. *script supervisor*: Jim Kelly. *sound recording*: John Hopkins, Clark Will, Sam Kopetsky. *wardrobe*: Nora Maxwell. *make-up*: Gen Mikels. *still photography*: James McEwen. *titles*: Pacific Title. *produced and directed by*: Ted V. Mikels. *running time*: 91 minutes. Color. *aspect ratio*: shot full frame and projected at 1.85:1. *shot*: 1967. *released*: 1968.

Songs: "Girl in Gold Boots," "For You," "Do You Want to Laugh or Cry," "Hello Michele," "One Good Time, One Place," *music and lyrics*: Chris Howard. "Lonesome Man" *music and lyrics*: George Eddy. "You Gotta Come Down" *music and lyrics*: Jody Daniel, Bobby Batson.

The Film

You're really hooked on this dancing, aren't you?—Buz from *Girl in Gold Boots*

In 1967, the biker film was really starting to rev up. Folks around Hollywood kept telling director Ted V. Mikels that he needed to make a biker film and that these things were going to be hot in the years to come. Released in 1967 were the highly successful *Hell's Angels on Wheels* and *Born Losers*. Then, between that time and the early 1970s, the biker movement and its celluloid reflection became virtually omnipresent. Just the same, Ted wasn't interested. "I simply did not want to do one," he explained. "I didn't have anything against them, and still don't, but it was something that I did not find to be that intriguing, subject-wise."

Motorcycle movies were simply everywhere, but in 1969 the most notorious of them all would be directed by Dennis Hopper: *Easy Rider*. Ted was propositioned by

Hopper's company to become involved in some capacity, and they sent some of their representatives to his office. As Ted headed down the hall he caught a whiff of something that he knew was illegal. He asked his secretary to see them out. Was Hopper in that bunch? Yep, he sure was, and asking Hopper to leave may have been an act even more audacious than cutting Peter Falk from *Astro Zombies*. Alas, Ted was not to become involved in one of the most popular motion pictures of all time, but the production team *did* rent some of his cameras and equipment for the shoot.

In no way swayed by the monetary potential of the burgeoning biker genre, Ted spread his creative wings and once again flew directly in the face of Hollywood convention. This time, upon landing, he turned up with *Girl in Gold Boots*, a Rock and Roll musical ... of sorts. Ted shot the film in late 1967 with about $6,800 in hand. The balance of the finances, explained the director, "were strictly on credit." Ted was so well liked and trusted around Tinseltown that everyone from the cast and crew to the optical lab signed contracts stating that they would work for a percentage of the returns.

The majority of *Girl in Gold Boots* was shot inside an L.A. nightclub called the Haunted House. The entryway was a hall of horrors, alive (or rather dead) with wax figures of Dracula, skeletons and the Creature from the Black Lagoon. Inside the renowned discotheque, lovely girls in shiny silver boots (only one in gold) danced to the music of a live band. Here, where the band plays, was the real centerpiece of the club. The stage was built inside a demonic-looking mouth. The creature's eyes glowed red, its nostrils spewed smoke and the band played on. This location was so striking that other movies have also filmed there, most notably Stephanie Rothman's *It's a Bikini World*, also shot in 1967.

Despite a balls-to-the-wall marketing campaign that included touring several major cities with the film's starlet, Leslie McRae, theater lobbies filled with promotional balloons, and countless newspaper ar-

Original one-sheet for *Girl in Gold Boots* (1968).

ticles, Ted's latest project was simply not destined for success. Also, within the pages of the film's press-book, an advertisement for a full-length soundtrack LP can be found; but, sadly, this promo item was never to surface. Not one single solitary copy was manufactured due to the disinterest shown the film by the moviegoing public.

In one instance, in Louisville, Kentucky, Ted and Ms. McRae, a 28-time beauty pageant winner, took the stage after the Beach Boys had performed. The two talked about the film and signed autographs, and, as Ted put it, "We really thought we'd done something there. Everyone was so receptive to what we were doing and what we had done." Little did they know: "We were opening against *Planet of the Apes*, and our picture sank like a rock."

Another angle of promotion involved a drawing for a free pair of gold boots. "You Can Be That Girl in Gold Boots!" promised the newspaper ads and theater lobby one-sheets. Ted remembers that they'd gotten the boots wholesale from a shoe company. The pressbook states that they were imported from Italy by the Nina Footwear Company of New York, and that they were a $60 value (a healthy sum for the late 60s). And at the Show-a-Rama Film Convention in Kansas City, Ted hired three females to don these pricey gold boots and dance on a table with Leslie McRae, all the while stomping and bursting balloons. This created such a stir

Promoting *Girl in Gold Boots*: director Ted V. Mikels, three unidentified dancers and actor Tom Pace.

that Ted's table was packed with onlookers while the major studios' displays went largely unnoticed. Too bad the interest in this exhibit didn't carry over to the box office.

So much capital was spent on advertising and promotion that the film never even recovered its $80,000 in print costs. As Ted recalls, the movie may have made $30,000 nationwide. It's a shock, really. *Girl in Gold Boots* is hardly a masterpiece, but for what it is, it's pretty enjoyable; and though the dancing isn't all that impressive, the girls look really good trying. The songs aren't bad (the Nicholas Carras pieces are standouts), and Ted even tried to placate the biker flick fans by having the protagonists do battle with a couple of cycle-riding thugs.

Eventually the ads were altered in order to concentrate on the subject of motorcycling. One original tear-sheet stated, "Vibrant! Unpredictable! *Girl in Gold Boots* Swings Into Action!" only to later become, "Groovy Chicks Hell-Bent for Kicks!" Then "New Hit Songs!" transformed into "Out of Sight Mind-Blowing Music!" Unfortunately, the moviegoing public weren't buying it, much less motorcycle gangs who were far more interested in living their lives than watching someone's cinematic interpretation of same.

As hard as they tried, *Girl in Gold Boots* simply vanished out of sight. In RE/Search's *Incredibly Strange Films* Ted told Boyd Rice:

> In *Girl in Gold Boots* we tried to do a picture that was non-violent and clean—no nudity, *no anything* that would keep it from afternoon matinees or daytime television. And it was so tame [laughs] that audiences wouldn't support it even though it has beautiful dancing girls. It

was a typical story of a young girl from the Midwest coming to Hollywood, meeting good elements, some bad elements, and being exposed to choice. After seeing a lot of the undesirable aspects of the "great life" in Hollywood, she chooses to lead the clean, simple life and leaves the area. So it had a moral, something to offer there.

All true, but Michele had to wade through quite a pile of human garbage in order to see that this wasn't the life that she'd envisioned. Take these instances into account before labeling *Girl in Gold Boots* purely harmless or "tame" (as the film's director puts it): Buz is a convict on the run, continuing his crimes that culminate in the brutal beating and murder of another man.

A *Girl in Gold Boots* tear-sheet ad highlighting the "Golden Boots" contest.

Haunted House club owner Leo McCabe is a narcotics dealer who has his lead dancer, Joanie, hooked on pills of some sort. At a party Michele experiments with marijuana. It's not quite as wholesome as Ted remembers it, and probably wouldn't fit too well into a Saturday matinee program for seven- and eight-year-olds.

While not as gonzo as Russ Meyer's *Beyond the Valley of the Dolls* or even *Valley of the Dolls*, at least *Girl in Gold Boots* is nowhere near as inane as the similar-in-theme *Showgirls*. *Girl in Gold Boots* was made nearly 30 years before *Showgirls*, and even with its shortcomings, Ted's film never approaches the stupidity that radiates from that Paul Verhoeven Hollywood potboiler.

The fact that the protagonists are in L.A. during Christmastime, and not at home with family and friends, should be a tip-off for the viewer. These characters are hard up. They're three desperate souls spending the Christmas holiday at a go-go dance club. The film never reveals that these people are entirely without loved ones in their lives, but this sequence certainly depicts them as despondent and willing to do almost anything to see their dreams come true, regardless of whether it is legal or not. It's a small nuance in amongst a bunch of fluff, but it does help to foreshadow some of our characters' peculiar behaviors.

As Ted has stated, the story is simple. Michele meets Buz, a small-time crook, and he wants a driving partner. Michele's alcoholic father and his behavior are just the catalyst she needs to help jumpstart her new life as a dancer. Michele accepts the invitation and away they go, but Buz has other plans for Michele, and they're of a sexual nature. Little does he know that she's merely playing him for the ride (car ride that is): Michele feels no physical attraction to Buz. Along the way they pick up a hitchhiker, Critter. Critter is a draft dodger on his way out West to hide from the government. Once in Hollywood, Buz directs the three to a nightclub where his sister, Joanie, is the lead dancer. Buz introduces Michele to Joanie,

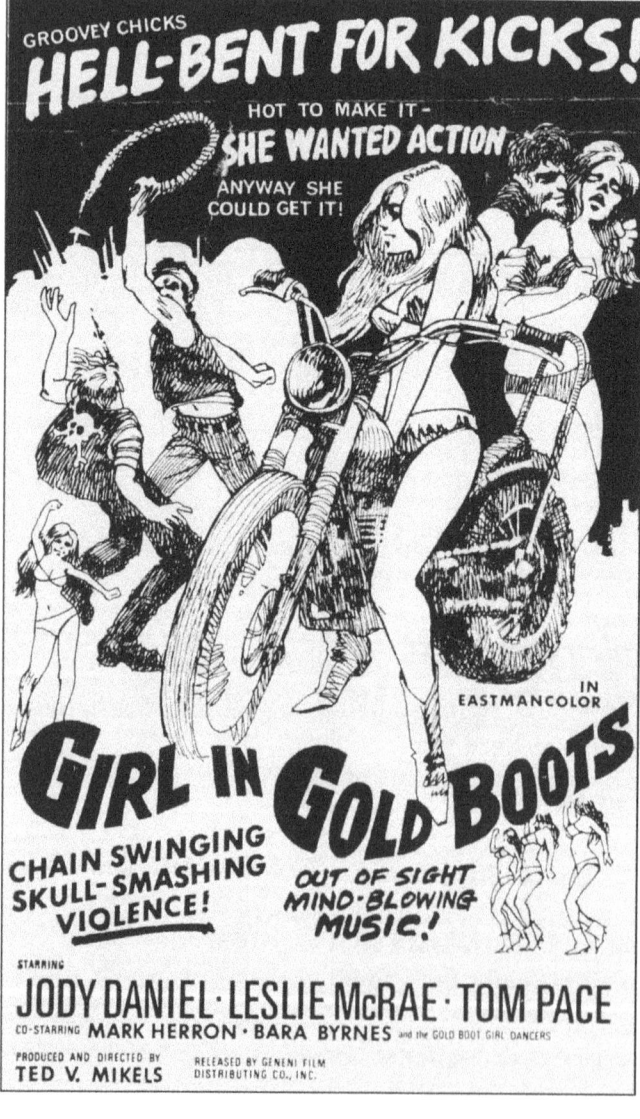

An example of altering the promotional materials in hopes of garnering a new audience. This particular version was aimed at fans of biker films.

The striking dancers from *Girl in Gold Boots*.

the current girl in gold boots, and the plan is for her to teach Michele the ropes. But are Michele's feet worthy of that shimmery footwear? Leo, the club owner, loves how Michele dances and hires her for the gig. Critter takes a job as a janitor and Buz joins Leo's narcotics syndicate. Michele is witness to it all, but continues to dance. All the while, Critter and Michele are falling more deeply in love with one another. Critter sees the evil of his surroundings, and Buz is still Buz, only out for himself. Critter and Michele flee. Buz and Leo are arrested, and all is well—or is it? At first it may seem okay, but if one were to look just beneath the surface of this shiny, and mostly happy, movie, then a whole lot more could be taken from this film.

Buz is turned over to the police and will be out on parole in no time, and it is likely that he will continue his life of crime. Joanie has a drug addiction to deal with; Michele has given up on her dream of being a dancer; and Critter has shed his anti-war sentiments. Is this really a happy ending? Buz is really a bad dude, and it's doubtful that a few years in the tank are going to change him much, if at all. Critter will be drafted, and if he doesn't become a war hero then he'll be wounded in some capacity, if not killed.

Ultimately, this allows Ted's frequent women-in-control theme to come into play, as Michele has effectively neutered Critter. He no longer holds onto his anti-war beliefs and concedes to do whatever it takes to make Michele the happiest. Critter is no longer thinking with the proper head—and who could blame him? Michele is quite the looker, but still she's pulling the strings that make Critter work. Michele is in control.

Nevertheless, where will this leave Michele when she finally realizes that she still wants to dance? The newness of the union will invariably wear off and she'll be faced with the reality of her actions. She has turned her back on *her* dreams and has manipulated Critter into something he wholeheartedly detests. If Critter doesn't return from the war physically in pieces, then his mental faculties are likely to have been blown to bits. Justly, Michele will probably wind up grooving on a stage at a county fair, a bingo rally or, more fittingly, the local VFW. Just food for thought.

Getting back to *Girl in Gold Boots* being a rock and roll musical (of sorts), the soundtrack to the film contained 14 numbers, but only seven were written for the film. Now, of those seven, only three move the storyline along, and one of those three is debatable.

Critter's acoustic piece "Lonesome Man" tells of his forlorn heart at the mercy of Michele, and then, of course, "Hello Michele" speaks for itself. The third tune doesn't move the story along in a dialogue sense, but rather in a physical sense. Critter is backstage messing around with a song he's written called "Do You Want to Laugh or Cry." Chris Howard, leader of the club's house band, the Third World, overhears this and offers to buy it from Critter. So while the lyrics don't really double as dialogue, the selling of the song does put cash in his pocket and allows him, and hopefully Michele, out of the dreaded clutches of Leo and his drug ring. *Girl in Gold Boots* isn't really a musical in the classic sense.

During the production of *Girl in Gold Boots*, Ted became involved with a man named Paul Burkette. Later, Burkette would help fund *The Doll Squad* and *Blood Orgy of the She Devils*. The two men met after Ms. McRae returned from her reading for *Girl in Gold Boots* and told Burkette that Ted Mikels was the *only* producer in Hollywood who didn't try to put the "moves" on her. Burkette was so impressed with this that he said, "I have to meet this man"; and so a long working friendship was born from Ted's ability to conduct himself in a professional manner. Besides, a man of Ted's considerable charms needs nothing as superfluous as a "casting couch" to bag his women.

Of further casting interest, the police officer who sits behind a desk and buzzes the door open for the prisoners was the original astro zombie himself, Rod Wilmoth, while Wilmoth's son turns up in a small part as the teenager who owns the dune buggy that Buz and Michele ride around in while on the beach. One odd fact is that while Buz, Critter and Michele tool down Hollywood Boulevard, a strange, squiggly cloud pattern can be

The sexy Michele Casey (Leslie McRae) posing in *Girl in Gold Boots*.

seen in the sky. Ted shot the scene merely because it looked fascinating. They later read that it was a NASA rocket gone awry!

Assistant cameraman James M. Farquharson supplied the vehicle that the three would drive across country on their way to their new lives, but this, in real-life, proved to be far more difficult than imagined. The darned car simply would not keep running. It was constantly breaking down and overheating, and the same was true for the motorcycles. More automotive hijinks involved the police car—or rather the faux police car. Unlike *Astro Zombies*, where the opportunity arose for them to film actual police officers and vehicles, the crew had to fashion some appliance to affix to the top of another clunker to "create" their top car. In the shot it looks authentic, but when described by Ted it seems unlikely that such a mish-mash of junk could come across so effectively. "I had merely mounted two cans shaped a little like lights, and a center can that could double as a siren, on a two-by-six board. Adding the sound effect sold it." Ted's certainly adept at making something out of nothing.

Girl in Gold Boots will never be the film that Ted is most remembered for, but at least the television show *Mystery Science Theater 3000* helped to expose millions to the movie world of Ted V. Mikels. When asked how he felt about the fun that the robots and Mike Nelson had at his expense, he replied, "I thought it was just fine, and some of it was really funny. Besides, I did get a bit of money out of it ... finally."

7. *The Corpse Grinders*

Synopsis from Pressbook

Sudden, inexplicable attacks by cats on their human owners, resulting in death and mutilation, surge through a metropolis. A young hospital intern, Dr. Howard Glass (Sean Kenney), and his nurse assistant Angie Robinson (Monika Kelly) seek the answer when her own pet feline assaults Glass without provocation. They theorize that an exotic canned cat food could be the cause after learning a fatally bitten woman's pet and Angie's ate the same brand. The food has turned partaking cats into man-eaters! Sleuthing eventually takes Glass and Angie to a dingy factory where the cat food is manufactured by two diabolical partners, Landau (Sanford Mitchell) and Maltby (J. Byron Foster). The basic ingredient consists of cadavers supplied by an accommodating but disreputable cemetery caretaker, Caleb (Warren Ball), and his wife Cleo (Ann Noble). It is in the factory that whirring power saws, red-stained chopping blocks, ominous cauldrons and a vociferous grinder transpose human flesh and bone into pussy cat puree. Desperate for fresh supplies of human flesh, Landau and Maltby ply skid row alleyways to fill the demand. For good measure they include the caretaker when Caleb insists on payment for his raw stock. Glass and Angie arrive at the factory on a ruse to get food samples for laboratory analysis, but are outsmarted by a suspicious Landau. A determined Angie, nevertheless, on her own returns late at night and sneaks in, but is trapped by Maltby, who, in the absence of Landau, is about to abscond with his withheld share of the profits. Angie is strapped on the conveyor leading into the grinder. Maltby's lecherous advances halt when Landau unrepentantly appears. A startled Maltby accidentally hits the controls and is dragged onto the running conveyor ahead of helpless Angie toward the flashing tips of the grinder knives. Meanwhile, Glass has alerted authorities. While he and the police, sirens screaming, converge on the factory, a maddened, fiendish Landau proceeds to aid his partner's demise. A freed Angie attempts to evade Landau's clutches as he himself is ironically caught and headed for the grinder, only to be devoured by a band of ravenous cats. Glass releases Angie.

Ticket-Selling Promotion (taken from pressbook)

1. "AMBULANCE in front of theater with sign 'For those who can't take the horror and shock of *The Corpse Grinders*.'"

2. "NURSE in lobby of theater with cot with sign 'Our nurse is available for our patrons who can't take the shock of *The Corpse Grinders*.'"

3. "MAN walking on street with head covered by long overcoat giving impression of being headless with sign 'I lost my head to *The Corpse Grinders*.'"

4. "MAN pulling donkey with sign on each side of donkey reading 'I'm going to miss *The Corpse Grinders* at _____ Theater ... and you know what I am!'"

5. "Run ads in the classified columns. Here is suggested copy:

'WANTED! Shock-proof people to see *The Corpse Grinders* at the _____ Theater.'

'WANTED! People with guts who dare see human bodies ground before your very eyes by *The Corpse Grinders* machine!'

'WANTED! People who dare sit thru the bloodiest-weirdest film ever made, *The Corpse Grinders*, now at _____ Theater.'"

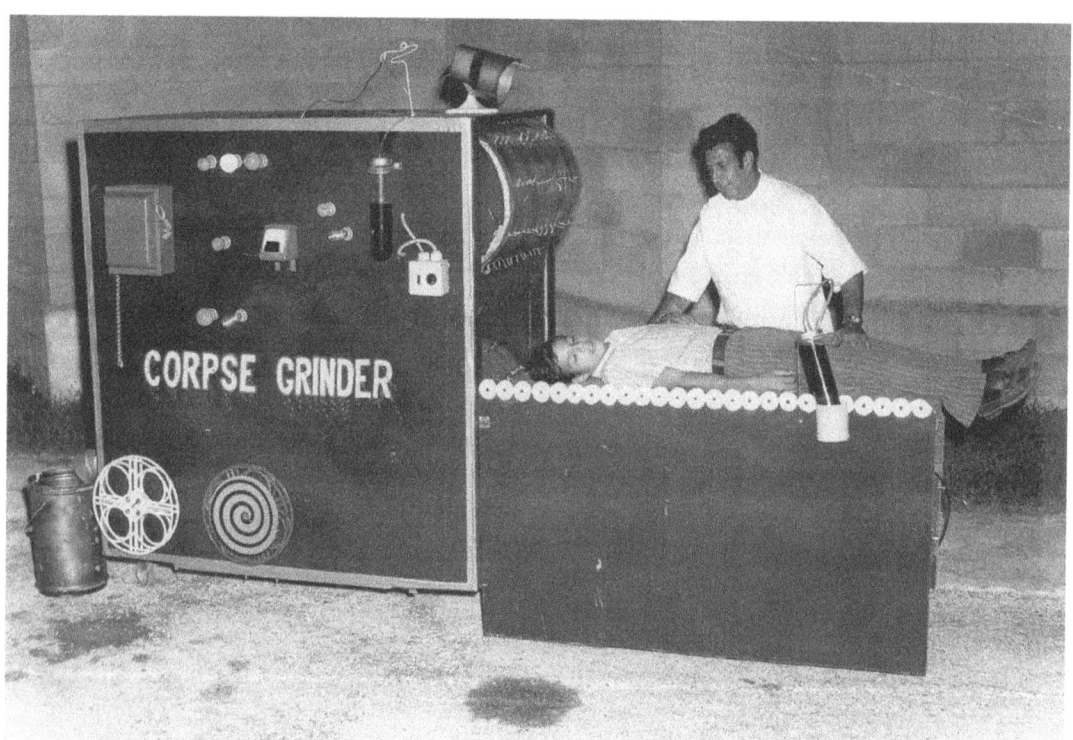

The Crest Theater in Hollywood, California, won the contest for building the most accurate replica of the corpse grinding machine. This was a one-off contest that took place during *The Corpse Grinders*' (1971) later, incredibly successful run under "The Final Dimension in Shock" banner.

6. "HAVE AN AD INVITING the first 10 people who dare sit thru a midnight screening of *The Corpse Grinders* (in a pitch black theater) be guests of the man who grinds the human bodies to shreds before their very own eyes in *The Corpse Grinders*."

7. "NO PATRONS dare be seated during the film until after the first human body is ground by the corpse grinding machine."

8. "Have man in Santa Claus costume walk in street with sign reading, 'I just had to come back to see the shocker of the century *The Corpse Grinders*, OR 'I just couldn't wait till next Xmas to see it!'"

9. "WHERE FILM plays in hot weather have man in raccoon coat and ear muffs on street with sign '*The Corpse Grinders*: left me freezing with fright. Chilled me to the bone.'"

10. "Have sound truck have record[ing] of grinding noise played thru speakers with announcement "You are hearing the shocking sounds of human bodies being ground to shreds in the blood curdling ghastly machine in *The Corpse Grinders* now at _____ Theater. Do you have the courage to see this gory sight? On the screen before your very eyes!'"

Credits

Cast: Sean Kenney (Dr. Howard Glass); Monika Kelly (Angie Robinson); Sanford Mitchell (Landau); J. Byron Foster (Maltby); Warren Ball (Caleb); Ann Noble (Cleo); Vince Barbi (Monk); Harry Lovejoy (the Neighbor); Earl Burnam (Mr. De Sisto); Zena Foster (Mrs. Babcock); Ray Dannis (Mr. Babcock); Drucilla Hoy (Tessie); Charles "Foxy" Fox (Willie); Stephen Lester (the Mortician); William Kirschner (B.K., mortician's assistant); Curt Matson (Paul, the Stranger); George Bowden (David, the Intern); Don Ellis (Factory Worker); Mike Garrison (Michael); Andy Collings (Dr. De Sisto's secretary, Donna); Mary Ellen Burke (Annie); Sherri Vernon (Wife); Richard Gilden (Husband)

Production: *produced and directed by*: Ted V. Mikels. *screenplay*: Arch Hall, Joseph L. Cranston. *cameraman*: Bill Anneman. *sound recordists*: Art Names, John Curran. *lighting*: Paul Wilmoth. *make-up*: Sherri Vernon. *set design*: John Robinson, Laura Young. *special effects*: Gary Heacock. *still cameraman*: Ron Char. *script clerk*: Carol Mancini. *assistant cameramen*: Curt Matson, John Anneman. *production manager*: John Curran. *editor—film, sound, music*: Ted V. Mikels. *music supplied by*: Music Industries. *filmed in*: EASTMAN COLOR. *Running Time*: 73 minutes. *aspect ratio*: shot at full frame and projected at 1.85:1. A T.V. Mikels Film Production. *released by*: Geneni Film Distributing Co., Inc. *released*: 1971.

The Film

Will you forget about pet food for just one minute?—Dr. Philip Glass from *The Corpse Grinders*

The Corpse Grinders is the perfect film by which to judge Ted Mikels' droll sense of humor. Make no mistake, Ted is very serious about the craft of moviemaking, but he's hardly taking himself seriously here (or at least we hope not). There are no artistic pretensions with this picture. The creator is fully aware of his creation and its exploitative trappings. He's winking at us with a devious grin, and we're going along with all the ballyhoo—hook, line and sinker. The film is a strange assimilation of neo-gothic horrors and campiness that's more akin to a spook house ride than anything remotely frightening. All the more, *The Corpse Grinders* gleefully waltzes onto the screen and successfully entertains for its cozy 72-minute running time.

Ted could never have known that such an absurd concoction of ideas would be so

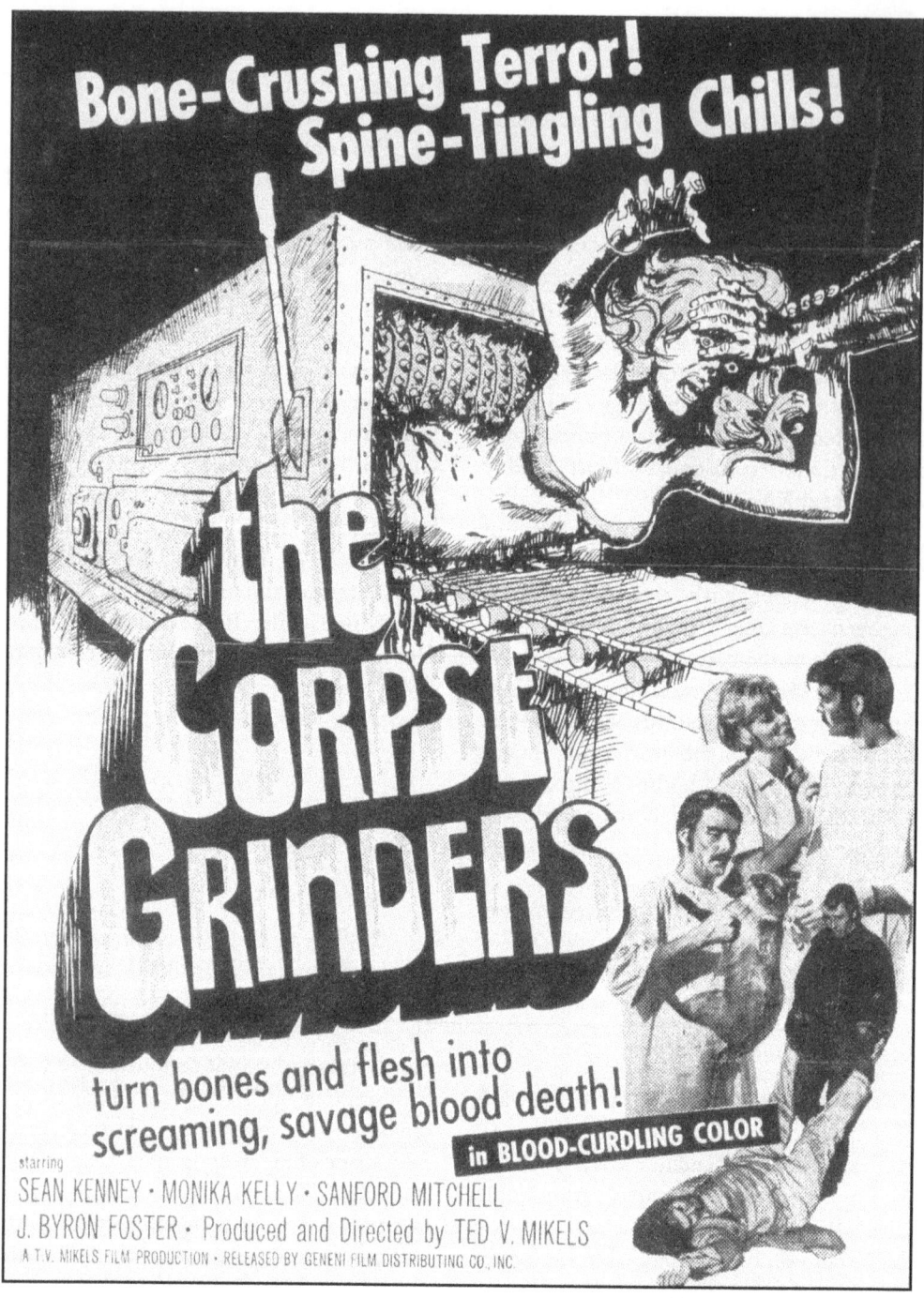

Original one-sheet for *The Corpse Grinders*. Notice that the victim is very much alive and not at all a "corpse," as the films title suggests.

incredibly successful, though he had been cooking it up for some time. A pet food company substituting USDA Grade-Z slaughterhouse floor sweepings for USA bottom-of-the-barrel human beings is a far-out concept that ranks up there with some of cinema's most curious. Domestic cats developing a taste for human flesh, and then wreaking havoc on their owners and their owners' lovers, ranks up there, too. It's enough to make you giggle; and, of course, that's exactly what Ted wanted us to do. However, consider the question wryly posed by Welch Everman in his book *Cult Horror Films*: "It makes you wonder why dogs don't attack horses, doesn't it?" Indeed.

But where did it all come from? In 1966 exploitation practitioner Arch Hall, Sr. presented Ted with a working script. It's odd that Hall didn't see himself producing the madcap project, as he had already helped make a number of low-rent cheapies, like *The Choppers*, *Eegah*, *Wild Guitar* and *The Thrill Killers*. Just the same, Ted soon fell in love with the piece whose original title (as Ted recollects) was *The Cat and the Canary*. Who knows what would've become of this fantastic slice of low-budget cinema had it carried such an insipid and largely misleading banner? As Ted recalls:

> Arch Hall brought me the script in 1969, and the re-writing began. I filmed it later that year, and was totally enthused with doing it. The movie actually hit the screen only a month or two after I'd completed it. It was the first time I paid back all deferments, and all bills including lab costs, studio rentals, and the cast and crew; and this happened all within five months after the release! We were already playing a substantial number of dates in hardtop theaters and drive-ins in 1970 and 1971, and out-grossing all the competition.

The Corpse Grinders cost under $50,000 to make and find its way to the big screen. Was it easy gathering all that capital? Ted didn't think so.

> Actually, to start the movie, I had managed to save up $1,700, and borrowed $2,500 each from four investors, so I had $11,700 to buy all the raw stock and pay labs as I went. Then I borrowed $5,000 more from one of my sub-distributors, and the total of $16,700 was all the cash I had to work with and finish the movie to an answer print. You know how tight that was to work with? I even scored the movie myself from a music library I had purchased outright from a German company. Ultimately, the ending cost was around $47,000.

When all was said and done, in excess of $10,000,000 exchanged hands, though not nearly enough was to pass through those of the film's prime mover. Ted's quick to point out that it earned those figures when movie tickets were only fifty cents, or even a quarter. That's somewhere in the neighborhood of $200,000,000 by today's standards! Not bad for a man whose career has been constantly belittled by Hollywood executives and film critics alike. Not bad at all. Even the haughty (oftentimes snooty) British publication *The Overlook Film Encyclopedia* gave the movie their seal of approval with the words, "An endearingly ramshackle exercise in bad taste...."

In keeping with his desire to maintain independence from the powers-that-be (ones that obviously did not share his vision), Ted built many of his sets on sound stages, and scouted existing locations for the remainder of his settings. The constructed scenery imbues some sequences with a surreal tone, while the real-life locales give the viewer something more tactile to hold onto or identify with. Monetary necessity was no doubt the culprit behind such a peculiar fusion of sensibilities, but it is no less effective in its ability to disconcert watchers, or at the very least keep them off-guard.

One impressive locality included Ted's very own home, or, better yet, his castle. This effective setting doubled as the fog-filled cemetery, and the "Farewell Acres" insignia on the wrought iron gate was, in reality, the entrance to Ted's estate at 3000 Sparr Boulevard, Glendale, California. Always eager to give his films that high-pro glow, Ted pulled some mighty lofty strings, and an even more massive dwelling made its way into the film. This particular mansion, and its grounds, belonged to the great Cecil B. DeMille.

Ted remembers an amusing incident on this day of shooting, which he related to in-

Caleb (Warren Ball) peering through the iron gates of "Farewell Acres" (Ted V. Mikels' castle entrance) in *The Corpse Grinders*.

terviewer David Konow for *Outré* magazine (no. 29) in 2002:

> Like I said, when you're shooting without money you never know who can't be there. Most of the time everybody was very loyal, and faithful. In any event, on *Corpse Grinders* we had permission to shoot on Cecil B. DeMille's estate. It was our first day of shooting; here we had about 40 people standing around and waiting to be told what to do. And here comes the cameraman yelling out so everyone can hear, "Hey Ted, can you come over here and show me how to load this thing up?"

One of the primary factors in the film's success is the cast's incredibly straightfaced and deadpan performances. It would have been all-too-easy for them to camp up their lines, but Ted wisely allowed the film's insane premise to do all *that* work for them. The actors deliver such doozies as, "Ah, maybe one day I'll can 'em," or, "I'm sick of your bones!" to Caleb's near-constant refrain of "No money! No Meat!" with authority— the type of authority usually reserved for more serious excursions in theater or film.

Naturally, no small credit should go to the highly-successful promotional angle; and who better to explain it than the man who helped contrive it? To wit:

> In the greater Los Angeles area, *The Corpse Grinders* raked in $190,000, and that was in only one week! It played against *Willard* and *Tora! Tora! Tora!* and successfully beat them out every time. We had a great ad campaign, though. When the movie began to get "legs," as they call it in the business, we began adding the promotional ingredients to make it fly. My sales manager at the time, Mr. Bob Kilgore, knew all the movie sub-distributors very well, and he recruited some talented folks to help round out a real and

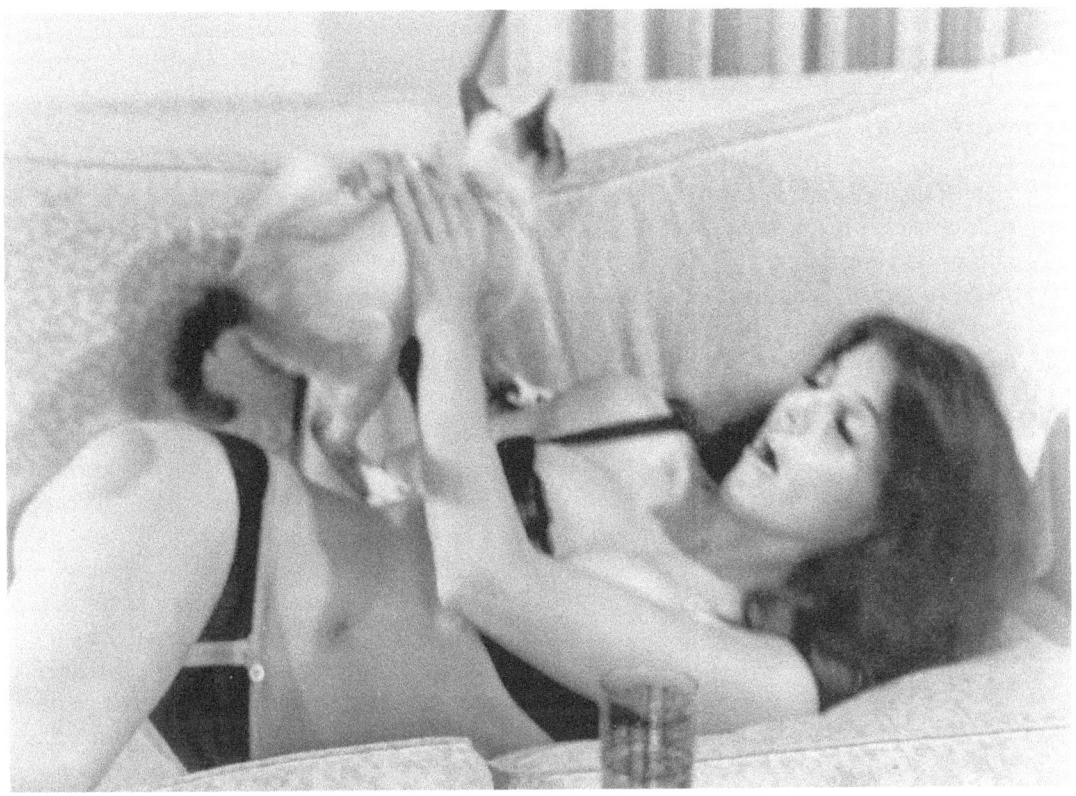

Donna (Andy Collings) suffers the dreaded cat-attack in *The Corpse Grinders*.

genuine sales campaign. At first, with the promotional things we did, the three movies were a hit; then we added "The Final Dimension in Shock," and we would not play any theater or drive-in that would not comply with our scheduling of radio, newspaper and TV ads. They also had to follow our demands of theatrical trailers on the screen for two full weeks before the play date. We even insisted they make patrons sign the "Certificate of Assurance." If the theater managements did not agree to follow all of our very successful procedures, we would not let them have the show. At first, some theaters refused to play the trilogy, so we passed on them. [Note: The other two films in question were *The Undertaker and His Pals* and *The Embalmer*.] Then, after the tremendous box-office successes we were running up, they all got in line—Pacific Theaters, United Artists, and others like them. They found out the grosses we were doing were often out-grossing their movies as our competition. The more gimmicks we used, the more successful the playdates were—like contests where theater managers built a corpse grinding machine for their theater's lobby, nurses taking blood pressure, ambulances outside theaters and loads of other fun stuff. The campaigns evolved from the original success of *The Corpse Grinders*. We eventually compounded the movement by adding the second and third movies to make the package as successful as it was, with "The Final Dimension in Shock." We kept it that way until we played the majority of the country. By then, I had purchased 100 or more prints of each of the three movies, totaling an outlay in prints alone of around half a million dollars, and my shipping cost to theaters was over one hundred and fifty thousand dollars. The income kept my offices, and staff of seven at Columbia Pictures Studios, then later Samuel Goldwyn Studios, for about three years before the income fizzled out.

One gem of a gimmick involved a mock-up radio show called "Solid Gold Countdown from the Wax Museum" hosted by Jolly Jack J. Posey. This 30-minute program had Jolly Jack spinning records from the "swinging 60s," with a wraparound of trailers from "The Final Dimension in Shock" and an interview with the film's producer, Lucius Fangstein. Fangstein is even more obviously bogus than Jolly Jack, as he talks of emotional unrest on the set of *The Corpse Grinders*, the importance of the on-duty nurses, and the signing of the "Certificate of Assurance." The over-dramatic Fangstein even goes so far as to explain the unusual origin of the corpse grinding machine. According to Fangstein, the contraption was manufactured in the early days of Hollywood, but the creators of the film that it was to be featured in were unable to bring themselves to use it. Of course, Ted and company were the *only* ones ready and willing to fire the sucker up.

This ridiculous broadcast was piped into the speakers of drive-in patrons as they awaited showtime, and while everything mentioned was completely preposterous, it worked. *The Corpse Grinders* was a success, becoming number 11 on the *Box Office* "Top Fifty Weekly"—not all bad for such a small production. Even the master of the modern horror novel, Stephen King, found himself drawn to the film, reminiscing in his book *On Writing: A Memoir of the Craft* (page 66): "When Tabby went into labor with him [son Joe], I was at a drive-in movie in Brewer with a friend—it was a Memorial Day triple feature, three horror films. We were on the third movie [*The Corpse Grinders*] and the second six-pack when the guy in the office broke in with an announcement ... [which] rang across the entire parking lot: 'Steve King, please go home! Your wife is in labor! Steve King, please go home! Your wife is going to have the baby!'"

Longtime fans of Ted's films are surely aware that occasionally his works become bogged down with entirely too many subplots. Even more, sometimes his subplots *have* subplots! Ted just has so many ideas that an hour and half isn't near enough time for him to execute his plan. It can certainly

Genini Distribution recycled *The Undertaker and His Pals* as a "B" slot feature for *The Corpse Grinders*.

be seen as a fault in regards to his filmmaking style, but that "fault" is an inimitable part of his charm. With *The Corpse Grinders*, however, Ted kept his "subplot temptations" at bay, and the film plays out fairly straight, with only one or two unexplainable surprises popping up at the end. Apparently, author Bill Landis felt the same, as he wrote in his book *Sleazoid Express*: "Little more than an hour long, *The Corpse Grinders* is a miracle of concision, and its garish colors and tawdry, precise sense of composition help make it a standout in the genre." Agreed.

The Corpse Grinders features future castle lady Sherri Vernon in her silver screen debut. Sherri mostly worked behind the scenes, but she did wind up being the first to suffer the dreaded cat-attack. Ted mused nostalgically of this incident. "She was so believable when I threw the cat at her, as she opened the door, that I myself jumped in front of the camera three times to save her, ruining the shot each time!"

Sherri was also chosen as the corpse grinding machine's inaugural victim, as she was the smallest person in the cast and crew. The grinding machine crushes Sherri (and all of its victims) at one end, flashes some red lights, and then spits her pink, pulverized flesh out the other. The concoction oozing from a drainpipe affixed to this plywood box of mechanized death? A ground beef and sawdust mixture—a mixture that Ted oftentimes points out was a large part of their minuscule budget.

Quite possibly the most infamous exploitation drive-in triple feature in the history of cinema: *The Corpse Grinders*, the old standby *The Undertaker and His Pals* and the Italian shocker (not so much, really) *The Embalmer*. Notice how the "Certificate of Assurance" takes up as much space as the graphics for the films themselves.

In the end *The Corpse Grinders* borders on parody. So many of the genre's ghoulish conventions are on display: dead bodies, heavy fog, full moons, cemeteries, madmen, and a diabolical contraption made for killing (er ... grinding). These very familiar characteristics are handled by Ted in a light-

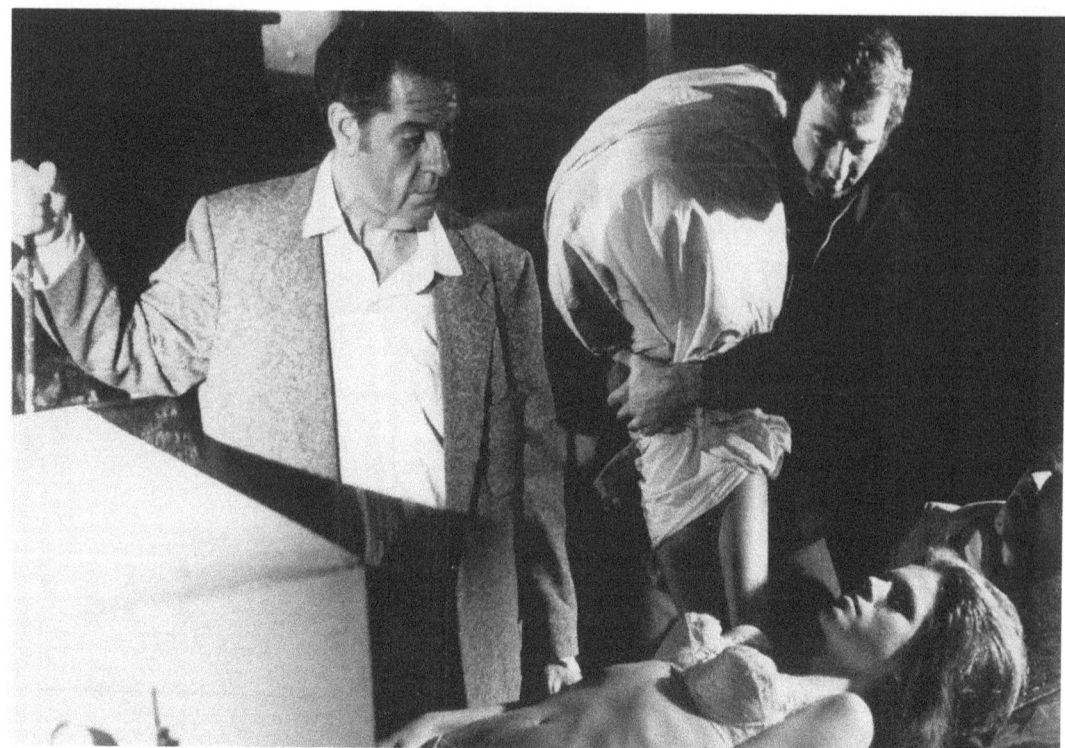

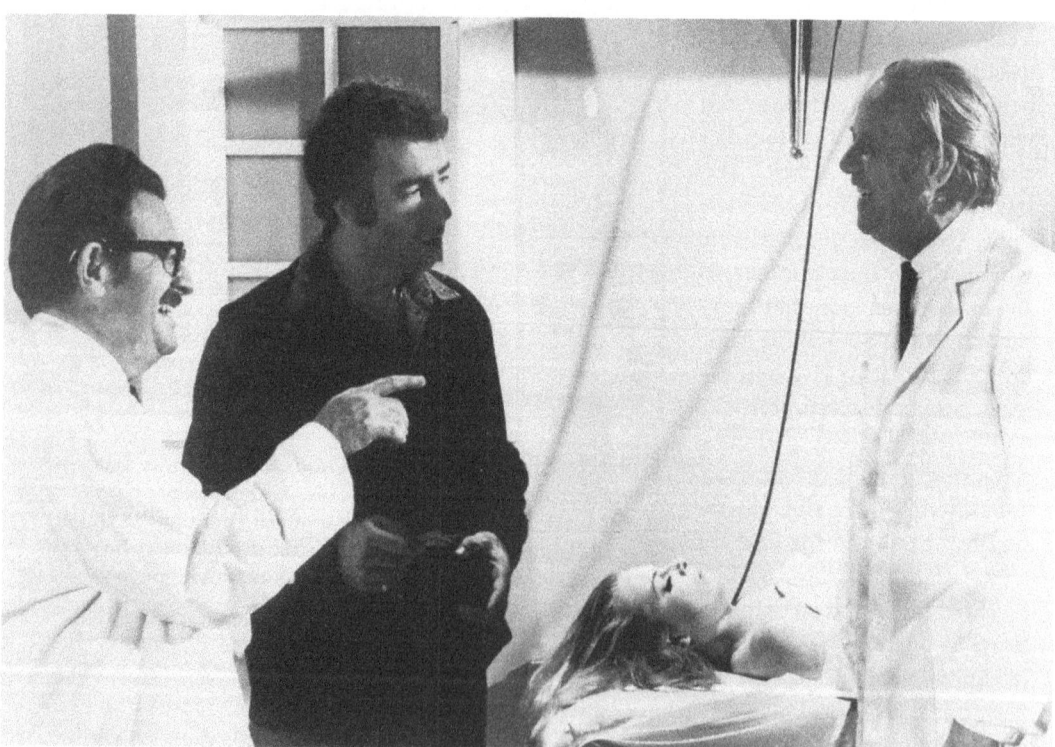

Top: A victim (Sherri Vernon) is being prepared for the jaws of the corpse grinding machine by Lotus Cat Food moguls Maltby (Byron Foster) and Landau (Sanford Mitchell) in *The Corpse Grinders*. *Bottom:* A scene in the morgue with morticians (William Kirshner and Stephen Lester), Landau (Sanford Mitchell) and an unidentified victim of *The Corpse Grinders*.

Top: A fantastic double feature that made its way through England, despite the best efforts of the British censor board. Notice that both films received an "X" rating. *Bottom:* While the stuffy British censor board found very little amusing about *The Corpse Grinders*, this small tear-sheet teaser ad is proof positive that director Ted V. Mikels did.

hearted, near-carnival fashion. Even the heavy use of colored lighting conjures up a midway-type atmosphere. Every step of the wacky way Ted keeps the movie appropriately zany and off-kilter enough to make one wonder just what the heck is going to happen next. The film is fiendish and funky, creepy and most certainly corny. Author John McCarty wrote in his book *Splatter Movie Guide Vol. II*: "At least Mikels had more brains than to take this all seriously; the same can't be said for the British censor, who ordered ten minutes clipped from the film's already scant running time." In this abridged version, *The Corpse Grinders* played second to Anthony Balch's *Horror Hospital*.

Still, *The Corpse Grinders* is not played for belly laughs, though it's difficult not to chuckle at the undertaker's use of chicken flavored embalming fluids. It's morbid yet totally ridiculous, and the entire film plays with the idea that morbid can, in fact, be funny. The ratings board didn't quite see it this way. Ted was incredulous when he received an R-rating. As recounted to Michael Weldon in *Psychotronic Video* number 32: I couldn't believe it, and called the man and said, "I can't believe you gave it an R. It's a campy joke, funny!" He said, "Sir, grinding up cadavers for cat food is not funny!"

8. *Blood Orgy of the She Devils*

Synopsis from Pressbook

Mara (Lila Zaborin), a "black" witch, practitioner of the occult, black magic and evil incarnate, is the leader of a coven of voluptuous, scantily clad beautiful young women who vent their sadistic love for passion and pain on helpless victims as they perform the body ritual of a hideously macabre dance of death, carrying aloft flaming torches and plunging spears into their human male sacrifices in a gory ceremony to titillate their pulsating pleasures and sanctify the evil desires of this Queen of the Witches. Mara is approached by Rodannus (Ray Myles), enemy agent of a foreign power, accompanied by his henchman, Barth (Paul Wilmoth), with the request that an Ambassador representative to the United Nations from another country be eliminated by means of her magic powers. During this meeting, Rodannus demands proof of her mystical power, and she causes a wine glass to shatter in his hands. When the enemy agent leaves, Mara keeps the bloodied handkerchief he had used on his cut hand. Lorraine (Leslie McRae), a newcomer to Mara's coven, persuades her boyfriend, Mark (Tom Pace), an unbeliever, to attend a séance. Astounded by the results, during which Mara has conjured up two spirit guides and a ghost, and worried about Lorraine's involvement, Mark decides to consult Dr. Helford (Victor Izay), a "white" witch or warlock, and an expert on psychic phenomena. After Mara has caused the Ambassador's death at a party, Rodannus fears that she may turn her powers against him, and sends Barth to kill both Mara and her high priest Toruke (William Bagdad). Barth also kills a young girl, Roberta (Linn Henson), but she manages to scratch his face before she dies. Meanwhile, Dr. Helsford agrees to help Mark. By means of witchcraft, Mara has caused Barth to kill a cat instead. She now restores Toruke to life, and, using Rodannus' bloodied handkerchief and Barth's scratched skin from the fingernail parings of the dead girl, Mara eliminates both Barth and Rodannus in a macabre and bloody manner. Mark and Lorraine are to attend another séance at Mara's residence, and they discuss with Dr. Helsford the possibilities of age regression under hypnosis, which Mark is to undergo. The doctor warns them of the dangers of dabbling in the black arts. He psychometrizes an amulet Lorraine is wearing which Mara had given her as protection against unfriendly demons. After the pair leave for the meeting, the disturbed Dr. Helsford, sensing an evil aftermath, enlists the aid of three other scientists interested in psychic phenomena, and they decide to visit Mara's home where the meeting is to be held. During regression, Mark is shown to have been killed by Indians in a previous life as a frontiersman, and now, drugged by Mara, he is to be offered up as a human sacrifice in an effort to conjure up Lucifer, the Devil himself. Mara and her coven of witches are soon terrified as an unseen presence takes over. The building rumbles and trembles as utter chaos reigns. The unseen terror possesses the bodies of the young witches, who turn against Toruke and kill him, and they then turn against each other. Outside, Dr. Helsford fights the evil within by means of exorcism and manages to restore order and sanity, driving the evil unseen presence away. When the quartet of scientists enter the building, all is death and destruction. Mark, Lorraine and all the others are dead. Only a bat clings to the ceiling, and, dislodging it, Dr. Helford, knowing its true identity, kills it and throws it on some burning coals. At last Mara pays for the consequences of evil, as her translucent, vaporous form floats upwards in a raging, screaming death.

producer: Paul Burkett. *production manager*: John Curran. *assistant director*: Joel Classer. *unit manager*: Phil Braverman. *still photography*: Ron Char. *sets and props*: Eric Nelson. *special FX*: Lee James. *film editor*: T.V. Mikels. *associate editor, sound effects*: James Christopher. *optical effects, titles*: Van Der Veer Photo. *ambulance furnisher*: Schaeffer Ambulance. *dance costumes*: Eros. *special electronic music*: Carl Zittrer. *choreography*: John Nicolai. *photography*: Anthony Salinas. *written, produced, and directed by*: Ted V. Mikels. *running time*: 79 minutes. Color. *aspect ratio*: shot full-frame and projected at 1.85:1. *shot and released*: 1972.

Credits

Cast: Lila Zaborin (Mara); Tom Pace (Mark); Leslie McRae (Lorraine); Victor Izay (Dr. Helsford); William Bagdad (Toruke); Ray Myles (Rodannus); Kebrina Kinkaid (Sharon); Paul Wilmot (Barth); Annik Borel (Witch Who Is Stoned); Curt Matson (Dr. Paxton); Linn Henson (Roberta); John Nicolai (Dr. Everest); John Ricco (Royce Littleton); Erica Campbell (Girl at Séance); Sherri Vernon (Witch Burned at Stake); Sean Shanna Day (Drummer); Dallas Beardsley (Dancer); Lister Shaw (Dick); Carla Green (Dancer); Sam Scar (Bishop); Brett Marriott (Bishop's Helper); Jeff Goodman (Bishop's Helper); Laine Karlos (Dancer); George Wilhelm (Gilbert DePlait); Kim Sudol (Dancer); Vincent Barbi (Indian Chief); Chris Capen (Member of Séance); Al Esbjorn (Guard at Dungeon); John Willard (Guard in Dungeon); Augie Treibach (Member of Séance); Lillian McBride (the Apparition)

Production: *assistant cameramen*: Curt Matson, Don Caldwell. *gaffer*: Paul Wilmoth. *grips*: Michael Argandar, Gary Shermaine. *sound recorder*: William Nipper. *script supervisor*: Dodie Warren. *make-up*: Sherri Vernon. *wardrobe*: Celine Mikels. *assistant to the*

The Film

WARNING! The producer warns against indulging or experimenting in occultism or the psychic sciences as presented in "Blood Orgy of the She Devils" without professional advice!—Tagline from the *Blood Orgy of the She Devils* one-sheet.

In 1972, Ted V. Mikels was still riding the financial wave generated by *The Corpse Grinders*, and he was about to embark on his most ambitious project to that point in his moviemaking career. This time, all the campiness of *Astro Zombies* and *The Corpse Grinders* was thrown completely out the window. Ted's cinematic offspring was going to be a fairly serious piece involving witchcraft and black magic: *Blood Orgy of the She Devils*.

Now, contrary to what has been written time and time again, Ted did not feverishly study the occult for two solid years in order to pen his screenplay. Actually, he attended séances and boned up on the subject rather infrequently over the course of those two years. He wasn't the slightest bit interested in practicing the black arts, and found himself merely curious about the subject. Lots of people are interested in the occult, and Ted figured it would make good fodder for another horror picture—and he was right.

One-sheet for *Blood Orgy of the She Devils* (1972).

Ultimately it was Ted's personal life that seemed to have a major influence on his desire to get away from the lighthearted, screwball stuff that he'd been making in the past. Ted was going through a divorce. Somehow he was keeping up the castle with Sherri Vernon at his side, and a home with wife Geneva in another place altogether. Such an arrangement could surely not last forever, and in light of Ms. Vernon's spitfire demeanor and jealousy, Mrs. Ted V. Mikels decided to terminate the marriage.

As mentioned before, Ted sublimated his giddy side in favor of something more heavy-handed for this film, and few, if any, scenes include intentional (or unintentional) humor. This is not to suggest that the movie is perfect or even close to perfect—it isn't.

The pacing is a little slow, and of particular note in the film-flubs department is a flashback sequence in which the turn-of-the-century witch hunters can be seen sporting black dress slacks. It's a minor complaint, but since those particular scenes are amazingly well handled for such a low-budget production, it's a shame that more attention wasn't paid to the wardrobe.

Another problem involves Dr. Helsford, played by Victor Izay. Helsford is a white witch and also a college professor of paranormal and psychic phenomena. During the course of the film he lectures two of his inquisitive students about the occult, at one point denouncing the practices of the witch hunters of old. But at the end of the film, he and his cohorts have absolutely no problems whatsoever dispatching the contemporary witches they've found residing in Southern California. It's another flaw, but it hardly ruins the picture.

It's not surprising that things of that nature went unnoticed, as Ted's head was in a whirlwind and he literally locked himself away for ten days to write the script. As he recalls, this was the only time in his career that he followed the screenplay to the letter. He didn't change one solitary thing about it. Maybe he should have, but once the words were on the page it was time to raise funds for the picture and get on with casting. Forty-three thousand dollars was the (black) magic number, and a large portion of the cast and crew from *Girl in Gold Boots* returned to help out their old friend, even though no one received a dime from their previous venture with him. So why would a group of young actors put their monetary livelihoods in potential danger a second time around? Ted's longtime friend Tura Satana knows why: "Ted is a great person to work with and is very stringent in his approach to the scripts, but he is also one of the most warm, wonderful and lovable men in this industry."

So, a standard five-week shooting schedule was underway, with the bulk of the picture being shot in Ted's beloved castle on Sparr Boulevard. So much of the film was lensed there that it almost becomes a guided tour of Ted's not-so-humble abode. The balance of the scenes were photographed on a Hollywood soundstage, and here Ted was able to utilize his directing skills to the fullest, as he had access to a 19-foot camera crane that allowed for some evocative overhead shots during the black masses. Other impressive scenes include the flashback sequences in which cute-as-a-cupcake Sherri Vernon is tortured, interrogated and finally burned at the stake for the practice of witchcraft.

Blood Orgy of the She Devils marked the first time Ted was able to employ special optical effects, such as lightning and evil green auras. Another first was his use of an electronic musical score composed entirely on a synthesizer. Not to leave his old pal Nicholas Carras out of the equation, Ted discussed his ideas for the soundtrack with Carras, and both artists agreed that a different composer would be needed to help Ted realize his aural vision. Carl Zittrer was called in for the job. Zittrer was an associate of Ted's in regards to Bob Clark's *Children Shouldn't Play with Dead Things*. Zittrer was handling the score for *Children*, and Ted's company Geneni was dealing with the film's distribution.

Just as *Blood Orgy of the She Devils* marks some firsts for Ted, it also marked the end of his working relationships with Leslie McRae, Tom Pace and Victor Izay. Fantastic character actor William Bagdad would hold on for only one more, *The Doll Squad*. When asked why he opted to no longer work with such a talented lot of performers, Ted replied, "Well, around Hollywood it is frowned upon to keep using the same group of actors and actresses. So, I decided to look for other talent when it came time to cast *The Doll Squad*."

As good as all these folks were in *Girl in Gold Boots*, they're even better here. Ms. McRae was really starting to warm up to the

It's curtains for Mark (Tom Pace) at the hands (er ... spear) of Lorraine (Leslie McRae), who's flanked by two of her fellow demon dancers in *Blood Orgy of the She Devils*.

Tanawaka. When confronted about this bit of silliness, the film's director stated:

> It was really difficult to get Lila in a trance-like frame of mind during those sequences, and she brought that Tonto-speak to the role herself. I had not written it that way in the script, but I was okay with it; and as hard as it was to get her to the point of being capable of doing those scenes, I wasn't about to call for a retake.

Of course, Ted couldn't leave out two of his favorite ingredients, and the first, the women-in-charge theme, is in full force here. Mara is most definitely in power for the majority of the film, and it doesn't hurt matters any that she has a vicious bevy of half-naked beauties, the she devils of the film, who dance one minute and stab men to death the next. These girls really know how to put their best foot forward. The second morsel that Ted threw in for his own amusement was the killing of a United Nations ambassador. Ted certainly has an obsession with spies, espionage and international intrigue, and if he can work some such subplot into his story, then he's going to do it.

camera, and apparently took some dancing lessons between 1968 and '72. Tom Pace seems more at ease on screen in *Blood Orgy* than in the past, and Victor Izay steals every scene he's in. His performance is genuine, and one can really tell that he believes in the material, the project and, most of all, his director. Ted couldn't have asked for more from any of them.

Newcomer Lila Zaborin turns in an especially impressive performance as Mara, the Queen of the Witches. Ms. Zaborin screams a lot and, when not testing her vocal capacity, manages to emit a creepy vocalization that helps the film overstep its low budget. The only questionable aspect of her portrayal is her Tonto-speak as the Indian spirit

One interesting footnote involves the casting of Kebrina Kinkaid as Sharon. Ms. Kinkaid was a well-known real-life psychic in and around Hollywood, with various Hollywood stars among her clientele. Another note worthy of mention is that during the dance segments Sean Shannaday, on the bongos, appears to provide the rhythm that the girls slink and gyrate to. In truth, they were dancing to a track that was performed and recorded earlier by Ted himself.

In the amusing mother-of-invention department, William Bagdad's character, the picture. Editors found it offensive and suggested that they run the ad with the truncated moniker *Orgy of the She Devils*, as opposed to its full handle. What the heck were they thinking? Their suggestion reads more like a porno title than a horror picture. Consequently, the movie was under-advertised and failed to match the financial success of his previous feature, *The Corpse Grinders*. What's really mind-boggling is that in the South, that very same year, Herschell Gordon Lewis re-sold his movie *Gore Gore Girls* to theaters as *Blood Orgy*, and he encountered no problems whatsoever.

Getting the film's entire title in the papers wasn't the only problem with the production of *Blood Orgy of the She Devils*. Perhaps the project was plagued—or cursed—by some supernatural entity that felt that humans were delving into a realm of the cosmos where they did not belong. Over the five weeks of shooting many fires broke out on the set, seemingly without rhyme or reason. The most frightening fiery incident involved the burning of Sherri Vernon as a convicted witch. Ted recounted:

Mara (Lila Zaborin) in a non-screaming moment during *Blood Orgy of the She Devils*.

> I wanted a raging fire in front of the camera, with Sherri in the background, thus creating the illusion that Sherri was really on fire. This is not a new concept or procedure. Lots of times directors would simply fill an empty film can with a flammable liquid, light it on fire and hold it in front of the camera during the take. Well, we were shooting outside, and I wasn't about to take a chance with the wind and it potentially kicking up at just the wrong moment. So I had my stage hands create a metal pan with chains attached to each corner so that the thing could be pulled away in case the wind did decide to blow in the direction of Sherri, who was tied to a stake and couldn't get away if something like that occurred. Well, guess what? Just as the scene was underway the wind blew the flames directly at Sherri, and I screamed for the stage hands to jerk the flaming metal pan away and they did. Sherri was so fortunate not to have been burned even a little bit. I am so glad that I had the foresight to have that special effect rigged in that way.

Toruke, sports some Viking-like head gear, complete with devilish-looking horns. As Ted divulged, "The horns on William's headpiece were fashioned from empty toilet paper rolls." Inventive indeed, and even the most observant viewer would never notice.

Author John McCarty points out in his *Splatter Movie Guide* that "The title of this film implies more than it actually delivers either in the gore or sex department, though there is some of both." Even writer Welch Everman noticed this, and states in his book *Cult Horror Films*, "No film could possibly live up to this title...." Indeed, while this incredibly lurid banner would have grabbed the attention of any fan of such cinema, the ploy backfired.

Later Ted would discover that most newspapers would not run the entire title of

One of the tear-sheets that newspapers refused to run due to the film's more-than-lurid title. Even so, the movie was rated PG.

Though Ms. Vernon didn't burn for real in the film, *she* burned *Ted* in one regard. At 79 minutes, *Blood Orgy of the She Devils* was and is one of Ted's shortest features. When asked if this was the full cut of the film, the director not-so-fondly recalled:

> The movie was about three or four minutes longer. I had worked so very hard creating dissolves and wipes to make the scene transitions. For instance, at the end of a scene I would zoom in on a chandelier while pulling the camera out of focus, and then go from an out-of-focus shot to an in-focus shot for the next scene. I really liked these transitions, but I guess Sherri didn't. While I was away she took it upon herself to edit those out. To my knowledge she hadn't even used my editing equipment before, but she got the job done, and I didn't even know until I was screening what I thought was to be the final print. To this day I have no idea whatever happened to that footage, and to be honest I was pretty damned pissed off at the time. It's funny now, but it sure as heck wasn't then.

With or without the wipes, *Blood Orgy of the She Devils* hit the silver screen in 1972 to a lukewarm reception at best. The Geneni Distributing Company was neck deep in the handling of Bob Clark's *Children Shouldn't Play with Dead Things*, and somehow, some way, Ted's film was lost in the shuffle. Ted wasn't happy about it, then or now. True to form, though, a masterpiece of a marketing campaign was launched that involved some of Ted's most hyperbolic advertising yet. "A Terrifying, Screaming Plunge To The Depths Of Hell!" screamed the one-sheet; or, even better, "Mara—Queen Of The Black Witches, And Her Wolf-Pack of Voluptuous Virgins Invade Satan's Tortured Realm Of The Unknown!"

In addition to the melodramatic written copy, ticket buyers were handed a postcard. This freebie depicted a psychedelic-looking eyeball, with the inscription, "Psychometry Test. Blow Very Gently Into The Hypnotic Eye. Hold The Eyeball Approximately 1½ Inches From Open Lips—Take A Deep Breath And Exhale Directly Into The Eye For Maximum Moisture Contact. If The Retina Turns Milky See Your Witch Doctor At Once. If The Retina Shows No Change It Is An Indication You Are Less Apt To Be Affected By The Metaphysical Powers Of Mara As She Casts Evil Vibrations From The Screen During Her Homicidal Rituals In 'Blood Orgy of the She Devils.'" Either

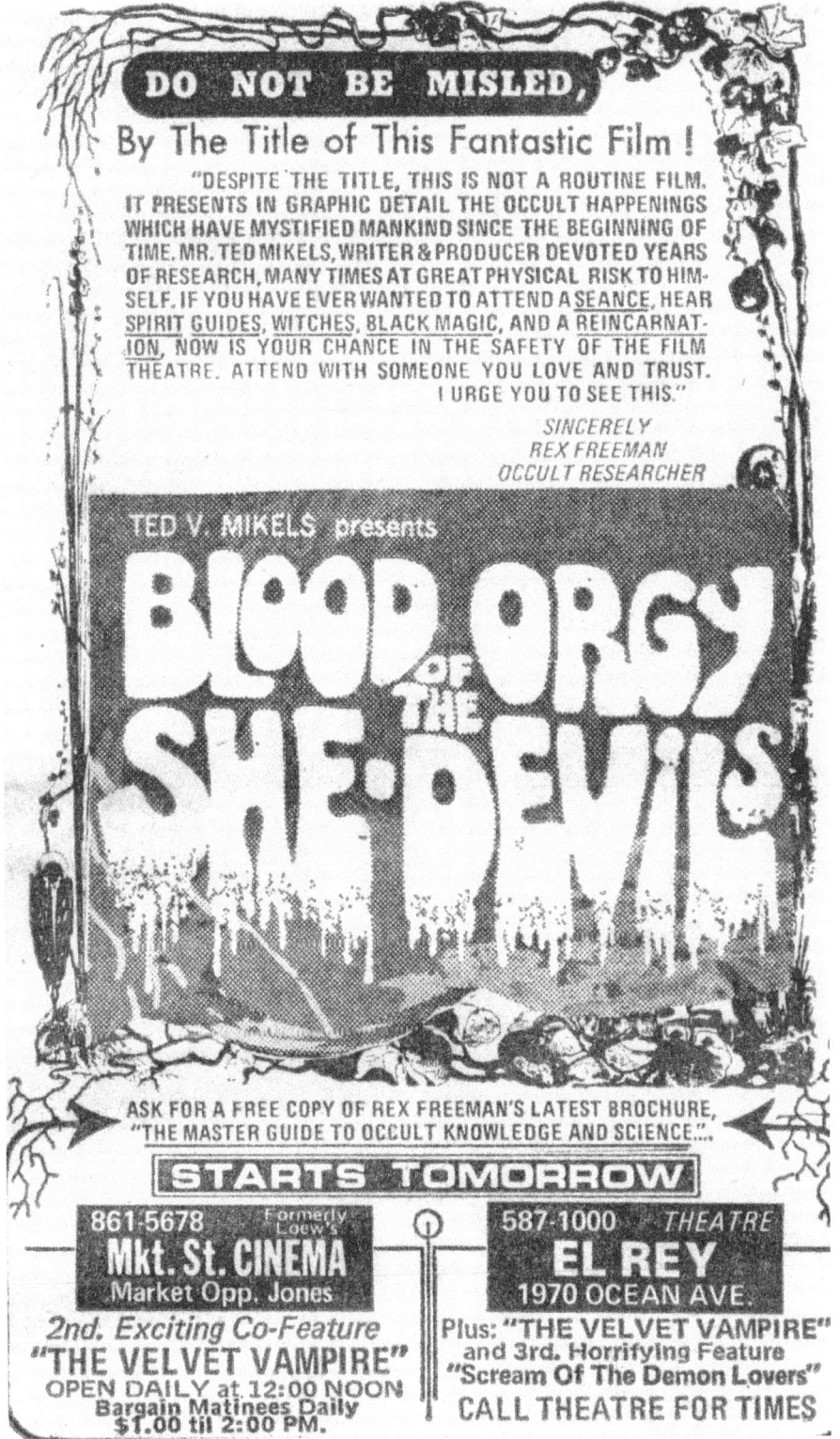

A *Blood Orgy of the She Devils* newspaper tear-sheet with a disclaimer from the bogus occult researcher "Rex Freeman." In real life, Freeman was William Thrush, a friend and later business partner of Ted V. Mikels.

that darned "eye" doesn't work properly or Mara is one lousy witch, as this writer has never seen that thing change to any color even remotely resembling "milky." Still, whatever its doubtful efficacy, such promotional tactics were worthy of fellow cinematic exploiteer William Castle himself.

Never fully satisfied, Ted wasn't about to stop the advertising juggernaut there. The one-sheets, the ads and the postcards just weren't enough. At the suggestion of friend William Thrush, a booklet was created called *The Master Guide to Occult Knowledge and Science*. Outlining many aspects of the Occult, the booklet included capsule descriptions of the casting of spells, séances, astral projection, reincarnation, psychometry powers, witchcraft, auras and protective amulets. Theatergoers received these gems of exploitation free with the purchase of a ticket.

Unfortunately, the odds were stacked against Ted and his team, and the film wouldn't really come into its own until the 1980s during the video rental craze. Just as newspapers wouldn't touch the title, so too did television stations reject it; so until VHS was unleashed upon the public, *Blood Orgy of the She Devils* remained largely unseen and unheard of for over a decade. Once the masses were hooked on viewing videos in the comfort of their homes, however, Ted's lost gem on witchcraft and black magic became one of his biggest sellers on DVD and VHS. In fact, it was so successful in its afterlife that one video company licensed the film from Ted and retitled it *Female Plasma Suckers*. True, it's a stupid title, but what the heck, Ted was finally getting some mileage out of a movie that was sadly and unfairly overlooked at the time of its original release.

9. *The Doll Squad*

Synopsis from Pressbook

Senator Stockwell (John Carter), monitoring the television launch of a Star-Flight-Twelve Saturn V Rocket, is joined by Victor Connelly (Anthony Eisley), head of the CIA, as the TV reception is interrupted by a distorted vision and an anonymous voice asking the Senator if "he is watching well?" and immediately cautioning him that "next time perhaps you'll listen!"

Video is immediately resumed, only to have the rocket explode in a tremendous, devastating malfunction. The two grim spectators immediately launch an investigation, calling on Sabrina Kincaid (Francine York), leader of a shapely and deadly coterie of female lovelies known as "the Doll Squad," to head the inquiry. Sabrina is intrigued by the voice of the unknown intruder, and except for the fact that future negotiations were to be continued by means of carrier pigeons, there are no other clues.

Sabrina enlists the aid of Carol Pierce (Carol Terry) and Cherisse (Brett Zeller), a karate operator and pathologist, respectively, but both girls are killed by Munson (Herb Robbins) and a trio of killers. Sabrina barely escapes with her life after inflicting a horrendous burn on Munson by means of a trick cigarette lighter.

Sabrina's investigations ultimately reveal that Nancy Malone (Lisa Garret), secretary to the Senator, has served as intermediary for Eamon O'Reilly (Michael Ansara), former CIA agent, previously reported dead, but who apparently is now heading this overt, treacherous action against the government.

Nancy's suicide apparently confirms this

knowledge, and Sabrina now reactivates "the Doll Squad," a band of female specialists, each skilled in a particular field and dedicated to the overthrow of America's enemies.

They are Sharon O'Conner (Leigh Christian), Cat (Sherri Vernon), Elizabeth White (Judy McConnell), and Lavelle Sumara (Tura Satana).

Sabrina has learned that Eamon O'Reilly is headquartered at a foreign island, and, now with her band, she sets off in pursuit.

Meanwhile, on the island, Joseph (William Bagdad), who works for O'Reilly, contacts a Kim Luval (Jean London), an uninitiated member of "the Doll Squad" who has been waiting for Sabrina's arrival by posing as a cashier at a local carnival, and dupes and captures her, replacing her with Maria (Lisa Todd), complete with replica mask and assuming the identity of Kim.

This ruse quickly fails when Maria is unable to answer Sabrina correctly. Sabrina overpowers Maria and drives off with her, leaving a frustrated Joseph to contact O'Reilly.

At their headquarters, the girls pinpoint O'Reilly's location from Maria, but in endeavoring to replace Maria for Kim, it is Maria who suffers a mistaken death in place of Kim. "The Doll Squad" sets out to track down O'Reilly, with Cat and Elizabeth pursuing an overland route by jeep, and Sabrina and her squad via boat.

After Sabrina and her group debark the boat and head for their assignment, Rafael (Rafael Campos), secretly working for—and in the clutches of—O'Reilly due to a drug addiction, misinforms Captain Curran (Curt Mason) into returning later than previously arranged for, then sets out after the girls and actually tricks them into capture.

Cat and Elizabeth reach the outskirts of O'Reilly's desert fortress, overpower and destroy the guards with a self-destructive alcoholic beverage, and press on.

At a meeting with all foreign representatives, Eamon O'Reilly now reveals his master plan: subjugation and overthrow of all foreign governments by means of artificial bubonic plague. All are to be inoculated against the disease, with twins Dr. Cahaymen and Dr. Cahaymen (Gustave and Bertil Unger) in charge of this phase of operations.

Cat and Elizabeth reach their objective just as Sabrina is taken by Rafael to meet for the first time with the ambitious O'Reilly. Sabrina quickly eliminates and kills the drug-crazed Rafael, then joins with Cat and Elizabeth in releasing the others. However, Kim is killed in this rescue.

Now Sabrina is free to follow through on her appointment with O'Reilly, as the rest of "the Doll Squad" continue on their assigned tasks: elimination of the balance of the armed guards and the implanting of dynamite charges to destroy the fortress and any and all agents. But Sabrina must first eliminate an angered Munson, who suddenly confronts her prior to her appointment.

In the meeting with O'Reilly, Sabrina and he discuss their former love affair, with each actually endeavoring to kill the other. Sabrina finally wins this battle of wits by means of a mace ring and a sword.

Dr. Cahaymen is eliminated as he attempts to escape via airplane. As "the Doll Squad" resume their journey to safety, the entire desert fortress is eliminated in a tremendous explosion. Only Dr. Cahaymen and a few guards now stand in their way, but these are eliminated by means of a bazooka.

A puzzled Captain Curran marvels at the insouciance, affability and carefree attitude of the somewhat bedraggled crew who stumble back aboard his boat. Sabrina reports her success back to Senator Stockwell and Victor Connelly, with the full knowledge that further adventures still await her and "the Doll Squad."

Credits

Cast: Michael Ansara (Eamon O'Reilly); Francine York (Sabrina Kinkaid);

Anthony Eisley (Victor Connelly); John Carter (Senator Stockwell); Rafael Campos (Rafael); William Bagdad (Joseph); Lillian Garret (Nancy Malone); Lisa Todd (Maria); Herb Robbins (Munson); Curt Matson (Captain Curran); Bertil Unger (Mr. Cahaymen); Gustave Unger (Dr. Cahaymen); Dru Landers (Nurse); *with* Richard Reed, Chris Augustine, William Bonano, and the All-Star "Doll Squad" Cast: Sherri Vernon (Cat); Carol Terry (Carol Pierce); Leigh Christian (Sharon O'Connor); Jean London (Kim Luval); Judy McConnell (Elizabeth White); Tura Satana (Lavelle Sumara); Brett Zeller (Cherisse)

Production: *cinematography*: Anthony Salinas. *special effects, production design*: Mike McCloskey. *associate producer*: Paul Burkett. *assistant director*: Lloyd Kino. *first assistant cameraman*: Curt Matson. *second assistant cameraman*: Jamie Anderson. *sound*: William Nipper, Scott Spencer. *lighting*: Brink Brydon, Mike Nussman. *script girl*: Jean Hewitt. *make-up, hair styling*: Sherri Vernon. *wardrobe*: Nickie Bernard. *still photography*: Ron Grover. *stunts*: Gregg Anderson. *production assistants*: Phil Tauber, Janine Mikels. *production manager*: J. Shannon Curran. *editor*: Ted V. Mikels. *assistant editor*: Sherri Vernon. *optical effects*: Van Der Veer Photo. *screenplay*: Jack Richesin, Pam Eddy, Ted V. Mikels. *music composed/conducted*: Nicholas Carras. *directed and produced by*: Ted V. Mikels. *running time*: 91 minutes. Color. *aspect ratio*: shot at full-frame and projected at 1.85:1. *shot*: 1972. *completed and released*: 1973.

The Film

Senator, sex and security don't mix. — Sabrina Kinkaid from *The Doll Squad*

In retrospect, it is fairly amazing to look back at Ted V. Mikels' filmography from his first feature release in 1963 to his ninth in 1973. That's nearly one movie a year, and as the productions progressed from one to the next, the quality and professionalism also moved steadily up the ladder. Even if his films weren't always as profitable as he would have liked, Ted was at least succeeding at being prolific. This is quite a feat by anyone's standards, and one has to wonder just when it was that he slept.

Countless chores and activities had to be completed in order for Ted to see any one of his pictures hit the silver screen, and *The Doll Squad* was no exception. Making a movie and seeing it released regionally, much less internationally, is a labor of love for the independent filmmaker. The following overview of film production, though by no means complete, will hopefully help illustrate the immense dedication needed to finish even the smallest of productions.

First an idea comes to Ted, and then a budget is proposed; from there a treatment of the story is composed. With these tools in hand, Ted hits the streets in search of potential investors. Once start-up monies are accrued, pre-production can begin.

At this point Ted prefers to concoct a series of scenarios that he would like to see in the picture. He jots them down on 3 × 5 note cards and tacks them to a cork board. He begins arranging the pieces—much like some directors would do with story boards. Eventually, the in-order scenarios will help make up the skeletal framework that will later become the script. When the script is completed it is time to round up the cast and crew. Interviews are conducted, agreements are made and contracts are signed.

Next up is location scouting, and simply finding the desired locale is hardly the end of the battle. Filming permits have to be acquired from the city at a fee, and it's seldom (if ever) cheap. Remember, they charged Ted hundreds of dollars a day to shoot on his own property! By this point rehearsals should be underway, along with the creation of props and wardrobe.

Film is then shot. Once principle photography has wrapped, and only after watch-

One-sheet for *The Doll Squad* (1973).

ing weeks of dailies, the editing process can begin. Audio and optical effects are added, as is a musical score. After everything is approved, the negative print is rushed off to the lab to be made into prints that can be played in theaters. (These prints cost nearly $2000 each, and that was in the 60s and 70s.)

Now theater owners, and sub-distributors, have to be convinced to rent the picture for a run on their screens. Promotional items are created to aid in the task of selling or renting the film to exhibitors, who in turn will be striving to sell tickets to theatergoers. Pressbooks, one-sheets, lobby cards, promotional photos, theatrical trailers, television trailers and even radio ads are among the ballyhoo involved in helping to make a motion picture a success.

Ted has been involved in all of these things on every one of his projects, but his 1973 production was to be his most ambitious ever: *The Doll Squad*. Always the showman, Ted didn't stop at the above-mentioned advertising tactics. He opted to accompany star Francine York on a national in-person appearance tour to help promote the film, much like he did with Leslie McCrae for *Girl in Gold Boots*. He also rented out the 20th Century–Fox theater in Hollywood at $1,500 for one night. There were movie stars and special guests in attendance, and champagne and hors d'oeuvres. But one *special* guest was to become quite a problem—television programming mogul and series creator Aaron Spelling. As Ted tells it:

> Tura [Satana] invited Aaron Spelling to a screening of the movie in hopes of landing some more parts. As I recall, Francine York took the script to Spelling also in hopes of getting some more acting parts. All the ladies are very aggressive when it comes to getting work in the movie industry. Anyhow, Spelling liked what he saw and a few short years later there was the very similarly, and successful, television series *Charlie's Angels*, and they even used my lead character's name, Sabrina, as *their* lead character's name!

Ted continues:

> After that show came out I was approached by numerous attorneys who claimed that we had a case and that we would win. I told them that I was not interested in lawsuits. I told them that I only wanted to make movies. I can make up idea after idea for a movie. I don't need to sue someone over just one of those ideas. Then when the *Charlie's Angels* movies came out, here come the lawyers again, and I had to tell them again that I wasn't interested in their propositions.

And here's the really sad part:

> Only two days after I'd sold international rights to the picture I was approached by MGM studios, who loved *The Doll Squad*. They were ready to sign a contract for foreign territories of *The Doll Squad*, and also a picture deal. I don't know how many pictures because the discussion didn't get very far, but if I'd only waited a couple of days I would have had a shot at being a contender.

Was the film a financial success?

> I'd have to say yes, even though we really didn't make any real money on it. You see, seven of our openings were wrecked by horrible weather conditions. There were snow and ice storms in places that had not had any in 100 years or more, and severe electrical storms in others. Oregon, San Francisco, Dallas, Houston and Florida were all a total loss; they were all hit with some horrible weather of some kind, and there was just no way that we could see it coming. It really hurt our finances in the advertising department because we had to pick up the theaters' losses. In Los Angeles we lost $42,000 alone. The reason that I say that the film *could* be considered successful is that in other territories it did fairly well and basically just barely kept its head above water. Had those openings not cost us so much then I've no doubt the film would have been a financial success. As it is, the film finally turned a profit around 1990. Better late than never.

That's the worst of it. The best part is that *The Doll Squad* is pretty darned slick for a Ted V. Mikels production, and when compared to other action films of the time it is right in line with them. The primary difference between most action films of the early 70s and Ted's is that his film featured an army of sexy women clad in skimpy, skimpy outfits wielding machine guns and spy gadgets.

Some of their weapons of choice include: grenades with time fuses, mini-cameras with instant developing, altitude bombs, breakaway rifles with scopes, lipstick recorders, signal homers, mace-filled engagement rings, cigarette lighters that double as blowtorches, and this author's favorite—"Sabrina's little nightcap, nitro-clite" ("It's odorless and it's tasteless; just mix it with alcohol—drink it and it's one for the road—all in little pieces"). By the way, this is supposedly the most powerful explosive humans had access to, next to the atom. Talk about putting women in control.

So with all of this in place it's easy to see that once again Ted had his tongue firmly planted in his cheek. But never before or since have the women of his films been more in control than in *The Doll Squad*. These ladies kick butt at every turn and at every conceivable time. They're hired female assassins, they mean business, and they look really good doing it, too. While smashing their enemies to bits they sport skintight black jumpsuits with one vertical white stripe from shoulder to toe that accents their ever-so-chic white patent leather go-go boots.

Of course, they don't always dress so snazzy. In fact, some of their outfits are downright painful to the eyes. Take, for instance, the scene in which Sabrina Kinkaid and her bosses find a stool pigeon in their very own office. Between Ms. Kinkaid and the secretary/snitch, Nancy Malone, a veritable pastel nightmare beams garishly from the screen. It's safe to say that Willy Wonka wouldn't be caught dead in these get-ups. Heck, even comedian Phyllis Diller might find her fashion senses compromised if asked to wear this garb.

Fashion and weapons aside, *The Doll Squad* boasts an effective cast—of both sexes. Star Francine York is perfect as Sabrina Kinkaid, head of the Doll Squad. She's quite striking looking, and exudes a motherly air that allows her to corral her cubs, so to speak, and get the job done. The adorable Sherri Vernon returns to the screen as Sabrina's second in command, Cat. The bewitching Tura Sa-

A newspaper tear-sheet ad focusing not only on the film's "World Premier," but also on special guest star Francine York. Note that Michael Ansara's head has been cut and pasted into the right-hand corner, since the picture of Francine York has been placed over Ansara's image from the original one-sheet.

tana can be caught dancing at the Fire and Flame nightclub, topless, with only a pair of tassels to get in the way of things. Most impressive.

Great character actor Michael Ansara turns in a fantastic performance as Eamon O'Reilly, the ex-secret agent who "...we think blows up rockets," and Ted V. Mikels regular William Bagdad gets in on the fun as well. Rafael Campos, from *Astro Zombies*, returns to the fold as bad guy Raphael, and O'Reilly's most interesting looking goons are the real-life identical twins Gustave and Bertil Unger.

As previous chapters have indicated, Ted has often found himself turning down the talents of stars and soon-to-be stars. In the past, Dennis Hopper, Peter Falk and James Caan were all sent packing, and the casting of *The Doll Squad* proved to be no exception to this odd rule. This time an unknown female actress tried out for *The Doll Squad*, but because she didn't fit what Ted felt was the "proper size and stature for a member of the Doll Squad," she too was sent away. The girl? Sissy Spacek. Three years later Canadian director David Cronenberg would also turn Spacek down for his lead in the film *Rabid*. He instead chose porno star Marilyn Chambers. What exactly could poor Ms. Spacek make of all this?

As the story of *The Doll Squad* goes, Eamon O'Reilly insists on being king of the world. How's he plan to do it? He plans to inject millions of rats with the bubonic plague and circulate them (the rats) throughout the world. Not exactly how most megalomaniacs would do it, but if it works for him and his elite gaggle of friends, then that's fine. Of course, he will inoculate himself and his cohorts against the dreaded sickness, but as things unfold we discover that he also wishes his ex-lover, Sabrina, to be his queen. The catch, and it's a big one, is that Sabrina and her gang of crime-fighting gals have been hired to take him and his disease-distributing pressure group out. This will certainly become a conflict of interests for Ms. Kinkaid.

The fun doesn't stop there, as a kidnapping takes place at a carnival, followed by some well conceived identity theft. In a very James Bond–like scene a girl's face is ripped from her head to reveal her as someone entirely different. It's a well-handled scene cinematically speaking, with only the somewhat hokey rubber mask to hinder the full effect of the sequence (but in the early 70s such hokeyness was mostly expected and easily accepted).

The next turn of events, however, was anything *but* expected: Ms. Kinkaid visits a psychic to help her determine what the heck is going on with bad guy O'Reilly. She gets quite the earful: "As a matter of fact, Eamon O'Reilly's psychological profile indicates occasional impotence, which seems to stem from an Oedipus complex, and any man who is thoroughly castrated by his mother is a prime candidate for some psychotic outburst, given the right circumstances to set him off."

Of course, Ms. Kincaid isn't given the opportunity to test O'Reilly's virility firsthand, and in the end, he and his thugs are apprehended, and the Doll Squad saves the day. Mission accomplished.

Ted shot *The Doll Squad* in late 1972 for around $156,000 dollars, with a final cost of $256,000. That's not at all a huge sum of money when one considers the sets, effects, cast and locations used in the making of the picture. But the film's original script was not entitled *The Doll Squad* at all, as Ted recounts:

> The script, as written by Pam Eddy and Jack Richesin, was called *Double Ought*. That story was nothing at all like *The Doll Squad* ended up, and only had some girls chasing a bad boyfriend of one of the girls to an island. The story did inspire me to do several rewrites, and then an added one, ghosted by the wife of Joseph Robertson, both my friends. She gave me her draft the morning we were leaving for location at the

Institute of Mental Physics, which played hell with the plans I had for scenes in my mind. Sherri Vernon and I worked together on one of the rewrites, saving some of the ideas.

The Institute of Mental Physics was one of the fantastic locations where a large portion of the film was shot. This is where so many of the shoot-out scenes occurred in what appears to be a bunker or a compound. In actuality, it was a place where people (with obviously too much time on their hands) went to learn and practice deep breathing exercises. Ted's associate producer, Paul Burkette, was a member of this organization and pulled the proper strings to get them this wonderful setting. Later, in the 90s, Ted would make a promotional video for this affiliation called *The Breath of Life*.

Another gem of a locale served as O'Reilly's home. The swanky kitchen and living room areas, along with the cave-like atrium and cavernous stone tunnels, were all parts of Zsa Zsa Gabor's home ... one of them, anyway. Ted even chartered a boat to Catalina Island, and in the rough choppy waters he and the captain were the only two not hanging over the side of the boat heaving from sea sickness.

A rather amusing incident involved actor Herb Robbins. Robbins and Ted had been friends for years, but for whatever reason this was the first time the two worked together on a film. After this incident one might wonder why Robbins would ever put himself in harm's way again. From Ted's recollection, this is what took place:

> What happened was, Herbie was supposed to come out with a patch over his eye, because, as you remember, Francine York had burned it out earlier in the movie with a flame-throwing cigarette lighter. So I wanted Herbie to come into the scene where Francine is alone, taking pictures with her spy camera. Well, I had Herbie hide in a broom closet, and I forgot about him while we were fixing the lights and everything. Any how, all of this was taking forever, and the whole time poor Herbie is patiently waiting in the closet for his cue. Well, I don't remember exactly what it was that we were having so much trouble with, but after a long time had gone by Herbie slowly poked his head out and said very quietly, "Can I come out now?" It was terrible that

A streamlined version of *The Doll Squad* promotional artwork.

I'd forgotten about him, but also very funny in a way.

It may come as a shock to some, but even with the number of ladies that Ted was involved with on the film (or had been involved with), very few problems arose. As Ted recalls, "On one instance Sherri suggested that she be the character to kill Eamon O'Reilly, but Francine York felt that *she* was the only one to pull that off as far as the story went." It's a small detail that might have changed the tone of the film, and it's amazing that Ted was able to wrangle so many of his lovely ladies without fostering a lot of jealousy and/or tension. But anyone who's ever worked with Ted knows that he brings out the best in a person. Besides, even if such an occurrence was on the horizon, there simply was not enough time in the shooting schedule to allow for such an episode to come to fruition.

Speaking of Sherri Vernon, despite her shenanigans in the editing bay during *Blood Orgy of the She Devils*, Ted once again allowed her to assist in the cutting room.

> Sherri's got a really good eye and feel for editing. I really like to pay attention to detail, and I want to lead people slowly up to what is about to happen, but Sherri would step right up and make it clear to me what needed to go and what needed to stay. Shanti is very good at it, too. [Note: Shanti, or, rather, Dr. Wendy O. Altamura, is a very close friend to Ted.]

Initially the film went out with a massive running time of 101 minutes. Ted felt that the picture was bogged down, and, in order to speed the pace up a bit, he called in the prints one by one and began cutting them down. As Ted recollects, dialogue was dropped, as well as some of the transitions/dissolves, bringing the movie down to 91 minutes.

> I had wanted these dissolves to be so unusual that no one would have seen any like it before. I had a kaleidoscope image between the two clips created from scratch, and it is an original effect. In my cutting minutes out of my edit, I had to remove several of these unusual effects, but there are several left in the cut. Even when I watch *The Doll Squad* today I think it should be about 80 minutes. I just feel that action films should move along a little faster.

Still, it's probably my most successful movie in terms of worldwide acceptance. During the early release in 1973 most of the countries of the world who were buying U.S.-made films acquired rights for their countries. Seymour Mayer, out of New York, was the sub-distributor who really helped us get *The Doll Squad* its massive international release.

A really fantastic thing happened to me around the time of *The Doll Squad*. I was driving down Hollywood Boulevard and noticing the movie marquees, and all at one time three of my movies were playing! *The Doll Squad*, *Girl in Gold Boots* and, I believe, *The Corpse Grinders*, though it may have been *Blood Orgy of the She Devils*. That was so much fun seeing that, and I don't believe any other director in the history of movie-making can say that three of their pictures were playing within just a few blocks of one another.

Even with his largest budget to date, Ted still had to take some unorthodox approaches in making this film. Ted told Jonathan Ross, host of *The Incredibly Strange Film Show*:

> I had an advantage of being able to use an automatic firing machine gun for one night. So I just, you know, went berserk. I'm sure the people on my cast and crew thought I was berserk, because it wasn't in the script. I made it up. I'd say, "You! You! Grab these machine guns and fire. You're firing over here in the direction of my hand. Camera's over here! Okay, the action is: you run in, you fire off camera and you run out." They'd say, "Who're we firing at?" [And I'd say,] "Don't worry about it." And so for about 12 hours, until daylight, I just had them running, and nobody knew what they were shooting at, or who was chasing who. There was no screenplay. I made it up.

Special mention should be given the musical score created by Nicholas Carras. Carras sat in with Ted and wrote the music to fit the rhythm of the film itself. Movie soundtracks are so often overlooked, and when they work properly they simply cannot be beat. Robert Fiedel wrote in the book *The Girl in The Hairy Paw* (in regards to Max Steiner's magnificent score for the original 1933 *King Kong*): "It is perhaps futile to attempt to determine the exact value and significance of the contribution of a musical score to any given film. Such an appraisal will always be relative to the critic's aesthetic criteria, musical knowledge, and personal taste." Agreed, and it's virtually impossible to ignore the power of Carras' music within the framework of Ted's film. As great as Carras' work was in the past, it almost seems like a dress rehearsal for his contribution to *The Doll Squad*.

The Doll Squad musical theme even made it into the top ten considered for an Academy Award for Best Movie Soundtrack. Unfortunately, the piece was nudged out of the top five. The under-appreciated Carras is not only responsible for the sounds of many of Ted's films, but also *She Demons, Dragstrip Riot* and *Frankenstein's Daughter*, all from 1958. In addition to those cult fan favorites, he also penned the music for *Date Bait* (1960), *Honeymoon of Terror* (1961) and *Omega Syndrome* (1987).

Three years after *The Doll Squad*'s release, a film exhibitor contacted Ted in order to obtain the rights to show the picture in his Texas territories. The company was working under the banner of Dinero Productions, Inc. The buyers were interested in changing the title, and Ted complied, with the only stipulation being that he be able to approve the film's new moniker. At least three different titles

and graphics were drawn up: *The Bang Gang!*, *The Female Connection* and *Seduce and Destroy*. Ted allowed them to use the latter, though he admitted, "I didn't really like any of them that well, but *Seduce and Destroy* did have the best looking artwork of them all.

So *The Doll Squad* opened to dismal weather and lackluster sales. Ted didn't get in on *Charlie's Angels* nor a shot at working with MGM Studios. And, adding insult to injury, the film's title track was unable to grab the much deserved Academy Award nomination. Ms. Tura Satana reflected:

> I know that he has given the public what they want in the entertainment industry. He should be a multi-millionaire for all of his work, but he is too trusting of his associates. Those are the ones that have bilked him out of millions. Needless to say, many have

One of Dinero Productions' submissions for the changing of *The Doll Squad* artwork and title. Ted V. Mikels nixed this version in favor of *Seduce and Destroy*.

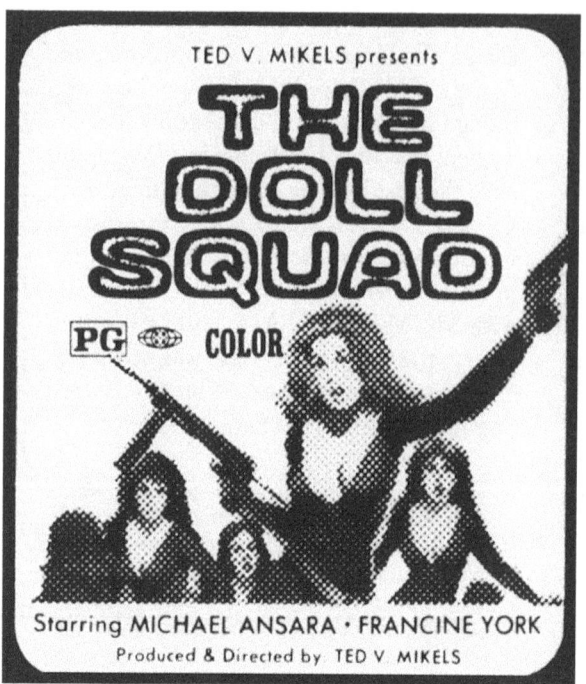

An even more streamlined version of *The Doll Squad* promotional artwork.

copied his work and his talent in his enterprises.

Many years would pass before *The Doll Squad* was comfortably in the black as far as profits go, but the film finally hit paydirt in terms of praise when Hollywood's outsider darling, Quentin Tarantino, divulged his love for *The Doll Squad*. Tarantino even said in numerous interviews that it was an inspiration to him in regards to the making of his incredibly successful *Kill Bill* movies.

Interviewer Theresa Duncan, for Artforum International, reported that

> While Tarantino is a fan of nearly all violent cinema, from mainstream directors like Peckinpah to spaghetti westerns to Hong Kong action films, he claims that the primary influence for *Kill Bill* was a string of decades-old genre and exploitation films. "I had a whole list of these films. *The Doll Squad* [1973] by Ted V. Mikels, Burt Kennedy's *Hannie Caulder* [1971], *I Spit on Your Grave* by Meir Zarchi [1978] — there are tons of them."

Indeed, when one watches both *Kill Bill 2* and *The Doll Squad*, the endings are conspicuously similar. Just as Bill and Beatrix were former lovers, trained in combat by the same master, so are Eamon and Sabrina former lovers with the same type of training. Both couples acknowledge this to one another, and in the end the girl wins. It was an unlikely turn of events for a Tarantino movie, as his films are predominately powered by males, but for Ted it was exactly what his fans had come to expect.

10. *Alex Joseph and His Wives*

Synopsis from Pressbook

The story you are about to see is true. The names have not been changed to protect the innocent. The film is based upon actual incidents and played by the people they happened to — Alex Joseph and his wives. All 105 minutes of color action were shot entirely on location in southern Utah — where it really happened. Never before has a drama with these ingredients been brought to the screen.

All this was accomplished without the cooperation of any federal bureau. The story is necessarily filmed under armed guard and carried forth despite the attempts of the U.S. Park Service to deny the right of access to public lands during filming.

In all respects, *Alex Joseph and His Wives* is a unique testimony to American ingenuity.

"The man who has raised the nation's eyebrows with his flaunting of the establishment, the man who claims 10 women—young, attractive, intelligent women—as his wives, the man who dares to do battle with the government...."

Now comes the true story of Alex Joseph, the one-man revolution whose devil-be-damned courage has arrested the attention of domestic and international press. Set to the long-striding pace of a man who walks through the world as though he owned it, the movie is filled with Joseph's romances and challenges, his friends and enemies. This man lives more in a week than most people do in a lifetime! The movie is laced with the adventures and escapades of the people who look for Joseph. Some of them are comical, some are deadly serious—but they all find out that whoever thinks he has an eye on Alex Joseph should look over his own shoulder to see who's really doing the looking....

An amazing portrait of an outrageous and beautiful family.... This true story is more incredible than any fiction. In outrage or admiration of this revolutionary polygamist lifestyle, you will be left wondering what will they do next?

Credits

Cast: Alex Joseph (himself); Dale, Margaret, Leslie, Lorraine, Carmen, Joanie, Pamela, Judy, Paulette, Melinda, Kitty, Carla (Alex's wives); Pius the Whirlwind Soldier (himself); Robbie Anslow (Minstrel); Mr. Vermillion (Bartender); Undein Hampton (Nora Grady); Noble "Kid" Chissell (Sheriff); Tommy Simmons (F.D.A. Man Floyd Perkins); Stuart Lancaster (Motel Manager); Patrick Wright (Barroom Rowdy); George Costello (Car Rental Agent); Mr. Blackmore (Assassin); Billy White Bird (Bobby Grey Fox); Beau Billingslea (F.B.I. Man Vernon Wood); Danny Scholl, Edmon Kaiser, Jim Gillings.

Production: *production manager*: John Curran. *director of photography*: Kolas Von Sternberg. *costume design*: Jackie Thrush. *editor, picture, sound effects, music*: Ted V. Mikels. *assistant cameraman*: Nick Peterson. *script supervisor*: Maureen Gaffney. *screenplay*: Rex Freeman, William Thrush, Ted V. Mikels, Alex Joseph. *music*: Nicholas Carras. *additional songs*: Bobby Worth, Stephen Witt, Robbie Anslow. *lighting*: Ron Batzdo, Mike Wasser. *props*: George Costello. *executive producer*: William Edward Thrush. *assistant executive producer*: Boyd L. Jentzsch. *produced and directed by*: Ted V. Mikels. *running time*: 103 minutes. Color. *aspect ratio*: shot at full-frame and projected at 1.85:1. *completed*: 1977. *released*: 1978.

The Film

Some people say he's next to God. Others think he's the Devil hisself. —Motel manager from *Alex Joseph and His Wives*

In the early 1970s, Alex Joseph bent the ear of the nation with his consistent (and persistent) defiance of the law. He virtually spat in the face of any rule or regulation that he did not see eye to eye with. It was odd behavior coming from an ex-policeman, but then maybe that's why he is no longer on the force.

Joseph had also served as a fireman and been a health food mail order guru. Joseph, a high school dropout, also went on to become mayor of his own town. Glen Canyon, Utah, was host to an unnamed area that Joseph bought and incorporated, and christened Big Water. But that wasn't what the government officials had their biggest beef with. Alex Joseph was a loud and proud polygamist who, over the course of many years, married 20-plus women. In Utah the prac-

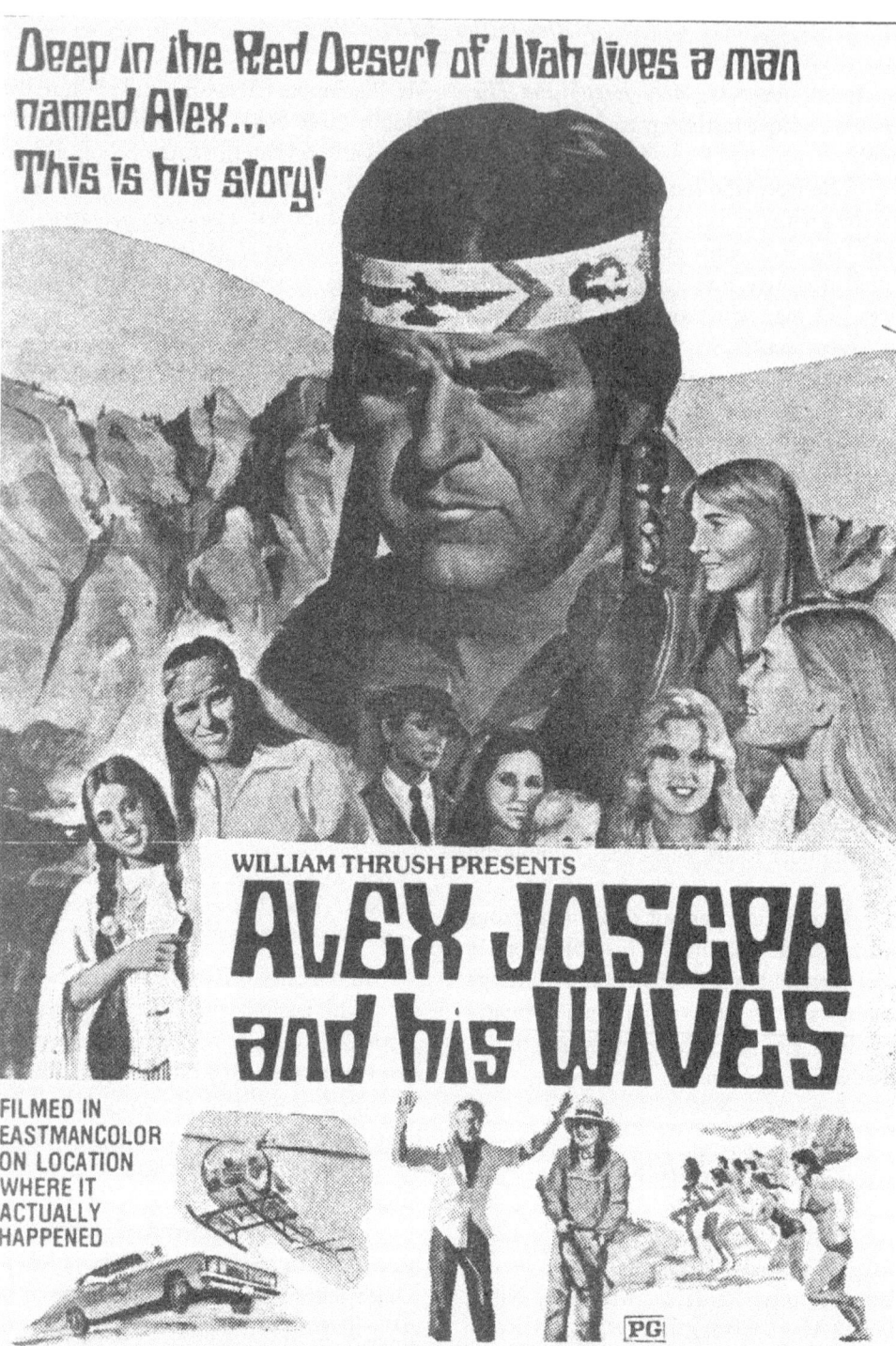

One-sheet for *Alex Joseph and His Wives* (1978).

tice of polygamy is not uncommon (especially 30 years ago), but it's still quite illegal.

Ted Mikels had become friends with a theater owner named William E. Thrush. Thrush was the man who took it upon himself to create the promotional booklets for Ted's 1972 feature *Blood Orgy of the She Devils*. Thrush also fought San Francisco newspapers who would not print the full title of the picture. Thrush was an ally to Ted, and in 1977 he hired the independent moviemaker to help him create the most unusual *Alex Joseph and His Wives*.

According to Ted, Thrush had become enamored of Joseph and his family set-up. Ted went on to say that "It was almost as though Alex Joseph was Bill Thrush's alter-ego." Perhaps Thrush was living one of his dreams vicariously through Joseph. In any case, Ted was enlisted to direct the picture for $100,000, plus a fee for editing and script writing.

The movie opens with the following prologue:

The film you are about to see was filmed on location in Southern Utah. The story is true, as told by Alex Joseph. Alex Joseph, his wives and followers appear as themselves. Professional actors fill the other roles. The producer neither condones nor condemns polygamy. This film reports the problems and joys of the lifestyle of Alex Joseph and his family.

This was not a form of contrived cinematic hype. All of the above was very real and very true. Alex Joseph plays himself, as do a good many of his wives. Dale, Margaret, Leslie, Lorraine, Carmen, Joanie, Pamela, Judy, Paulette, Melinda, Kitty and Carla were all married to Joseph, and perform in the film their everyday doings, goings-on and happenings. Some work in the town restaurant that Joseph owns, while others maintain the homestead. Carmen, in particular, is quite the career girl, as she studied and later became a successful lawyer who still practices in her chosen field to this very day. Carmen, and her knowledge of the law, became an incredible asset to Joseph, as he would spend a large portion of his life

Alex Joseph's wives in *Alex Joseph and His Wives*.

fighting for what he felt were his unalienable rights as an American citizen.

So, with all of that in mind, the tone of the film is very pedestrian, if one accepts polygamy and law-fighting as the norm. Joseph sectioned off a portion of Utah as his own, acquired a helicopter (for a time presumably stolen), firearms, a restaurant and a group of renegades who the town sheriff refers to as "...his [Joseph's] posse." Joseph goes about his business of cultivating health foods, mostly ginseng, and peddling them through mail-order. He also spends a great deal of time dealing with the authorities, whether they be local, the F.D.A. or the F.B.I.

All of this activity revolves around the fictitious hub of the film, wherein a female reporter from London's *Women's World* magazine comes to interview the cowboy-like harem keeper. *Women's World* is "...devoted to the interests and needs of the modern woman." A feminist and a polygamist ... well, there's a powder keg aching to go off for sure. The reporter? Nora Grady.

Not only is Ms. Grady sent to debunk Joseph's lifestyle and report to the world that it is unwholesome, but she also strives to prove that Joseph is a misogynist. Joseph is not a misogynist and treats his wives equally and fairly. They are all there of their own accord, and only the laws and boundaries of bigotry threatens to keep them apart. Their lifestyle, as Burt Brandon wrote in the *Salt Lake Metro*, "...was one based more upon personal autonomy for the wives as well as the husband than upon the absolute (and often abusive) authority husbands wield over wives in fundamentalist communities like Colorado City."

Once Grady recognizes this she shifts gears and "hits on" Lorraine in an attempt to uncover some lascivious behavior in the form of lesbianism. The attempt fails, but Grady does ask Joseph the obvious: "Alex, what gives you the right to have so many wives?" To this he replies: "The law gives me that right. I have a lawful right to have as many wives as I please and to be married to whoever I please. I translate that right into responsibility, and I'm making that demonstration."

It's an interesting sentiment, but the fact of the matter is that it *is* against the law in America to have more than one wife. Whether it is immoral, amoral or just plain wrong is left to the discretion of all those in tow. As history has stated, Utah was not allowed into the Union until they abolished polygamy once and for all. Joseph found this ruling unjust and based the decision of his lifestyle on the very idea that Utah was "forced" into outlawing polygamy in order to become a "recognized" state. It was a loose argument that was full of holes, but it did allow him to continue his way of living, in and out of court, until his death.

Now, while Joseph was demonstrating his right to be a polygamist he also felt the need to demonstrate his right to be a racist. Early on in the film, he jokingly refers to his Native American Indian friends as "savages," while they refer to him as a "racist honky." It's all amicable, or at least consensual, but when actor Beau Billingslea shows up as F.B.I. agent Vernon Wood the tone drastically changes. During an arrest Wood tells Joseph, "I was beginning to think you didn't like me." At this, Alex Joseph replies, "I don't like niggers." Vernon snaps back, "I'm black!" And Joseph retorts, "I don't like niggers, no matter what color they are." Later, during a routine interrogation by Agent Wood, Joseph offers him a cup of coffee. Wood peels his eyes from his paperwork to say, "I thought you didn't like niggers." Joseph steps up and offers his hand and says, "Well ... I like gentlemen, no matter what color they are."

That's Alex Joseph. He was a no-nonsense kind of man who made no excuses for himself or his behavior. But the fact that Ted V. Mikels made a film with a racist tone is in stark contrast to his sympathetic portrayal of the blacks in his incredible and telling feature *The Black Klansman*. Said Ted:

> I didn't want that stuff in there. Bill Thrush and Alex Joseph really wanted to show things as they were, regardless of the entertainment factor. I never wanted to be controversial, but these guys were putting up the money, so my hands were tied. It was the same deal with all of that political crap in the middle of the movie. I didn't want all of that in there. I tried to keep it out, but ultimately I was out-voted.

The "political" scene that Ted speaks of is a makeshift town meeting where landowners and movers and shakers get together and talk about the follies of the American government. This scene is not only inappropriate in a film of this type, but it also sticks out like big fat sore thumb. It adds nothing to the film's narrative and could only serve as an intermission sequence for those uninterested in such political topics, but Joseph and Thrush wanted that material in there.

Not to leave Alex Joseph in a bad light, one of his wives had this to offer Brandon Burt, of the *Salt Lake Metro*:

> "Big Water is about freedom," Boudicca said. "Alex was always about freedom and choice. He moved out here in the desert to get away from people because he didn't want to oppress his neighbors with his lifestyle."

Burt continued:

> It is that freedom that seems to be Alex Joseph's enduring legacy—everywhere you go in Big Water, people talk about freedom, whether it's freedom from crime, from high taxes, or from excessive government regulation.

That's pretty much all there is to Joseph's story and the film. Joseph was embroiled in a constant struggle to be himself. Reporter Nora Grady finds no conclusive evidence for her feminist article, and in the end, she herself longs to be a part of Joseph's life. Of course she cannot so easily tear herself away from the trappings of her own life

The *real* Alex Joseph in *Alex Joseph and His Wives*.

and work, and so makes her way back to Merrie Olde England.

The story concludes with this epilogue:

> Federal Marshals forcefully removed Joseph and his followers from public lands on December 3, 1975. They were later found in contempt of court. On October 2, 1976, the charges against Alex Joseph for stealing a helicopter were dropped. The Homestead Act was repealed on October 21, 1976. Alex Joseph is presently pursuing a Hollywood movie career.

Joseph's movie career never materialized, but he did continue to own Big Water in a number of ways, though troubles with the law were to follow him to his grave. However, because of his policy of open-mindedness the town now has its first ever openly gay mayor, Willy Marshall. It's all baby steps.

Ted reminisces fondly:

> I had a wonderful time on that movie. I got to direct on horseback, and that was great. I felt like the real wild-man in me was able to come out. Here's something fun. Everyone there was "packing." You know, they were armed. Well, we were taking a break and

A striking and scenic shot photographed in Big Water, Utah, for *Alex Joseph and His Wives*.

someone set up a beer can on a post and no one could hit the thing. I walked up, drew and fired, and hit. I smugly put my pistol back and walked away, laughing to myself. No one questioned whether or not I was carrying that pistol for show or not. Another instance with the firearms involved two or three of the cast who were wanting more money for their parts. Apparently they got drunk and shot up Bill Thrush's trailer one night, but thankfully no one was harmed, but I have no idea if they received the money that they felt they deserved.

Bill Thrush seemed to have been the recipient of bad vibes, as Ted continues:

> Alex Joseph was a legend of sorts to Bill Thrush, and in the beginning they got along very well. But as the project went along they began fighting over petty things that were probably rooted within the money aspect of the movie. Alex Joseph had put up 40 or 50 thousand dollars, and he felt that he should have a stronger voice in the production, but Bill Thrush thought otherwise. They became belligerent on the set, and both of them asked me to choose sides. I would not, and ultimately I remained very good friends with the both of them.

As it was, the movie went nowhere fast. Ted lost control of it for monetary reasons. William Thrush tried distributing it as *The Rebel Breed*, and then Alex Joseph wrapped his paws around it and re-titled it *Obadiah 18*. All of the title changes made no difference. The film just wasn't selling well to the public, which is too bad, because as far as cinematic quality goes, it ranks up there as one of Ted's finest. The acting is sketchy, as more than half of the cast were non-actors; but that aside, Ted really did a bang-up job with this one.

With the exception of the racism issue, Ted did like Joseph and his company:

> He came to the castle on several occasions. I didn't really have the "castle ladies" until I'd made that movie. A few of the girls said that my personality leant itself to the idea of polygamy, so I went back to the coast and upped my numbers from two or three to seven or more.

Ted and William Thrush weren't the only ones taken by Joseph's way of life. Outlaw country singer David Allan Coe visited Joseph in the mid-80s and was interested in polygamy, but as Joseph reported, "Coe just wasn't any good at it. It's not a lifestyle for everyone." Later, Joseph would visit Coe in Nashville, and while Coe had given up on the idea of plural marriages, Joseph left the capital of country music with yet another wife. Coe's album *Darlin' Darlin'* is dedicated to Alex Joseph.

The film ran way over budget at $300,000, and, as Ted remembers:

> Bill Thrush and Alex Joseph wanted to feed the cast and crew multiple times a day. They were bringing these steaks and burgers, and there just wasn't any money in the budget for it. Everybody ate really well, but the food cost alone was at least five times what they were expecting.

With that sort of unrestrained spending it's not at all surprising that Ted never received the $100,000 promised him for directing the film, but he *was* paid for his editing duties. When Ted asked Joseph's son, Billy, if he could release the film, he was told that Billy would rather not see the picture released, and that, frankly, he'd rather the movie had not been made at all. Conversely, Joseph's widows are all for the idea—as long as they are in on the take.

Alex Joseph was born June 24, 1936, and died at the age of 62 on September 27, 1998, from liver cancer. He insisted that his occupation on his death certificate be listed as "pirate." If nothing else, Alex Joseph was an eccentric.

The helicopter that Alex Joseph was accused of stealing (he was later found innocent of the charges). From *Alex Joseph and His Wives.*

11. *10 Violent Women*

Synopsis from Pressbook

Ten lovely young ladies, all shapely and beautiful, tired of the conventionality of office work and miscellaneous boring jobs, band together to mine gold in the mountains. They are nearly killed inside the mine when an irresponsible dynamite man, "Tom the Atom Bomb," detonates a charge, trapping some of the girls under falling debris. Once safe, they pounce on Tom with flailing fists, especially furious since he had attacked one of the girls, with intentions of rape. The girls announce they are tired of "busting their asses" the hard way and getting nothing, now they will do it "with class."

A little later, dressed to the hilt "with class" and a borrowed limousine, they stage a jewelry-store heist with precision timing. They make off with a million dollars in jewels, including a sheik's collection and his sacred scarab ring from the vaults. The sheik and his man, "Achim," are put off outside the store by pretty girl decoys, but are soon hot on the trail of the escaping girls, along with the police.

After a quick change of clothes and vehicles in an alley, the girls stop en route to Las Vegas for a refreshing rest at dusk in an animal park. Here, after loud and ambitious talk, they pair off for a shoot-out with their automatic pistols and revolvers. Instead of spitting out death to each other, the guns spit out water, and we learn that the girls are using water guns in the heists, and amid howls of laughter and shrieks of delight they douse and wet each other down royally.

In Las Vegas they meet furtively at a disco joint with an underworld fence who takes them to his boss's mansion. Here, Leo tries to take their jewels and trade them for cocaine. They refuse him, and in a violent physical confrontation during which one of the girls, Beth, is accidentally shot and badly wounded, the girls barely escape with their lives. Sheila, a little more vicious than the others, stomps the life out of Leo with her heels after flattening him with a whisky bottle, while the others race to their cars. Sheila now has Leo's real gun, and a million dollars in "coke" with her, and the other girls are not aware of this.

Later at a roadside park, after a blouse-tearing-bosom-baring fight between Sheila, who now stays constantly drunk with tequila, and the beautiful black girl Carol, two of the girls, Sam and Maggie, take over as leaders of the group. Two of the girls take a new look at the serious developments, and leave, taking Beth with them to get her medical help for her wound. As police drive through the park checking vehicles, our girls panic after narrowly escaping questioning. As they pull out of the park, they are followed at a discreet distance by the sheik's man, Achim, in his Mercedes. He is determined in his pursuit to regain his master's jewels and sacred scarab ring.

To acquire a new car, the girls force a man to strip off his clothes in secluded wood, and, with their menacing "pistols," "cool" him as they drive off in his Mark Four, leaving him naked, wet, and screaming in anger.

The girls stop at a flamenco club after first hiding the jewels in a nearby culvert. While patrons in the club join in with the dancer, keeping time clapping and stomping to the beat of the flamenco rhythms, Sheila offers to sell cocaine to a couple of gentlemen who had bought the girls a drink. Outside, in back of the club, Sheila learns in the attempted sale that the men are narcotics officers. Sheila is shot and killed when she levels Leo's gun at the man. The girls inside, still unaware of the shooting, the real gun and the cocaine, are arrested and taken to a nearby women's prison facility.

Meanwhile, Achim, who has been constantly following the girls, has recovered all the jewels from the culvert—that is, all except the scarab ring. In prison the girls find their dignities somewhat ruffled. What originally started out as a lark has now become a desperate struggle for survival. Here, they find themselves forced to fight violence with violence. After several weeks of beatings and quirt-whippings by lesbian guards, and shower-fights with tough female inmates, Sam and Maggie become closer together, and, with Jill and Liz and two other new-found friends, plan to escape. Using every form of trickery, physical attacks, and enlisting the coordinated assistance of the girls' boyfriends on the outside, the plan gets underway. They incapacitate the guards, trick the cruel section matron with the promise of sex, and obtain the keys to unlock the cells and successfully escape.

Once outside the prison gates and across the tracks to freedom, the two friends take off with their waiting boyfriends, and Sam, Maggie, Jill and Liz are picked up in a Mercedes driven by none other than the sheik's man, Achim, dependable in pursuit of his master's ring. Achim tells the girls that he is the manager of a traveling show and that he can arrange for a night's lodging at the hotel where the troupe stays. The girls are terribly distressed when they ask Achim to drive them to where the jewels were hidden, and find them missing. Sam, having been allowed to wear the ring instead of leaving it with the other jewels, tells the others that she hid the ring in a flowerpot in the flamenco club as they were arrested. Outside the club, Achim's eyes grow big as he sees the huge and heavily-jeweled ring on Sam's finger as she returns to the waiting Mercedes and the excitement of the others. Achim must not give himself away and spoil his chances of ever recovering the ring.

That night in the hotel, after a scrumptious meal of gourmet delights, Sam and Maggie are terrified as a figure in the darkness steals into their room and attempts to remove the ring from Sam's finger as she sleeps. Petrified, but afraid to call police or security for assistance, the girls sit up for the rest of the night playing cards.

In the morning, Jill and Liz announce to Sam and Maggie that the "manager" bought them nice gifts, but told them there was room for only two girls on the show, so they plan to go home. They called and found Beth had recovered, and the others were awaiting their return. In the hallway, Achim is seen listening to an unknown voice coming over the receiver. "You are to escort the girls to the docks, where I will have a proper reception waiting. Avoid police and notoriety."

In the room, Achim tells the girls he can get them on a cruise yacht to the Mediterranean if they are willing to work. The girls meet the yacht steward on the dock, and are asked if they can dance. They most emphatically agree they can, and are escorted to the lavishly Middle-Eastern decorated dance floor of the pleasure boat. Here they are costumed and awkwardly fake an attempt to belly dance along with the other dancers. A gong is struck by the attending guard and the sheik enters with a policeman. It is the sheik's yacht, after all. Taking a look at the girls, the sheik announces that he has recovered all of his jewels, and the jewels that did not belong to him were returned to their rightful owners, and now that he has recovered his sacred scarab ring, he would drop all charges against the girls. Sam reluctantly hands the sacred ring to the sheik, and the policeman leaves, saying, "You no longer need me." The sheik, in the tongue-in-cheek manner of the entire escapade, leads the girls off the dance floor, inviting them for a drink to "prepare for whatever lies ahead" as the yacht sails out to sea.

Credits

Cast: Sherri Vernon (Sam); Dixie Lauren/Doreen Ross (Maggie); Sally Alice Gamble (Sheila); Georgia Morgan/Joan Hannan (Bri Terry); Jane Farnsworth (Madge); Melodie Bell (Jill); Christina de Gattani (Liz); Paula Ian (Beth); Sherry Hardin (Joanie); Kelly Lancaster (Carol); Peggy Hayes (Robbins); Juanita Morgan Copeland (Jackie Kent); Eileen Lee (Doris); Julie Wakefield (Pam); Leigh Reynolds (Donna); Lynn Culver (Ms. Cameron); Sonja Knowlton (Warden Clark); Claire Gable (Guard); Ted V. Mikels (Leo "the Fence"); Anne Gaybis (Vickie); Lyle Peskin (Dude); James Emery (Danny); Steve De France (Mob Man on Phone); Sigfried Von Conanburg (Jock "Man with Mark IV"); Frank Washe (Jeweler); Jack Dees (Jewelry Store Guard); Johnny Hawk (Jewelry Store Policeman); Sal Hasbun (Yacht Steward); Bertrand Levesque (Sheik's Guard); Michael McCloskey (Sheik's Man "Achim"); Charles Gorgano (Sheik); Neil Hays (Policeman on Yacht); Samra, Cheryl Jensen (Belly Dancers); Lani Silver/Kalani Satana (Attacked), Loretta "Irish" McCarthy, Linda Holmes, Nayra Perez, Debra Ryan, Laura Bonn (Other "Gold Mine" Girls); Thomas J. Manning ("Tom the Atom Bomb"); Marie De La Rosa, Tamasiro Kiyoro, Sato Kaworo, Joan and Jerry Keehr, "Jackie" (Other Jail Prisoners)

Production: *directed and produced by*: Ted V. Mikels. *written by*: James Gordon White, Ted V. Mikels. *music production, music supervision*: Nicholas Carras. *additional music performed by*: The I.C.'s. *director of photography*: Yuval Shousterman. *editor, pictures, sound, music*: Ted V. Mikels. *legal council*: Neal Baseman. *production design*: Michael McCloskey. *camera operator*: Miles Blum. *production manager*: Steve De France. *assistant director*: James Desmarais. *second assistant director*: S.R. Sirot. *sound recordist mixer*: Vernon Lombard. *script supervisor*: Alison

Cobb. *make-up artist*: Nancy Blair. *special effects*: Neil Hays, Jack DeWolfe. *assistant editor*: James Jaeger. *still photographer*: Robert Vose. *second unit production manager*: Thomas J. Manning. *first assistant cameraman*: Varouj Balian. *second assistant cameraman*: Tony Balderama. *gaffer*: Jim Watkins. *electricians*: Colin Spencer, Tom Plant, Rick Endelson, Roger Brown. *production assistants*: Kelly Dellagatta, Michael Glicksman, Will Klapp, Troy Mikels, Yoram Joshua, Steven R. Barry. *casting*: Doreen Ross. *running time*: 97 minutes. Color. *aspect ratio*: shot at full-frame and projected at 1.85:1. *shot and completed*: 1978. *released*: 1979.

The Film

Adventure and women's lib is one thing, but this is quite another.—Maggie from *10 Violent Women*

After a minor setback with *Alex Joseph and His Wives*, 1978 found Ted Mikels up to his old tricks again, and the women of *his* life were about to find their way back to the silver screen. In truth, it was those very ladies, the castle ladies, who prompted Ted to make his next feature film:

> We'd finished working with Herb Robbins on *The Worm Eaters*, and the girls wanted to get busy with another project. I had a script by James Gordon White, *The Violent Sex*, which was strictly a women in prison story, and I bookended it with the caper part to lend a reason to how the girls wound up in prison.

And so, Ted's eleventh film in 20 years, *10 Violent Women*, was born.

The film follows the exploits of eight attractive ladies who've had it with the 9 to 5 gig. They seek their monetary gain through more unconventional means than the largely unsatisfying and dreaded grind of

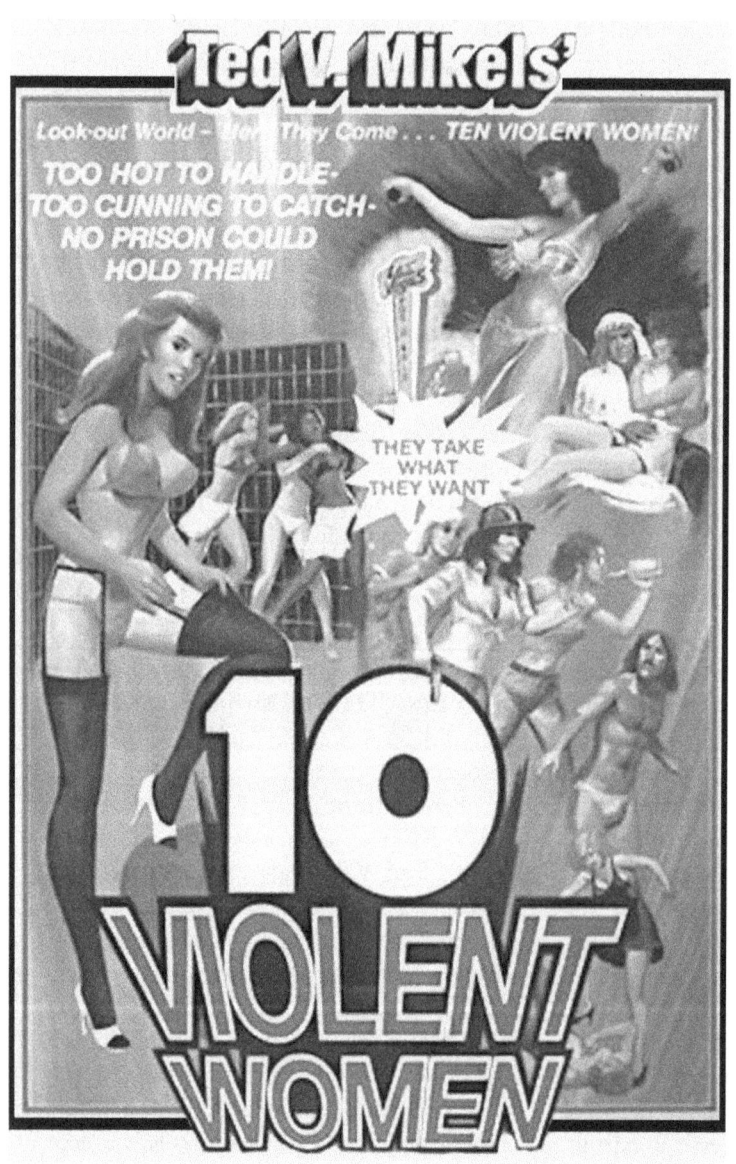

One-sheet for *10 Violent Women* (1979).

office work or its ilk. Any employer would do well to *not* hire these ambitious but nonconformist gals. Wrangling these females to execute dull and monotonous duties might prove to be too much for even the most hardened business owners or people pushers.

10 Violent Women opens with the title card "...in the beginning," and here we catch the girls mining for gold in an effort to remedy their money woes. "Tom the Atom Bomb," not quite the explosives expert he makes himself out to be, accidentally blows up the wrong wing of the mine and some of the girls are trapped and/or injured. The butterfingered pyromaniac is relieved of his duties and, in lieu of three weeks' back pay, he attacks and mauls one of the girls in an attempted rape. The rest of the gals beat him senseless and decide, "We busted our asses the hard way and got shit. From now on we're gonna do it the easy way ... with class." Incidentally, the topless victim of Tom's hormonal rage was none other than Kalani Satana, daughter of the notorious Tura Satana. Here she was credited as the less conspicuous Lani Silver.

And Mommy Satana thought:

> As for my daughter Kalani and her role in *10 Violent Women*, I am very proud of her. I had always taught my daughter to feel free to do what she thinks is right. Since I was an exotic dancer for so many years, she thinks nothing of showing her breasts. Granted, the scene always makes me cringe, but I thought that she did a great job. Also, I know that Ted would never demean her in any way, because of me.

Tura Satana's daughter, Kalani Satana, is mauled by "Tom the Atom Bomb" (Thomas J. Manning) in *10 Violent Women*.

After the mining experience literally blew up in their faces, "...a short time later with class" the lasses try their hands at armed robbery. An unassuming jewelry shop is their next stop, and with water pistols and a carefully devised plan they turn over the store and make away with the booty. Unfortunately, part of the gem collection belongs to a sheik, who considers a stolen sacred scarab ring to be his prized possession. The girls have gotten far more than they bargained for. They flee the scene of the crime, and within minutes the Arabs are in hot pursuit. The destination? Las Vegas—and "...the plot thickens." While in Vegas, Sherri Vernon's character, Sam, falls in love with the scarab ring, and the rest of the girls agree to let her wear it, figuring that there is plenty of loot to go around. Sheila, the most aggressive of the bunch, sets up a meeting with Leo "the Fence," played by Ted Mikels himself. The girls believe that he will give them a fair price for the jewels, but Leo has other plans.

Earlier in the film, Leo was scolded by his boss for not moving an allotment of cocaine quickly enough, and so he offers it to the girls in trade for the jewels. They're not interested in the least, but with the Mob breathing down his neck, Leo pulls a gun and insists that they take the deal, "While you're still healthy!" Writer Bill Landis points out in his book *Sleazoid Express* that this stands in very stark contrast to the

Leo (Ted V. Mikels) and Vickie (Anne Gaybis) in a scene from *10 Violent Women* that hit the cutting room floor.

everyday Ted Mikels: "Ted plays the blustering, nasty heavy one, twirling his mustache ... and doling out bags of flour masquerading as cocaine—a far cry from the gentle polygamist he is in real life." So true.

The gang's leader, Maggie, opens a packet, pretending to test the goods, and blows a cloud of the white stuff directly into Leo's face and eyes. A whiskey bottle is smashed over the crook's head, but in the scuffle one of the girls, Beth, is shot and wounded. They make it out with their jewels; however, they left one small bit of business unfinished ... Leo. Sheila returns to take care of the culprit. She stabs him to death by repeatedly stomping her spiked heel clean through his chest. Bill Landis also makes mention of this most violent display: "He [Ted] winds up with a heel in his stomach, just like the iconic image from his 1960s movie *One Shocking Moment*." Ted revisited this powerful imagery in 1998 with *Female Slave's Revenge*.

Ted laughs:

> All the girls wanted to kill Leo! Kelly Lancaster especially wanted to do the killing. She was the real pretty black girl who played Carol. As her character was written, it just wouldn't have worked out for her to have done it. I will say this, though, that was the moment in which a seed was planted for my 1998 movie *Female Slaves' Revenge*. In that picture a whole group of lovely black ladies torture and kill their slave owner, who is played by me.

In the story, Sheila is clearly the most determined of the bunch and not at all satisfied with the latest turn of events. She nabs the cocaine (1.5 million dollars worth) and Leo's gun. She even goes so far as to rip Leo's boar's tusk necklace from his throat, then maliciously smashes it to the floor. This girl means business. All of this is unbeknownst to the others, who are more concerned with getting Beth medical attention *and* getting as far away from the scene as possible.

Once the girls have escaped from Leo's compound, the high-strung Joanie cracks under the pressure and begins to cry uncontrollably. Sheila, having no patience (and also being quite nervous about her earlier doings), smacks her silly. Carol comes to Joanie's rescue, and the film's first cat fight is underway, with much screaming, scratching, kicking and clawing.

At this point some of the girls decide to split, but Sam, Maggie, Liz, Jill and Sheila stay on course, and at a nightclub Sheila tries to move the cocaine. Unfortunately for Sheila, the marks are undercover narcotics agents. In an act of desperation, she pulls Leo's pistol on them, but they beat her to the punch and gun her down in the parking lot. Sam witnesses this, and dumps the scarab in a planter and warns the others. But it's too late: "...BUSTED!!!" The girls have been caught red handed, and it's off to prison for these dames.

Once in prison, the balance of the ten violent women of the film's title are finally introduced. Bri Terry, the "sadistic and psychotic" warden, and her right-hand woman Madge make up number nine and ten of the violent women. The Bri Terry character was played by Joan Hannan, credited here as Georgia Morgan. Ms. Hannan, as stated before, was the inspiration for the bisexual character of Joanie in *One Shocking Moment*, but here she gets to display her on-screen talents by laying on an over-the-top portrayal of a cruel and perverse lesbian prison head.

Ms. Terry takes a liking to Sam, but Sam isn't responding to her affections. Ms. Terry tries seducing Sam, and when that doesn't illicit the proper response, various tortures are in order. Everything from mental torment to freezing cold showers to whippings are employed in an attempt to break Sam down and bend her to the will of the egomaniacal Bri Terry. Ted remembers an incident with Sherri Vernon during one torture sequence:

> It was during the scene where Joan was to put a metal bucket on Sherri's head and beat

Sam (Sherri Vernon) and Maggie (Dixie Lauren/Doreen Ross) are behind bars in *10 Violent Women*.

it unmercifully with a riding crop, thus creating an almost unbearable amount of pain upon her ears. Well, Sherri wanted the room cleared, and I couldn't ask everyone to leave because I had to have people there to help me get the shot. Anyhow, as it happened, Sherri flipped out and ran completely out of the prison and into the street. I had to chase her down and coax her back onto the set. You see, Sherri's not a disciplined actress. I think she did really well in the film, but she just doesn't have the discipline that it takes to act under any circumstances. She really wanted to get into the part, but she didn't want all those people around. I was able to clear the room of a few of the people, though. At least enough in order to make her feel more comfortable about the scene.

While the jewelry store robbery with the water pistols came across a might lighthearted, once the film moves to the prison setting, all bets are off. Ted doffs his gloves and gets down and dirty. Loads of abusive behavior is displayed by both the authorities and inmates. The film features shower room cat-fights, lots of nudity, drug usage and, unusual for a Ted V. Mikels production, very vulgar language. In fact, the MPAA slapped this baby with an R-rating based solely on the use of the "F" word. Without a doubt, *10 Violent Women* contains the highest content of questionable or offensive material of all of Ted's films.

At one point Bri Terry is questioned as to why she allows the girls to behave so wildly. She answers, "Well, I believe it's psychologically healthy for my girls to release their inhibitions, their aggressions and their

Sam (Sherri Vernon) is being reprimanded (to put it mildly) by the sadistic, lesbian warden Bri Terry (Georgia Morgan/Joan Hannan) in *10 Violent Women*.

frustrations." Now that's an interesting angle to running a women's prison. Most jailhouse administrators would do everything within their power to curb that type of behavior, but in a Ted V. Mikels film things are very different. It's probably also worth mentioning that the prison sequences really shift his "women in control" fixation into overdrive, as women are controlling women! There's little doubt as to the immense pleasure Ted must have derived from creating those scenarios. However, Ted doesn't stop the debauchery there.

Bri Terry's henchwoman, Madge, is a brow-beating Christian. Many of the girls suffer severe persecutions and floggings at the hands of this fundamentalist beast of a woman. The devil must be beaten out of them, and it's this religious fanaticism that takes the film into nunsploitation territory. *10 Violent Women* really is quite grim and dreary, and Ted's deft use of lighting, especially in the darkened cells, gives the full-color film an almost monochromatic look that works famously to its advantage.

Oddly enough, Ted's assistant director, Jim Desmarias, felt entirely different about the movie, telling the *Seal Beach Journal* on August 23, 1978, "There's very little violence actually, only one person dies. There's hardly any sex either. For a film of this type, it's really quite tame." It's possible that Desmarias may have changed his tune as shooting progressed; but if not, it makes one wonder just what the heck he might consider violent.

Eventually, we come to "The Escape."

With the help of two new allies, the girls cook up a scheme to break out of the joint. They succeed, but the Arabs are waiting. They've recovered the bulk of the jewels, but the scarab is still missing, and they'll not rest until they have it. Sam returns to the nightclub where she hid the ring, and the Arabs lure her and Maggie to a ship with the promise of work as dancers. Once the girls are aboard the boat, the Sheik takes back his ring; he decides not to press charges, since he has retrieved all that he had lost. The Sheik, Sam and Maggie walk off-camera together. The mind reels at what the Sheik may have in mind for those two lookers once he got them back to his room, and "...so they sailed off into the sunset, living happily ever after."

Ted shot *10 Violent Women* (sometimes known as *Woman's Penitentiary*) in 1978 and released it in 1979. A mere $145,000 was needed to bring it to the screen. Real locations, like an abandoned L.A. prison, were utilized, along with the Seal Beach police department and a Ramada Inn. Ted's films really come alive when he uses existing locales rather than fashioning some sort of set on a stage or in a warehouse. When working on a soundstage the look and feel of the interiors are dictated by the shot list, whereas when using actual locations, as Ted does, the genuine site dictates the shots. Ultimately, depending on the room and the space, a lot of the photography is improvised on the spot. It's that sort of freewheeling sensibility that helps make independent features so endearing and charming.

Composer Nicholas Carras turned in yet another fantastic piece for Ted. The title track is simply sublime and ranks right up there with his piece for *The Doll Squad*. Of course, Ted was short on capital, so Carras had to recycle some of his other compositions

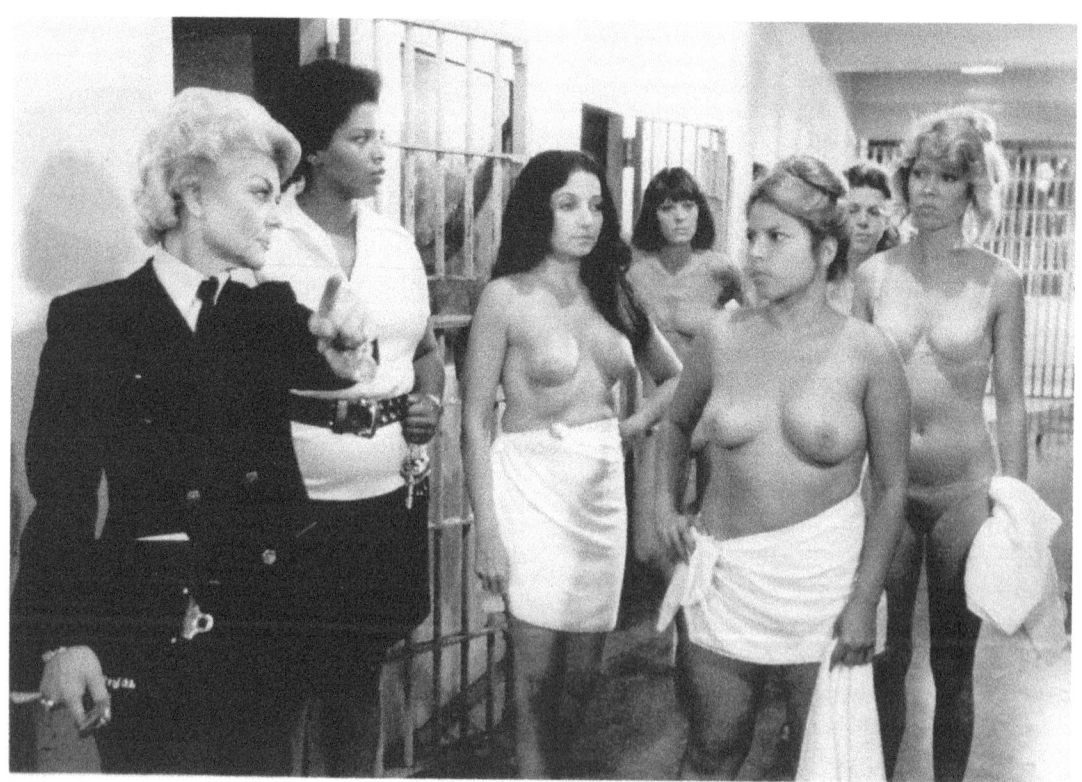

A topless line-up from *10 Violent Women*.

for the incidental music and chase sequences. But still, his *10 Violent Women* theme is worthy of many a listen, even if it does stand in odd contrast to Ted's bleak tale.

When asked about the grittiness of the picture, Ted remarked, "That's what exhibitors and distributors felt would be marketable; I simply wanted to make a picture that would entertain and hopefully make its money back, and then some." Unfortunately, as had become all-too-common for the independent filmmaker, *10 Violent Women* did not make any money at all ... at least not for its creator:

> Of all my movies, that's the one that gets to me the most. I had made a deal with Terry Levine of Aquarius to show the picture. He had several theaters in New York City up and down 42nd Street. I sent him eight prints and the movie ran for weeks. It was very successful. I have letters from Terry telling me how much he liked the movie and how well it was doing. He said people were lined up around the block to see it. Then when I inquired about my portion of the money he turned on me. He actually had his attorneys send me letters stating that their client did not even know who I was. This really hurt me. The film was successful, but I never saw a dime from it, and all the people who invested in the picture didn't get a dime from it either. These days it's my third best seller on DVD.

Author Bill Landis, a longtime Ted V. Mikels fan, apparently caught the show while living in New York and had this to say: "*10 Violent Women* exceeds the sum of its parts and stands out as one of the most eccentric of the female rough-trade films." Agreed.

12. *War Cat*

Synopsis

(Note: There was no official pressbook developed for the promotion of *War Cat*. This synopsis was created by the author and then approved by Ted V. Mikels.)

Pretty Tina Davenport relocates to her deceased father's hometown in order to write a book about him. While waiting at the bus station for her ride, she is approached by an uncouth man, Manny, with obvious sexual intentions. He offers her a "ride," and Tina promptly turns him down with a "No thank you." So incensed is Manny that he attacks an elderly woman selling homemade baked goods, knocking her basket of breads to the ground. "Pedal your shit somewhere else!"

Tina's escort arrives, and she is taken to a small cabin in the woods. Tina really knows how to live off the land. She spears a fish in a river, and guts and cleans it before roasting it over an open fire. She's also physically fit, and jogs and hikes when not working on her book.

Manny follows Tina into the woods, but he is stopped short once again. This time, rather than a polite "No thank you," the perpetrator is threatened with the business end of a fishing spear. Manny retreats once more, but not for long.

Back at the cabin, Tina works on her writing, and a drunken Manny glares at her through a window. The peeping tom routine gives way to breaking and entering, but Tina's too quick for him. Tina smashes his head between the door and the door frame. She calls the police and Manny is arrested. He vows to get back at her!

The film now shifts to a military compound that is manned and operated by a group of gun-handling outlaw survivalists preparing for war. Meanwhile, Manny is escorted from the court house, a free man. He is met by the leader of the military organization, Major Hargrove.

Major Hargrove drives Manny to the desert, nearly running over a motorcycle rider, and reprimands him for his attempted assault on Tina. Then a bit of Manny's sordid past is revealed—he spent six years in prison for a sexual offense. Manny is a bad man.

The motorcyclist and his gang, Thrill Killers, make their way to the desert to teach the Major a lesson, but Hargrove is not fooling around. He pulls a machine gun on one of the bikers. "What the hell is that for!?" demands the punk. "Killing mostly," the Major informs him. For the moment, the bikers flee.

At the compound, more plans for survival are discussed, and the training continues. The Thrill Killers, having failed to learn their lesson and now tanked-up on booze, descend upon the survivalists' territory. This time the fire power is employed, and the bikers go down one by one.

One biker is attacked, but takes out the gunman by head butting him with his motorcycle helmet and then twisting his head, snapping his neck. Two captured bikers, one male and one female, are interrogated, and when they fail to answer the Major's questions satisfactorily, he unceremoniously blows their brains out. One captive girl, Linda, is handed over to Manny as some sort of a reward. Manny locks her in a cell, roughs her up, and leaves her with the words, "Think about the snake pit. Think about the snake pit."

Later, while in town, Manny spots Tina jogging and kidnaps her, taking her back to camp. The Major is not at all pleased with Manny's decision to bring Tina to the compound and flogs him with a bullwhip for his infraction. Tina is put into the cell with Manny's other plaything, Linda.

In another part of town two rough looking thugs, Zach and a partner, turn over the Bullet and Blade Trading Post, killing the store clerk. They declare that they're sick of "city life" and retreat to the mountains, whooping and hollering the whole way.

In time, Tina is unmercifully bound to a bed and repeatedly raped by the soldiers, while one member, Pierre, sits idly by, sipping coffee and listening to classical music on a portable tape recorder. Finally, it's Manny's turn, and he gets what he's wanted the whole time. Somehow Tina finds the strength to maintain her composure.

Once in the mountains, Zach and his partner pay a visit to Bo and Meg. Bo had been chopping wood, and Zach's cohort lays Bo's own ax into his back. Zach shoots Meg, and the two derelicts leave the scene of the unnecessary and brutal slaughter, but not before killing Bo and Meg's pet bunny rabbit. Zach and his companion are really bad men.

Back at the compound, Manny pays a visit to Linda in her cell. Linda smashes a bottle over his head but is unsuccessful in her attempt to knock him out. Manny pulls a switchblade on the helpless girl and presumably kills her.

Tina is taken to the Major to be assassinated, but before he can kill her she calls him out on his suspected sexual impotence. "I know now why you didn't take me last night; that gun is the only prick you've got!" Tina eventually convinces the Major to set her free so that he and his men can hunt her down and kill her like an animal. This plan obviously gives Tina a chance for survival, but the major and his men are convinced that they will win.

The Major allows Tina a two hour head start, while the boys load weapons, sharpen knives and arrows, and contemplate and plan their methods of pursuit. Tina takes to the mountains. After the two hour waiting period, the Major sets his "animals and anarchists" loose on their unarmed prey. Jake, played by the film's producer, Jeffrey C. Hogue, is the first to locate Tina, and he fires off a bazooka in her direction, but she narrowly escapes.

In another part of the mountains, Zach and his buddy continue their killing spree by shooting a picnicking couple and then making off with their sports car.

Tina is still on the run and getting tired and thirsty. She pauses at a creek for water and a rest. Jake is now pursuing her with a crossbow. He levels his weapon, aims and fires, but again the sly Tina escapes unharmed. Tina then lures Jake to her; and just when he thinks he's got her, she stabs him directly in both eyes with two broken tree branches. One down and five to go, but now Tina has Jake's weapons.

Tina sets a snare trap and snags Pierre, and then blows him to bits with a hand grenade, leaving only a single chunk of bone and some mangled flesh hanging from the rope. Having heard the explosion, the others surmise that Pierre has gotten her. Two down and four to go.

Tina hides high in the mountains and ambushes a member of the militant organization, kicking him to his death hundreds of feet below. Three down and three to go, and now Tina has an automatic machine gun.

Tina uses Jake's crossbow on one of her stalkers, and the Major and Manny flee back to the compound. Four down and two to go.

Also returning to the compound, Tina goes to rescue Linda but finds her dead, with her throat slit from ear to ear. Manny had indeed killed her. Tina then goes back to the mountains to plan her revenge on Manny and the Major.

Tina fools Manny by recording herself singing on Pierre's portable tape recorder. While a confused Manny stares at the tape recorder, Tina gives him a taste of his own medicine, slicing clean through Manny's throat with a knife. Five down and one compound and its leader to go.

Using all of the weapons that she'd acquired on her human scavenger hunt, Tina levels the outlaw camp. An exciting crescendo of fire and explosions ensues. Once the smoke clears, Tina apprehends the Major and throws him into Manny's secret snake pit. Rattlesnakes reside in every crack, crevice and corner of the pit. Tina gives the Major a pistol with one bullet, and leaves him to die with the words "Snake against snake."

While walking along the highway, Tina is approached by Zach and company. The two murdering sleazeballs offer her a "ride" just as Manny had done at the beginning of the picture. Rather than turning them down with a polite "No thank you," she says, "Sure, why not?" However, what Zach and his boy do not see is that Tina is clutching a live hand grenade behind her back.

Credits

Cast: Jannina Poynter (Tina); David O'Hara (Major Hargrove); Macka Foley (Manny); Carl Irwin (Ron); Jeffrey C. Hogue (Jake); T. Craig Keller (Craig); Pierre D'Augusto (Pierre); Ron Jason (Don); David Collins (Kid); Gary Hodge (Ace); Pat Kerby (New Guy); Jason Holt (Zach); Ed Walters (Zach's Partner); Linda Eden (Linda); Joe Wilkerson (Motorcycle Gang Leader); Monty Perlin (High Rider); Jennifer Collins (Biker); Maria De La Rosa (Biker); John Stewart (Biker); Carson Heal (Biker); Rocky (Biker); Lee Neske (Gun Shop Victim); Bo Richards (Woodcutter); Shelagh Talbot (Woodcutter's Wife); Danny Owen (Picnic Boy); Denise Barras (Picnic Girl); Jerry Carroll (Sheriff John Lester); Mary Bee (Old Lady); Katherine Coon (Lady Lawyer); Maria Domingo (Major's Girlfriend)

Production: *screenplay*: Gary Thompson, Jeffrey C. Hogue, Ted V. Mikels. *additional dialogue*: G. Wayne Caro, Garry Hodge. (California Crew): *second unit direc-*

tor of pyrotechnics: Paul Staples. *production manager*: Carl Irwin. *cameraman*: Hal Schwartz. *first assistant cameraman*: Jennifer Collins. *second assistant cameraman*: Rick Ties. *sound recordist*: Maria De La Rosa. *boom man*: Elston Leonard. *script supervisor*: Katherine Coon. *make-up*: Mark Williams. *production assistant*: Wyetha Lee Janes. *key grip*: Pat Kerby. *grip*: Joe Wilkerson. *location editing*: Chris Wells. *special effects (pyrotechnics)*: Hollywood Special Effects. *prop master*: Jerry Carroll. *catering*: Nancy Weatherman. *location scout*: John Heston. (Nevada Crew): *cameraman*: Pat Kerby. *first assistant cameraman*: Jennifer Collins. *second assistant cameraman*: Mark Farmer. *sound recordist*: Jim Mingo. *gaffer*: Bill Allen. *best boy electrician*: Rick Husted. *set designer*: Rick Strelak. *set construction*: David Vlasak. *production assistants*: Wyethat Lee Janes, Jeff Hill. *script supervisor*: Diane Bowers. *special effects*: Kelley Kerby. *make-up*: Joe Klein. *snake wrangler*: David Upton. *editor—picture, sound effects, music*: Ted V. Mikels. *assistant editor*: Diane Bowers. *negative cutter*: Charles Hammon. *editorial consultants*: Calvin Floyd, Elston Leonard. *master mix facilities*: Quality Sound, Inc. *sound mixers*: Irwin Hafshun, Steve Hafshun. *Foley mixer*: Lloyd Keiser. *music continuity coordinator*: Christi Hogue. *original music score composed and performed by*: Chuck Dodson. *closing theme "Take Me Home" written and performed by*: T. Craig Keller. *titles and opticals*: Hollywood Optical Systems, Inc. *director*: Ted V. Mikels. *associate producer*: T. Craig Keller. *producer*: Jeffrey C. Hogue. *running time*: 78 minutes. Color. *aspect ratio*: shot at full-frame and projected at 1.85:1. *shot*: 1986. *completed and released*: 1987.

Promotional artwork for *War Cat* (1987).

The Film

You'll never learn, will you, creep!?—Tina from *War Cat*

By the end of the 70s the film industry was taking a turn for the worse in regards to costs. It was becoming increasingly more and more difficult for the independent filmmaker to keep his or her head above water, and between 1979 and 1986 Ted Mikels had a rough go of it. 1979 saw Ted releasing his last feature film to the theaters, *10 Violent Women*, and after that he started no less than three projects that either were impossible to complete or would take years to do so.

Chad, a precursor of sorts to Ted's 2005 project the *Heart of a Boy*, was shelved after a large portion had been completed and a major character, the grandfather, died while on an operating table. *Space Angels*, one of his most ambitious projects, could not secure proper funding because Hollywood execs said, "Even Ted V. Mikels can't make this movie for under two million." Then *Mission: Killfast* was underway, but monies ran out for that one as well, and it would take nearly a decade to see that film to completion.

Once *Mission: Killfast* had been on the back burners a while, Ted was coaxed into leaving his beloved castle. Las Vegas, Nevada, was the destination, and the relocation was in hopes of a more stable and lucrative financial future. The filmmaker recounts in John McCarty's *Sleaze Merchants*:

> In 1985 I was given great encouragement, by a man who did a lot of international business, to move here and start a studio to make films. He promised to finance both the studio and the pictures, and said I'd get a check for $600,000 the day I finished moving here to get the studio started. But, of course, nothing came of it. The guy meant well. He was a mover and a shaker, but he couldn't put it together.

Ted had spent a lifetime working outside of the Hollywood system, and now he found himself living far far away from it. Fellow exploitation filmmaker Ray Dennis Steckler also lived in Las Vegas. Steckler had been responsible for some real drive-in doozies, not least of which were *The Thrill Killers*, *Wild Guitar*, *Rat Pfink a Boo Boo*, and the infamous and unforgettable *The Incredibly Strange Creatures Who Stopped Living and Became Mixed-Up Zombies*.

Practicing attorney at law Jeffrey C. Hogue was a long-time film buff and wanted to get involved in the industry. In the early 80s he contacted Ted about an action film project called *Angel of Vengeance*. The film would involve a rape/revenge plot line, a military outpost setting, a motorcycle gang, and lots of guns, bombs, gore and explosions. Ted concocted a quick budget of two-hundred-and-forty-thousand smackers. This was too rich for Hogue's blood, so he approached someone he thought would be the next best man for the job, Ray Dennis Steckler. Steckler surmised that he could bring the film in at 20 grand. Hogue was impressed. Hogue signed Steckler for the job.

The film was to center on a character, Tina, who had relocated to a small-town cabin in order to write a book about her father, who was a successful military man. While in town she is approached by a brain-dead Neanderthal of a man (aptly named Manny) who has ideas of a sexual nature in mind for himself and the cute Tina. Of course, Tina declines, and later in the film she is repeatedly raped by Manny and his cronies. Tina is a fighter and a survivor, and

Original title and artwork for *War Cat*.

one by one she takes her revenge upon her attackers. The plot of the film is not at all unlike Meir Zarchi's 1978 scorcher *I Spit on Your Grave*, where a young, and presumably innocent, Jennifer Hill retreats to the country to pen a novel and is repeatedly raped and brutalized by a gang of miscreants.

Rumor has it that Steckler spent the first two days of the production shooting 16mm footage of locations and streets and passing cars. Steckler, a charming and endearing director in his own right, is certainly capable (and often guilty) of padding his films with this type of "time capsule" footage. Jeffrey Hogue, however, was quite sure that travelogue scenes of Las Vegas was not the ingredient necessary for a successful exploitation film. As Steckler recalls, "I was hired to do a Ray Dennis Steckler movie. Hogue wanted a Jeffery C. Hogue movie. I gave it to Ted."

In addition, Steckler's projected budget had increased drastically when the location was shifted from Las Vegas to Northern California. Also, a larger cast and crew were employed, making Hogue and associate producer Craig T. Keller extremely unhappy, as the changes were putting them in a difficult financial position. The businessmen were about to shirk their businesslike demeanor; but, fortunately, the answer to their problems was waiting in the wings. Ted Mikels was on the set.

Steckler and Ted had been friendly for some time, and Steckler had asked that Ted join the project as production supervisor in order to make sure that all went smoothly. When things went awry between Steckler and producer Hogue, Ted was asked to step in. Ted recalls:

> I told them that I would only do it if Ray said that it was okay. I went to him and said, "Ray, they want me to take over directing this movie, but I won't do it without your good graces." He said, "Ted, we'll be out of here by tomorrow afternoon. Good luck with the movie." That was it, I was in charge of directing *War Cat*, which at the time was still under the working title *Angel of Vengeance*.

Of course, the budget escalated higher than anticipated in the beginning, but with Ted's knowledge and experience, Hogue literally handed over his checkbook. From Ted's recollection, he was personally responsible for spending around $150,000 of the film's $350,000 final cost. Hogue and Ted had a fantastic working relationship, and that was fortunate too, as Hogue was not only acting as producer of the film, but also as one of its antagonists. He portrayed "Jake," who gets his eyes gouged out by the determined and Rambo-like Tina. As Ted remembers:

> Jeff [Hogue] was a joy to work with, and he was very friendly on a personal level. Gary Thompson, who'd written the script, and there was very little of it, had written for the television series *Vegas*. But as I said, there was very little to the script of *War Cat*, and every morning, at breakfast, Jeff and I would talk about that day's shooting. Jeff would say, "Can we do such and such?" and I'd say, "We can do anything you want to do." He was the man with the money, so whatever he wanted I did. I even did the executions, which I was not, and still am not, fond of. It was too cold and calculated. The revenge stuff involving the leading girl was fine, but the gunshots to the heads of the Thrill Killers was something that I would not have put into a movie of my own making; but it was Jeff's movie, so I did what he asked.

The Thrill Killers that Ted speaks of were one of the very few things left intact from the brief period that Ray Steckler was in charge of the production. Steckler apparently decided to give a nod to his 1964 feature by christening the renegade biker gang of the film "the Thrill Killers." It was a nice, though no-less-shameless, touch that reminds fans of the genre that the film once belonged to another beloved director of independent cinema. Regarding Steckler, Ted related:

> I'll tell you this, and I'm not really proud of it, but it did happen. On my first day of

shooting, after I'd taken over the project, the girl playing Tina literally got on her knees, kissed my hand and thanked me for taking over directing the film. It was the scene where her character begs for a chance to escape by making a deal with the Major to have his men hunt her like an animal, kind of like that movie *The Most Dangerous Game*. Again, I'm not proud of this, as Ray is a friend, but it did happen that way. But I did appreciate the fact that she was pleased to have me as director of the movie.

One half of the film was shot in the mountains of North California near a town called Independence—an ironic choice, given that the film concentrates on a group of militant outlaws bent on surviving an impending war and invasion. But the other half of the picture was photographed in Ted's very own backyard. The area that Ted had purchased in Las Vegas had three smaller houses upon several acres of land:

> The scene where Bo the woodcutter gets murdered along with his wife was on my property. The buildings where the Major and his men are planning all of their attacks were all mine too.

Ted has very fond memories of the shoot. "I did 117 camera set-ups in one day with only one camera. That has to be some sort of a record!" But despite Ted's enthusiasm for the project, he was not fully paid for his duties. He only received $15,000 for editing, directing and the rental of his equipment. In those days his editing fee alone was $22,500, and the cutting of this specific picture was far more of a chore than he had anticipated:

> Initially I wasn't supposed to edit the film, but Jeff really wanted me to do it. The film had been shipped here and there and when it finally arrived it had been magnetized by having gone through all of the airport screenings. I had to go in and place the sound back in frame by frame. I had to use a magnifying lense in order to see the actors' mouth movements and get the sound synched up as closely as I could get it. I tell you, that was the hardest editing job of my entire career. If I had it to do over I

The Rambo-like Tina (Jannina Poytner) in *War Cat*.

wouldn't do it for a cent less than $50,000, and that was in the mid–80s.

As Ted mentioned, *War Cat* contains some pretty grisly scenes and images, particularly the rape scenes and the point blank execution of two Thrill Killers. In fact, the executions are handled so dryly and in such a deadpan fashion that the sequences take on an almost snuff film–like quality. As Ted recalls, "Hogue wanted all that rough stuff in there. Personally, I wasn't comfortable with it, but he was the one signing the checks."

Once the picture was completed, it enjoyed a fairly successful run in the South. To date, it is Ted's last movie to receive a theatrical release. In the end, the film's director feels very little affinity for the final product, even if it did contain the empowered female angle that he loves so dearly. "It wasn't my picture. I was hired to do the work. That movie belongs to Jeff Hogue. I feel closer to *Worm Eaters* than I do *War Cat*." Even so, *War Cat* successfully showcases Ted V. Mikels' penny-pinching filmmaking talents

Producer Jeffery C. Hogue gets his in *War Cat*.

ing for the magazine *Brutarian*, quite liked the film, recognizing its dark and near hopeless tone:

War Cat has been pared by Hogue and Mikels to a mere 78 minutes, excising the dross of exposition, character development, and all but the most rudimentary dialogue. What remains is an almost unbearable series of tableaus depicting little more than depravity and graphic violence. This strategy on the part of the filmmakers serves to strengthen the viewer's growing sense of horror and dislocation as the story unfolds, yet it also leaves the viewer with the burning question: why would anyone bother fighting for survival in such an increasingly brutal and psychotic environment? This is, however, not a major failing; those cineastes who enjoy the kind of sensibility displayed in films such as *I Spit on Your Grave* and *Fight for Your Life* will not want to miss *War Cat*.

as well as, or better than, some of his more popular features. Dominick J. Salemi, writ-

13. *Mission: Killfast*

Synopsis from Press Materials

Nuclear detonators stolen from a United States military installation fall into the hands of unscrupulous international weapons dealers. The detonators are transferred to highly mobile terrorists in training camps in a third world country, where they are being used for nuclear blackmail.

The CIA put many of the weapons dealers out of business through placement of "moles" into the energy centers of the terrorist operations. Several of the agents, working undercover, are found out and killed after locating the weapon warehouses and penetrating the strongholds of these camps. The illegal and deadly shipments continue.

Models for a *Playboy* type magazine entertain foreign buyers in a ploy to hide the supply-line of shipments from a large manufacturer.

A hit-man is brought in to eliminate any agent suspects.

Hoping to avoid a full-scale military incident, the CIA and agents from British Intelligence enlist the services of an ex-agent, Tiger Yang, and his trained team of fighters to spearhead activities to stop the shipments and retrieve the nuclear detonators.

Yang and his men, with the support of government agents, penetrate the terrorists' strongholds and succeed with their mission to halt the arms-dealing and possible nuclear calamity by demolishing the encampments and returning the detonators to U.S. Intelligence.

13. Mission: Killfast

Credits

Cast: Tiger Yang (Tiger); Sonny King (Murak); Ronald Gregg (Harry Bremen); Sharon Hughes (Catherine "Catt" Valone); Myron Natwick (Nick Julius); Kyle E. Cranston (Shannon D'Apolito); Harry Pugh (Ansemino D'Apolito); Rex Ravelle (Cocoa Charlie); Chuck Alford (Fike); Ron Dwart (Blake—CIA); Robert Legionaire (Pritchard—CIA); Wendy O. Altamura/Shanti (Chantelle—CIA); Perry Genovese (Mario); Fred De Florentis (Terrorist Chief); Carol Stein (Slavitza); Charles McLaughlin (Valone); Sandra Browning (Maria); Gary W. Hodge (Lacey); Jewel Shephard (Miss August); Freddie Bell (Freddie the Informer); Michael J. Patton (Limo Driver); Hector Garcia (First CIA—Parade); Mark Beach (Second CIA—Parade); Nedra Cooper Scott (Female Terrorist Aide); Jack Streeter (CIA Office Agent); Linette Cobb (SCAM Magazine Model); Stan Yale (Poolside Sheik); Deborah Ann Howell (Model with Sheik); Kelly Elkins (Parade Sniper); Sharae D'Antona Jonak and Susan Aller (Murak's Girls); Timothy B. Davis (Poolside Second Photographer); Mike Garrison (Aide to Camp Commander); Behrouz Vossoughi (Terrorist Camp Commander); Sue Yang and James Yang (in parade); Paul Yang, Jerry Dupuis, Paul Cheng, Steve Moles, Ali Jafar, Howard Kay, Behzad Khodaverian, Von J. Roy, Najib K. Khoury, Mark E. Crews, Lisa Kee, Greg Linsmeire (Moo-Yea-Do Black Belt Members); Ron Jason, Joe Azzato, Reece Harrison, Ken Schultz, Ricky Davenport, Marya Grant, Katena Gardener, William Stone, Ted V. Mikels, Jr., Pierre Mzadeth, Bernard Peter Williams (Camp Terrorists); Danielle Stiles, Guy Ferraro, Colleen Cocks, Jill Johnson, Ramona Thrower, Chuck Terrell, Bobbi Petroni, Aly Cusumano, Lee Garland, GiGi McAllister, Ed Purcell (Pool Party).

Production: (Reno Crew): *martial arts choreographer*: Grand Master Tiger Yang. *Las Vegas stunt coordinator*: Perry Genovese. *stuntmen*: Roy Kieffer, Nick Prvulov, Larry Scott, Wally Hawkins, Stephen Boccason, Michael Delcarpini, Keith Johnson, Gary Roberts, Joel Scudder (crossbow). *cinematography*: Miles Blum, Ron Vidor. *first assistant camera*: Mark Ludwig, Scott Smith. *second assistant camera*: Joel Soisson, William Guttentag. *camera assistants*: Richard Pomeroy, Jennifer Collins. *gaffers*: Ken Wiatrak, Doug Cragoe. *best girl electrician*: Beth S. Stiller. *gaffer/grip*: Steve Gero. *sound recordist mixer*: David Sonnenshien. *boom grip*: Maria De La Rosa. *grips*: Mark Settles, Karey John Watson. *first assistant director*: Bill Moroni. *second assistant director*: Michael Morse. *production manager*: Mark Ratering. *talent coordinator*: Pierre Mzadeh. *script supervisor*: Kathryn S. Louis. *special effects*: John Eggett, the Court Wizards. *wardrobe*: Jennifer Michaud. *make-up*: Dale Gilespie. *sets/props*: Linette Cob. *Reno stunt coordinator*: Tony Snegoff. (Las Vegas Crew): *cinematographer*: Patrick B. Kerby. *first assistant camera*: Maurice McGuire. *gaffer/key grip*: Dan Owen. *second unit camera*: John Higgins. *sound recordist*: Jim Mingo. *boom grip*: Gary Seidman. *driver grip*: Ted V. Mikels, Jr. *grips*: Lyle Maulsby, Joel Scudder. *first assistant director*: Garry W. Hodge. *second assistant director*: Scott Weimer. *production manager*: Arnie Bartz. *script supervisor*: Art Lynch. *make-up*: Michael Keavin. *props/sets*: Ron Jason, Michael J. Patton. *special effects*: Chuck Alford. *production equipment*: Cinema Features, Inc. *craft food services*: Jackie Mindell, Polly Montgomery. *medical attendant*: Wm. G. Stone, M.D. *editor—picture, sound, music*: Ted V. Mikels. *assistant editors*: Wendy O. Altamura/Shanti, Russell Kingston. *re-recording mixers*: Irv Nafshun, Steve Nafshun, Screen Music Lab. *titles and opticals*: T and T Optical Effects, Inc. *film laboratory and prints*: Hawk Film Lab. *music*: Nicholas Carras, Jack Cookerly. *screenplay*: Ted V. Mikels, Hugh Smith, Don Rene Patterson.

executive producer: Patrick J. Shannon (in association with Cinema Features, Inc.). *associate producers and additional story material*: Wendy O. Altamura/Shanti, Gerald W. Carroll. *directed and produced by*: Ted V. Mikels. *filmed in*: color. *Running Time*: 97 minutes. *aspect ratio*: shot at full frame and projected at 1.85:1. A presentation of Claddagh Holdings, Inc., and TVM Global Entertainment, Ltd. *partially filmed*: 1982. *completed filming*: 1990. *released*: 1991.

The Film

I wait for no one!—Tiger Yang from *Mission: Killfast*

Mission: Killfast may not be one of Ted V. Mikels' more well known projects, but it certainly scores high marks for being one of his most technically adept. Arguably, the acting, editing, cinematography, script and storyline are as well done as any he'd made since *The Doll Squad*. Nonetheless, Ted wasn't entirely thrilled with the outcome. He laments:

> As I view the film these days, I wish I would have shortened it by 12 minutes or so. I have a Beta copy that I made for myself, and it moves a lot faster. It's an action movie! I cut out several scenes of unnecessary dialogue, and it's just a better film for me. Unfortunately, I edited the work print, and in order to re-cut the film for the market, I would have to have another made and that would cost thousands.

One contributing factor that has kept this action-thriller from the public eye is a multitude of title changes that confound the brain and memory alike. Only the film's creator could possibly recall them all; *some* were: *Cocoa Charlie* (in regards to the film's antagonist), *Catt and Cocoa* (in regards to the film's heroine), *Alias: Cocoa Charlie, Omega Assassins, Operation Overkill* and, finally, *Mission: Killfast*.

However, another obstacle was in place—the city in which Ted lived. California had become increasingly more and more difficult to film in, even going so far as to charge Ted $200 a day for shooting on his own property! Even more, the hustle and bustle of the metro area was added aggravation that Ted didn't need to deal with in regards to getting his cast and crew to the locations on time; wall-to-wall traffic, automobile accidents, time delays involving "this and that" could hinder, or prove fatal to, a low-budget production. The solution? Charter a bus, herd 'em up, and head 'em out ... to Reno.

Ted more or less kept his cast and crew prisoner for a large portion of the shoot, and it worked famously in his *and* their favor. They all stayed in the same hotel, ate at the same restaurants, and, in effect, had a working vacation away from the madness that is Hollywood. The friendly atmosphere on the set, coupled with the quasi–stress free environment and working conditions, could only be advantageous to all involved. Conse-

One of the many titles that Ted V. Mikels used for the film that would eventually be called *Mission: Killfast*.

13. Mission: Killfast

Promotional artwork for *Mission: Killfast* (1991).

quently, this luxury—the lodging, the meals and the isolation—would total in excess of $26,000, a sum that was considerably higher than a good many of Ted's films had cost to make in the first place.

Still, seemingly perfect accommodations and a comparatively inflated budget didn't nip all problems in the bud. Budgetary constraints was still the order of the day, and soon much of the initial financing began to fall through. Ted knew the drill. He knew it all too well. Corners had to be cut and footage had to be dropped, as the frugal filmmaker recalls:

> We tried to "blow up" the bad guy's Cadillac, which was, in actuality, my own car. The weather was so cold in Reno that the naphthalene and the fire pan threw the crystals into the air when the explosion was to take place, and the crystals floated down between the camera and the car like snowflakes. The fireball that was supposed to take place would have obliterated the vision of the Cadillac, but, alas, it didn't, and that sequence was never shot.

Corner-cutting involved things like shooting all the helicopter sequences in as few as two hours, since that was all that could be allotted by the film's budget. Another was that many of the cast died multiple times on screen, and Ted laughs about this one:

> At the wrap party, which was at least 40 people, my very close friend Shanti asked, "How many have been killed at least once in this film?" Everyone's hand went up. "How many were killed a second time?" Once

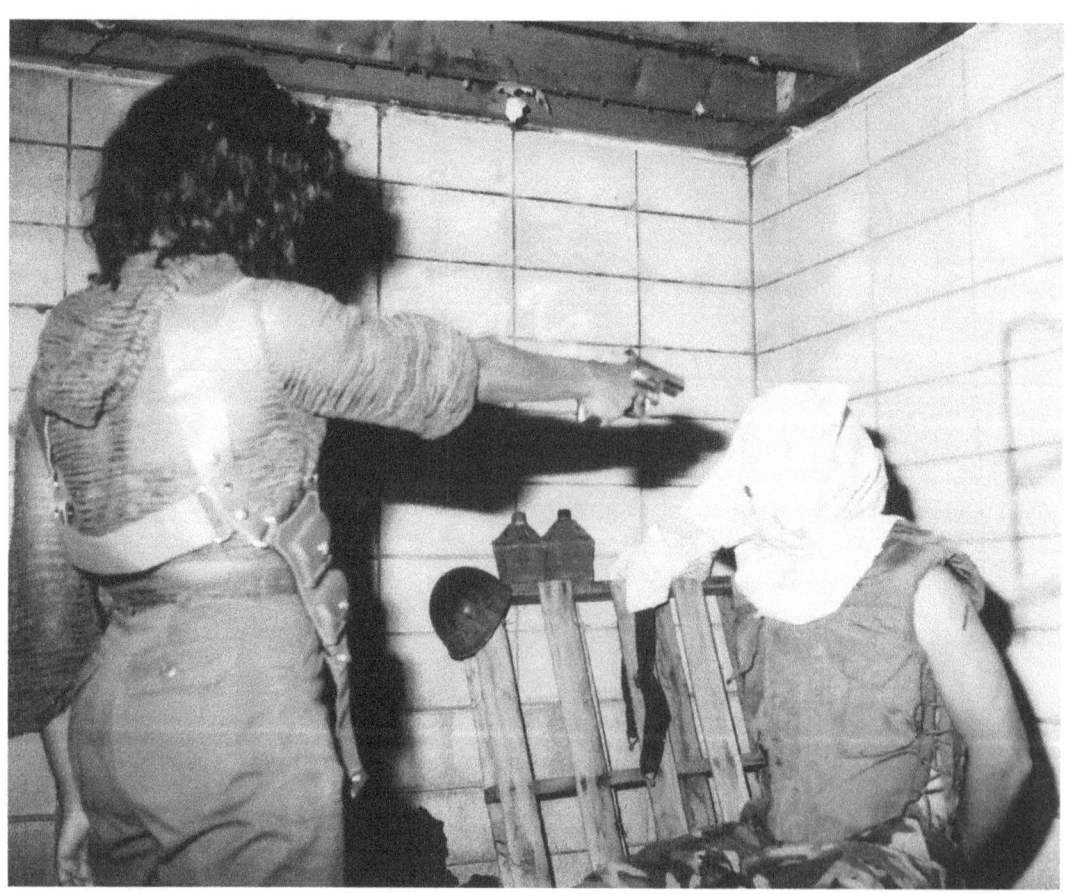

A bleak scene from *Mission: Killfast*.

On the set of *Mission: Killfast*.

again, all hands were raised. "Three times!?!" And still some raised their hands. The reason why they couldn't be killed more times was that there wasn't any cloth left on their uniforms which could be shot to heck. We had to film the cast from varying angles so the other bullet holes would not be visible.

Another part of the "Ted V. Mikels corner-cutting package" involves his willingness to accept favors from his accomplices. Again, all things have to be utilized in order to keep the project rolling along as smoothly as possible. One fellow offered his services as a camera repairman, and Ted was, no doubt, thrilled at having his Mitchell tuned-up for the shoot; but something went awry, as he explains:

> The guy took the Mitchell apart, since he was a service tech at a Hollywood repair place. He replaced the claw pull-down levers at the wrong place in the gear-box, so the time when the exposure was to be made, the film was blocked from the aperture, and when the aperture was open, the film was moving with the claw motion, so all we had for that long night's shoot of delicate scenes was a continuous blur. The entire shooting session had to be re-done later when we again had access to the setting in a vacant house. In other words, the exposure and the film movement timing was off.

Luckily, none of this affected the topless scenes of the wonderful and lovely B-movie queen Jewel Shepard. Nudity in Ted's films is a real rarity, but a wholly welcomed one just the same. Though it is amazing that it happened at all. Ted has said time and time again that he is not one for sex and nudity in film, and, according to Ms. Shepard in her book *Invasion of the B-Girls*, neither is she (note: Ms. Shepard is not speaking specifically of *Mission: Killfast*): "It was a painful experience to have to take off your clothes just to keep food on the table, but I didn't have anyone or anything else at that moment."

It's unfortunate that Ms. Shepard felt forced to compromise her ethics and pride, but Ted recalls her being very easygoing about the scenes. To his recollection, she even seemed comfortable in the pool sequences where anyone in the complex could have seen her. But why include nude scenes at all if they're not necessary to the plotline? Further, why demand them when the very folks involved are uncomfortable with the situation? Ted sets the record straight:

> At the time I did *Mission: Killfast* it was said that any film available for the world market, and rated R, whether for violent action, sex or whatever, had to contain nude scenes, or it probably would not be sold. Hence the nude shots, albeit done tastefully, I think.

Interestingly enough, in his 1982 interview with V. Vale for *The Incredibly Strange Films* book, Ted revealed that *Mission: Killfast* (known then as *Operation Overkill*) would differ from many of his other films in that a strong female lead would not be present. Initially, Ted wanted Tiger Yang to take the spotlight, but "Ted the ladies man" couldn't resist. The temptation was just too great, and Sharon Hughes' character Catt became the proverbial headstrong woman that Ted is so well known for creating, exploring and exploiting. It's all to the credit of the film, too; Catt is sharp, sexy, believable, able-bodied (to say the least) and hell-bent on avenging her father's death.

It's astounding, but *Mission: Killfast* literally took nine years, and over $500,000, to complete. If finished on time in 1982, the film would have surely found its fans. The syndicated program *Kung Fu Theater* was all the rage and in full force. This poorly dubbed but hi-octane broadcast was helping expose millions to the wonderful world of Asian cinema and all of its high-kicking, chopping and socking mayhem. Youngsters and adults alike were indulging themselves in Eastern culture by purchasing butterfly knives, throwing stars, samurai swords, ninja

Catt (Sharon Hughes) with Ted V. Mikels and crew preparing for another shot in *Mission: Killfast*.

outfits and maybe even a chopstick or two. *Mission: Killfast* had a built-in audience.

Now, Ted has been adamant and outspoken about his aversion to Chop-Saki cinema, and he wanted something altogether different for his film. Rather than depicting the martial arts in a cartoon-like fashion (as was not only customary but expected of Chop-Saki), he longed to make a film where the executions of kung fu and karate were more realistic than super-hero–like. To a large degree he succeeded.

Moreover, the less than campy violence could be chalked up to his very real, and very discouraging, dissatisfaction over the trials and tribulations of finishing the film and getting it to theaters. Whether aware of it or not, the barrage of bombings, shootings and tortures displayed over and over again in the picture were quite possibly a celluloid manifestation of Ted's heartaches and frustrations. More than ever, *Mission: Killfast* is a testament, yet again, to a man who is a walking, talking, breathing marvel of patience and persistence.

Author and enthusiast of this form of movie Michael Weldon was appropriately impressed, as he stated in *Psychotronic Video* number 34:

> Jewel Shepard has the standout nude scenes.... With lots of explosions, a flaming man, Ted's voice on a car phone, important faxes, and typically overdone sound FX. It was filmed in Las Vegas and Reno. If released when new, the Korean Yang could have been as famous as Leo Fong!

Whether or not Tiger Yang would have, or could have, been thrust into the same ranks as Fong is debatable, but Yang's strengths and abilities are undeniable. Yang still has several schools dedicated to his chosen sport, and just as many (or more) movie credits to boot. And he is a two-time holder of the world championship of martial arts. Still not impressed? Take in this account from Ted:

> Tiger and I were headed down the highway towards Reno, and we stopped off for a minute. I came back to the car and found Tiger in a small river bed assessing a large rock. I told Tiger that it was time to go, but he looked up at me and said, "I break." I said, "C'mon Tiger, you'll hurt your hand and we'll never be able to do the movie." To which he replied, "I break! I break!." Tiger smashed his fist two times into this rock and broke it into 3 pieces. It really had to be a mind over matter kind of thing. It was amazing! I picked up the pieces of the rock and put them into the trunk of my car.

Another point worth mentioning is that the film's antagonist, Cocoa Charlie, was portrayed by world famous body builder, and Mr. California 1940, Rex Revalle. He had a short career in movies, but reportedly turned up as a stunt man and stand in for Johnny Weissmuller on a few of the *Tarzan* films. Ravelle also owned a health club and spa in Hawaii.

Mission: Killfast is Ted's last foray into *film*making, as skyrocketing production costs have led him and his cohorts down the less expensive route of video production. Video has become a necessary evil for many of the independents. Lots of things have changed over the years. Conglomerates have successfully swallowed up the little man, and now several of those conglomerates are being swallowed by even *bigger*(!) conglomerates. It's pretty sickening, and Ted's not at all happy with it either, as he confessed to Michael Weldon in *Psychotronic Video* number 32:

> When you do something 35mm, you like to play theaters, but you couldn't buy your way into a theater right now at any price. A million dollars would not put you into a theater. The loss of drive-ins was devastating. And an even bigger loss was from the tax laws changing, so that there was no longer a tax haven, sometime near 1980. That was the end of getting an investor, because he couldn't even write off his investment.

All in all, *Mission: Killfast* is a small gem of independent genre cinema. The film moves along competently, with the ups and downs all in their proper places. The photography is telling, and the performances

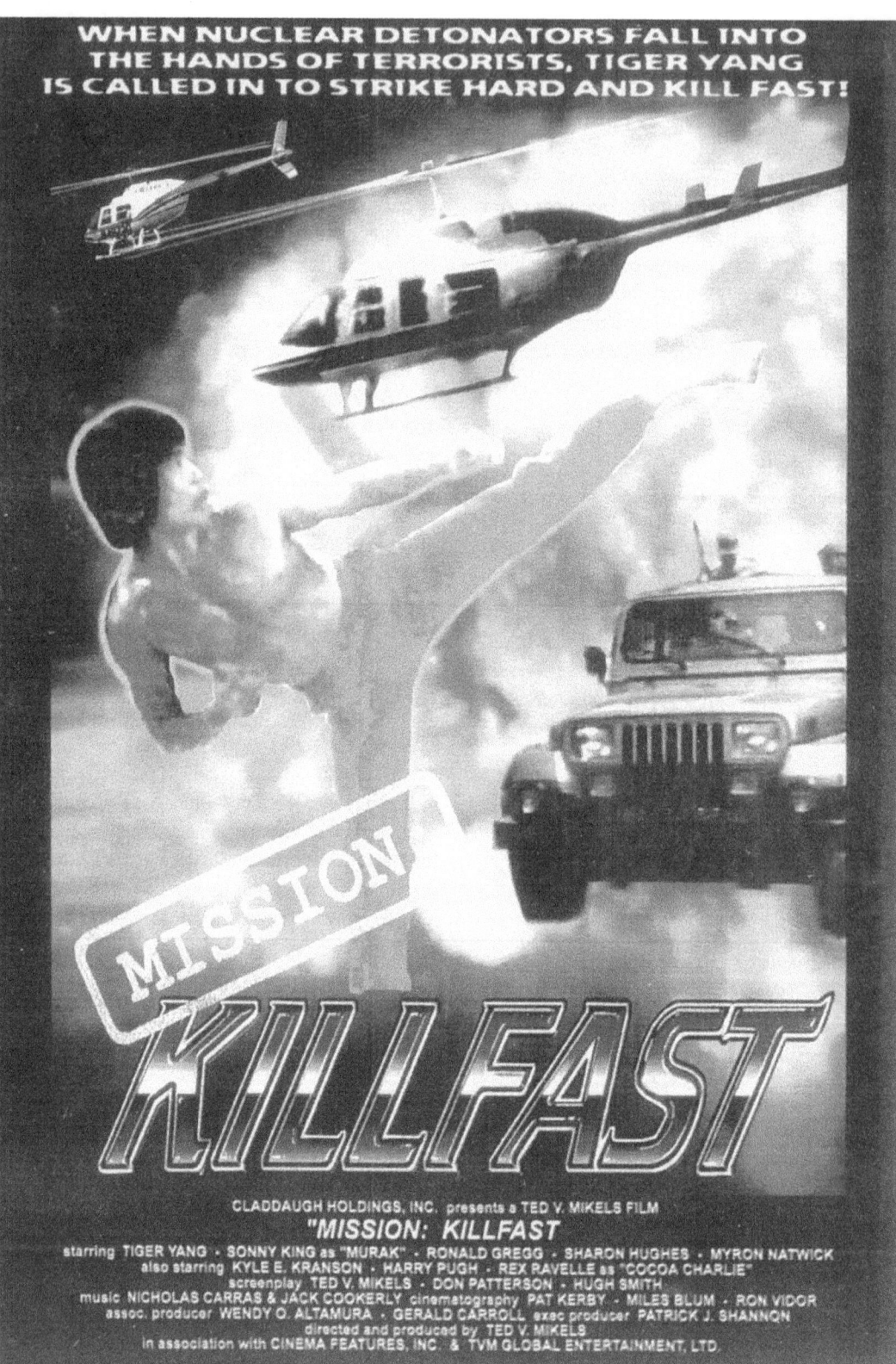

Alternate artwork for *Mission: Killfast*.

Ted V. Mikels (in foreground) with Shanti (seated, wearing helmet), awaiting the next take in *Mission: Killfast*.

are handled quite well for this type of low-budget picture, but it's hardly flawless.

For all of its strengths, *Mission: Killfast* contains its share of shortcomings. Of note are a few of the bunker explosions (during the nighttime battle) that were clearly shot in the daytime. Contrastingly, in the audio commentary of the DVD Ted points out some of his day-for-night shots (and vice versa), which are completely undetectable to this writer's eye. He did a fabulous job of lighting and matting *these* scenes properly, so why allow an obviously day-lit shot in a nighttime sequence? The answer is simple. Ted has entirely too much on his plate to be able to catch every single solitary incorrect nuance. This one-man-band approach does not spring from any type of vanity or ego trip, however, as he explained to Boyd Rice in the book *Incredibly Strange Films*:

If you want to be a filmmaker, it's like: if you want an automobile and all you've got is a junkyard full of parts and pieces; if you don't have any other way to get it, you build it. If that means you have to learn how to paint the car when it's through, you do that too. It's the same with making a film: I don't *like* having to write, produce, direct, raise the money, shoot, be director of photography, cameraman, work with the drama teacher, do the make-up and special effects, do all the editing, put on every sound effect, do all the music, handle it through the answer print, then start out with the film under your arm, selling it.... I don't do that because I *want* to; I do it because sometimes there's no other way. *I do whatever it takes*.... It would be nice to be able to just hire someone and have all these bits and pieces done. In a way it's an advantage to do it yourself, but it's also a disadvantage because it takes so much time. You start writing, end up with your first answer print, and it's a year out of your life.

One year is understandable, but nine years is something altogether different. Simply put, *Mission: Killfast* became a labor of love for Ted. A labor of love that was seemingly plagued with problems from beginning to end. It's a wonder Ted didn't develop an ulcer from this particular incident:

> Since I was overwhelmed day and night doing everything I had to do, and dealing with the pounding on my motel room door all through the night by folks who were wanting answers to the next day's shoot, as I had no functional production manager, I had little or no sleep for a month. I had given my checkbook to one of my assistants to handle for me. He forgot to record one sizeable check paid out for negative film raw-stock, and I was faced with getting my entire cast and crew back from Reno to Los Angeles with no money left. I hocked my prize Angenieux 35mm zoom lens for six thousand dollars to get everyone back home again. It took a long time to get it back.

With this picture Ted exercised his filmmaking urges, while at the same time exorcizing his frustrations with the film industry. New friendships were born and old ones were rekindled, as was the case on many of his productions. When all was said and done, Ted had created an enjoyable and exciting action-adventure movie filled with "international intrigue, spies, terrorists and martial arts." A movie that he could, would and should forever be proud of having made.

PART TWO

The Videos of Ted V. Mikels

"Ted was unique in our field, and his pictures are very memorable. In addition to that, he is one of the warmest and most lovable characters in the exploitation industry that I have ever had the pleasure of meeting."— Producer David F. Friedman (*Blood Feast* and *The Defilers*)

Introduction

Nineteen eighty-six saw the final (to date) theatrical release for a Ted V. Mikels staging, *War Cat*. 1990 was witness to Ted's final (to date) 35mm film production, *Mission: Killfast*. As mentioned in the previous chapter, the late 80s were very difficult for the independent moviemaker. Changes in tax laws and the death of the drive-in theater were wielding the proverbial axe that would behead the exploitation cinema of old. Video tape and video production would be the next frontier for movie creators such as Ted V. Mikels.

In compiling this book, it seemed only fair to separate the "films" from the "videos." There is a different process in producing and bringing video to the screen, whether it be the big screen or the small screen. It's also worth pointing out that video productions lack the grainy and tactile sense and warmth that 35, 16 or even 8mm films contain, and should be judged accordingly. Video tape almost always brings a stark and unusual quality to a movie, and Ted's latest six features are no exceptions.

Still, some of these "qualities" are not always desired ones. The lighting can be harsh and unforgiving, allowing every facial blemish to beam. Audio-wise, the soundtrack and/or dialogue can be muffled and, at times, downright inaudible. Cinematically? Looking-like-a-soap-opera is the best way to describe it, and depending on one's palette, or patience, for such characteristics, Ted's later features may or may not satisfy.

Additionally, movie production on video tape can (and does) carry the "anybody can do it" baggage, and *that* baggage is a big hump to get over. It's a "hump" that not only the moviemaker has to deal with, but also the fans of this type of cinema. While Ted recognizes the differences between the two mediums, he maintains that:

> People obsessed with making movies will make them any way that they can, and people who like these types of movies are going

to like them whether they are shot on video or on 35mm film. If they like the story then they'll like the movie. I honestly don't think they give a poop what it's shot on. Making movies is an obsession of mine, and I just always hope and pray that I can make at least *some* of the money back to recoup my costs.

However, be forewarned that, no matter the medium, these are still very much Ted V. Mikels' productions. The visage and feel is different, but quirky characters and oddball situations abound. Subplots weave wildly in and out and around themselves, while strange monsters and villains, and even strange heroes and heroines, find their way into these videos. Ted continues to steer clear of formulaic moviemaking, and, regardless of his newer and more inexpensive manner of creation, his latest half-dozen pictures are certainly worthy of a look-see or two.

Ted V. Mikels hard at work on *Corpse Grinders II* (2000).

14. *Dimension in Fear*

Synopsis from Press Materials

A pretty and talented television weather reporter, Dedra Hagan, en route to a new assignment in Las Vegas, Nevada, from Texas, encounters a psycho-killer who has escaped from prison. He has vowed to murder everyone who testified against him. While traveling mountain roads, Dedra's car breaks down, and no one will give her a ride except our killer. After escaping, he has committed several murders and stolen a car. A chase on the high desert ensues when the stolen auto blows a tire. Dedra has sprayed pepper spray into the killer's eyes during the chase. She encounters rattlesnakes and scorpions while trying to hide from the man. She collapses into the sand as the killer abandons the chase. He vows to kill her when he finds her again. After killing nine people, he is about to make Detective Mays and Dedra the tenth and eleventh. The killer has kidnapped Dedra after shooting the detective who was trying to protect her. The killer intends to kill her and sink her body to the bottom of Lake Mead by weighing her down with chains. The ending is shocking and leaves lingering thoughts. A suspense thriller filmed in and around Las Vegas and other Nevada locations.

Credits

Cast: Ron Jason (Cal Lewis); Ron Jason (Ralph Lewis); James Lee Roberts,

John Cornett, James Monllos, Rob Swifel (Arresting Troopers); Robert Southerland (Jail Captain Moore); Colby Miller, Michael Scott (Jail Guards); Denise Alford (Jail Captain's Secretary); Gene Ellison Jones (Detective John Mays); Henry Wood, Michael Eric Van Hoose, Shane Gorrell (Jail Prisoners); Chuck Alford (Head Jail Guard); Margaret Cadera (Police Telephone Operator); Scott Miller, Crystal Smith-Wright (Television Newscasters); Nicole West (Dedra Hagen); Delores Fuller (T.V. Station Owner); Liz Renay, Sherrie Tady, Perry Lewis, Jerry Olenyn, Bunny Suttle, Donald Laws, Carol Holboke, Philip Chamberlin, Chris Henkel (Station Party Guests); Terry Donahue (Homeless Drunk); Liz Renay (Monique the Psychic); Nancy Williams (Woman on Train); Arnie Bartz (Rancher Cal Lewis Kills); Barrie Bailey (Rancher's Wife whom Cal Kills); Elissa Finale (Rancher's Daughter whom Cal Kills); Sherrie Tady (Mother of Dedra Hagen); Veva Roberts (Boy's Mother in Restaurant); Kenneth James Ebner (Little Boy in Restaurant); James Peck (Bob, Driver Picking Up Cal); Helen Baker (Marsha, Bob's Wife); Keith Grimes (Mechanic at Desert Garage); Kenneth Bolling (Second Mechanic); Vincent T. Altamura (Man Giving Dedra Ride); Dudley Boleware, Mary Boleware (First Rest Stop Couple); Tony Rome, Nancy Lee Romanaco (Second Rest Stop Couple); Donneda Bindues (Village Store Clerk); Frank Davis (State Trooper at Bodies); Shanti (Dr. Anjhí); William Garbaz (Plainclothes Officer at Dr. Anjhí's Office Door); Ted V. Mikels (Motel Desk Clerk); Melody Kinney (Cocktail Waitress Witness); Tracey Roweth (Second Cocktail Waitress); Mike "Sluggo" Woltman (Bartender at Lounge); Chris Gomez, Julie Y. Jones (Dirt Bike Couple); William Stone, M.D. (Quick-Care Medic); Candace Morrison, Foster Boom (Quick-Care Nurses); Scott Paolera (Quick-Care Janitor); Eddie Smitz (Detective Smith); Joni Boyer, Judy Coady (Hookers); Alice Williams (Motel Desk Clerk); Patrick Carter, James Vahovick (911 Police Guards in Motel); Art Lynch (Television and Radio Voice-Overs)

Production: *director, producer, cinematographer*: Ted V. Mikels. *story*: Ted V. Mikels, Gerald W. Carroll. *co-executive producers*: John F. Willuhn, Don B. Lewis. *associate producer*: Thoma D. Vidmar. *story consultant*: Wendy O. Altamura, Ph.D. *production manager*: Arnie Bartz. *location manager*: James Lee Roberts. *music, sound*: Glen Grayson. *editor*: Ted V. Mikels. *assistant camera*: Adam Lane, Steve Silvas, Daryl Blakely, Gabe Campisi. *key grip*: J. L. Roberts. *sound*: Chris Henkel. *production assistants*: Gerald Wilcox, Alan Palmer, Pete Jonas, Sandra Clory. *electronic/video engineer*: Gene Larson. *video consultant*: Harlan Hill. *running time*: 1 hour and 49 minutes. Color. *aspect ratio*: full-frame. *completed and released*: 1997.

The Video

Dirty little bitch! If I find her, I'll kill her.—
Cal Lewis from *Dimension in Fear*

Direct-to-video films inherently have a hard go of it. Promotional angles are streamlined and minimized. Few television commercials are aired to make the public aware of its existence, and only a small amount of paper materials are produced to help bolster the production. There are no theatrical trailers, theatrical one-sheets or, most importantly (and most damaging), theatrical showings.

Direct-to-video films, even those backed by the major Hollywood studios, go largely unnoticed or ignored. So it should stand to reason that direct-to-video *videos* will have an even harder time finding the movieviewing public. *This* difficulty was one that Ted V. Mikels was fully aware of, but Ted's love for the production of movies completely superseded his doubts and reservations about the plight of the independent

Artwork for *Dimension in Fear* (1997).

moviemaker. As Ted's friend and fellow filmmaker Ray Dennis Steckler attests: "Ted V. Mikels loves making movies! It's what he does."

The maverick moviemaker was determined to move on, despite the disheartening climate in independent cinema production. In 1997 Ted stepped back into the ring. The fruits of his labors? *Dimension in Fear*. This was Ted's first feature-length production since the completion of *Mission: Killfast* seven years early in 1990. So what was Ted doing during those 7 long years?

> Well, I was shooting commercials. I opened the studio. We were doing a lot of music demos. I'd written *Revenge of the Lady Ninjas*, and nothing came of that, and I was trying to get the money together to finish my pet project, *Chad*. We were also doing music videos at the studio, and I did a full 12-minute promotional video for Chris Rock, and I believe it did very well for him and helped land him some jobs. The Nevada State Film Commission referred Chris Rock to me. I just did dozens and dozens of music videos and promos. There was a lot of activity going on other than the actual shooting of a movie. I'd also written a piece called *Two Feathers and Little Hawk* about an Indian boy, and then another called *Girl Power* about female athletes that were weightlifters and in beauty contests and all of that. Anyway, I'd written several screenplays, and then we, Shanti and I, took some trips. We also had Shanti's dear friend Nancy with us, and we'd take 10 days at a time and go to Paris and Rome and London. I think we went to Paris twice, and we visited Stonehenge and Loch Ness and all of those places. I was also doing free film lectures at the studio for students of film and video production. Then it was time to shoot a feature and I decided upon *Dimension in Fear*.

Dimension in Fear follows the exploits of escaped convict Cal Lewis as he tears, swears, swindles, steals and murders his way across the Nevada desert. His motive is a simple one: he plans to kill all those who helped put him in the slammer. Unfortunately for pretty little Dedra Hagen, he sets his sick sights on her after a confrontation with the blonde-haired vixen ended with Lewis being kicked in the groin and blasted with pepper spray.

After round one, Dedra takes to the desert and collapses from heat exhaustion and dehydration, and is later rescued by a couple of bikers. Meanwhile, Lewis seeks medical attention for his injuries at a Quick Care Center. As fate would have it, or as a Ted V. Mikels narrative would have it, Dedra is taken to the very same facility. Lewis spots her, but his attempt to apprehend *his* attacker fails, and Dedra is on the run yet again from *her* attacker.

Along the way Lewis continues to kill indiscriminately. Lewis hates everyone he comes in contact with, including himself. Before each murder he mutilates his own face for some unknown reason. It's certainly a display of sheer madness, but it's also an obvious

Mikels-ism. The viewer simply does not know why the killer does this, and the narrative is not about to reveal it either. Cal Lewis is insane, and that's all Ted wants us to know. It's an interesting approach to modern day storytelling; most directors would bend over backwards to explain such actions away, but not Ted V. Mikels. Ted really does seem to revel in the idea of smearing the viewer's nose directly in his cinematic stew no matter how implausible it may or may not be.

Dedra eventually finds her way into the custody of Detective John Mays. From here, near-endless phone conversations ensue, and Detective Mays sweats a lot. Cal Lewis opts to kill (er ... spend) an evening at a disco, and all seems to be going well for our heroine, even though her assailant is still on the loose.

During the run of this cat-and-mouse routine it is revealed that Cal Lewis has a twin brother, Ralph. Ralph's a successful businessman, and brother Cal is jealous and vows to kill him as well. Detective Mays locates Cal at the Roosevelt Hotel and unwittingly allows Dedra to accompany him. Once there, Cal shoots Mays in the leg and pursues Dedra into the basement. Brother Ralph also knows of Cal's whereabouts and follows him and Dedra into the basement of the Hotel. Dedra cannot tell Ralph from Cal, and screams when Ralph attempts to help her. The police, thinking that it is Cal, shoot Ralph dead and take Dedra away to safety—or so they think.

Detective Mays bids farewell to the lovely Dedra, and no sooner than he is out of the frame, Cal steps in and captures his quarry. Apparently, there was no investigation, nor even an I.D. check, of Ralph Lewis, as the authorities seem convinced that they had gunned down the right man.

The shooting of the twin was an inventive twist, but the authorities' assumption that Ralph was indeed Cal is a major plot hole. Plot holes, when dealing with corpse grinding, blood orgies and the creation of astro men, are just fine, sometimes even charming (if not altogether amusing). But when dealing with a quasi-serious character study of a sociopath turned psychopath, a heavier hand should be employed in the plot and narrative department.

However, this incongruity is, in part, excusable in light of Ted's peculiar method of operation on this particular picture:

> As I'm shooting, if I dream up something else that should belong, then we switch things around. *Dimension in Fear* was a strange undertaking, and it was one of my first where I tried to do the entire movie improvisational-style, based on scenarios that I set forth in an orderly manner, or at least what I considered an orderly manner. I would set up the scene and then say to the actors and actresses, "Say what you would say in this circumstance." Usually when I write a script I'll try and follow it to the letter, but, as it always seems to happen, locations need to change. You need to substitute a gas station for a coffee shop and stuff like that. So I stay very loose and fluid, because when you're working with highly limited funds you have to be fluid and open to any necessary on-the-spot changes.

Dimension in Fear was shot and completed in four weeks in 1997 for a paltry 75,000 smackers, a far cry from his one-half-million-dollar budget on *Mission: Killfast*.

> Most of the cost of my movies is keeping up the equipment availability in my studio. Keeping up all the payments. My studio rental alone is around three thousand dollars a month. Of course, all that has to become part of the ongoing cost of the movie. Further, getting any money for *any* production is next to impossible. I don't even look for it either, and I'll tell you why. You can't promise anything in return—except in my case, where I have a proven track record and I've never had to supply a completion bond. The only thing that I can ever guarantee is a completed movie for marketing.

As mentioned before, Ted had to move from 35mm productions to video—Beta SP, to be exact, though Ted admits that some footage was shot on Super VHS and then transferred to Beta SP. While the VHS sequences fused seamlessly with the Beta, one distinct scene did not. While in the desert, Dedra happens upon a rattlesnake pit, and this footage was left over from *War Cat*. *War Cat* was shot on 35mm film, and the insertion of this sequence is disconcerting to the viewer, to say the least. There is a marked difference between the brightly lit video scenes and the dark and grainy film footage. Still, Ted maintains that it's all part of the magic of making movies. So what are some of the differences between shooting film and video? Ted explains:

> Mainly it's the medium and the size and experience of the crew. I shot every frame of *Dimension in Fear* myself, except for the helicopter shots and the sequence where I'm the hotel desk clerk. With film you just can't do that. You can't direct from behind the camera. If I'm director of photography on a film I usually have a three or four man camera crew. I always did the operating, but I liked to have a first assistant, a second assistant and so on. The assistants would load the film and put the lens on that I called for, position the camera in the exact spot I'd laid out and so forth. I'd also have a focus puller, who was usually someone other than the slate person. So you see, when shooting film you need a crew. On *Dimension in Fear* I didn't have a crew. I didn't need anyone to load film or change lenses or pull focus. So the primary differences between shooting film versus video becomes the camera, the crew and the monetary cost, and that's about it, but the monetary difference is severe. I used to figure that it cost a dollar and a half a second to shoot 35mm film, and that's excluding the renting of special lenses. The raw stock, the processing and the daily printing and so on would average a buck and a half a foot. So just imagine shooting 5,000 feet of film a day. That's 7500 dollars, and you're gonna do that for 20 days?! So the cost of 35mm film and the processing of it was more than the entire cost of shooting a video with the cast and crew and all.

Funding, shooting mediums and time constraints aside, Ted was still able to assemble a pretty good cast, with some familiar faces for genre fans—most notably Liz Renay and Delores Fuller. But how does a man with such limited funds manage to coax actors and actresses into his productions?

> Usually what happens is people will say, "Ted if you have any parts that will fit me I'd sure enjoy doing it with you." I get that a lot. I even get these offers from other countries. People will fly in, at their own expense, because I cannot possibly pay them or their way, but they come just to work with me and to be in one of my movies. I'd worked with Liz many years earlier in 1965 on *Day of the Nightmare*. Of course, I've known her all these years, but we did kinda lose touch with one another. Then when I came to Las Vegas I found out that she lived here, and it was Ray Steckler who said, "Let's go see her." So one evening we made the call and went over and visited her. Of course, you know, she'd done *Thrill Killers* with Ray in 1964. Then she did two more with me after *Dimension in Fear*, *Corpse Grinders 2* and *Mark of the Astro Zombies*. I had also known Delores Fuller for some time. I met her through her husband Bill. I'd done some shooting of them involving some product that they were trying to sell at the time, and I can't even remember exactly what the product even was. Anyhow, I thought it would be a delight to work with her. She's written hit songs for Elvis, and, of course, everyone knows now that she worked with and was Ed Wood's girlfriend.

Ted's more astute fans will recognize actor Ron Jason, who portrayed the good and evil twins in *Dimension in Fear*, from a bit part in *Mission: Killfast*, where he can be spotted brandishing a rifle while playing a mercenary. Jason had a larger role in *War Cat* as the militant outlaw Don. Ted is quite fond of Jason: "Ron Jason is dependable, capable and he looks the part. That I very much like. Ron takes direction very well, and he's very cooperative and, like I said before, very dependable."

Early press materials showcased the heroine from *Dimension in Fear* as singer-turned-would-be-actress Marlowe Capone. Ted explains:

> Marlowe had some mouth surgery just as we were about to start shooting. She was supposed to play the part of the woman who is pursued by Ron Jason's character Cal

Lewis. She was very sweet and very pretty, and this would have been her first movie. She was warm and endearing, but I don't know that she would have done any better of a job than Nicole West did. Nicole had more experience than Marlowe, but Marlowe was a singer. She was a very sultry singer and had a beautiful voice, and I was gonna somehow put some of her music into the movie. We did get some scenes completed with her, though. Like the sequence with Liz Renay in Liz's home. Those are Liz's paintings on the wall, too, she's really a marvelous artist and she does wonderful work. Anyhow, we'd completed some scenes, but then she had the mouth surgery and just couldn't continue. I can't remember exactly what the surgery was, but I do recall that it was a surgery-gone-bad type of instance. It swelled up her mouth and it swelled up her cheeks and we just couldn't go forward with her. We actually put off shooting for a month, but it didn't work and she wound up going back home to Chicago.

For many reasons, some completely out of the creator's control, *Dimension in Fear* sank into obscurity, but not before a stab at foreign sales:

> I had a distributor who was dealing with foreign territories, and he wanted to change the title to *City in Terror*. He insisted that people in other countries would not understand the word *Dimension*, and so he changed the title. I didn't mind one way or the other. So I made a poster that cost more than 100 dollars to print so that he could take it along with him in hopes of getting some foreign sales. I also used the artwork for the VHS jacket, even though it never officially came out that way. Honestly, I don't know if he ever even made it to Europe. I know he did make it to New York, but, alas, no sales were brought about by any of it.

Alternate artwork for *Dimension in Fear*.

It's unlikely that *Dimension in Fear* will ever set the world afire. For Ted's diehard fans it's simply too pedestrian when compared to some of his more gonzo efforts. Still, it's an interesting footnote in the oftentimes mercurial career of a man seemingly gone mad with a movie camera.

15. *Female Slave's Revenge*

Synopsis from Press Materials

In a distant country where blacks outnumber their minority white rulers many hundreds to one, an uprising takes place. In the takeover of control, slaves are freed, and white landowners are ordered to surrender their lands, plantations, farms and mansions to the servants, workers and slaves who were owned or subordinated to them. Men are off fighting the war as ten black mistresses, household maids and servants capture an evil and murderous landowner who has refused to leave his ill-gained wealth and holdings. Empowered by the new order, he is cast in chains. Jurors and witnesses testify to his evil deeds. The female court sentences him to death and executes him in a most brutal and bloody manner.

Credits

Cast: Jennifer Dove (Queen—Mistress Wateesah); Rachel Powell (Butra the Prosecutor); Ted V. Mikels (Landowner); Sandra Young (Belahsa); Zia Brunner (Sellahlie); Helen Sellers (Raybutta); Delvera Spears (Etrosef); Viola Brown (Petrinah); Starlita Burton (Fleurlilli); Beverly Spears (Wishtofti); Suyen Mosely (Suhya); Patrease Ashley (Imposter Sister Mary Ellen); Helen Baker (Landowner's Wife); Billy André (Limo Driver); Leavon Smith (Military Commander); Bernard P. Williams (Military Officer); Melody Kinney (Mansion Servant); Raymie Chatman (Slave Girl); Amber Washington (Slave Girl); Nancy Web-Williams (Kitchen Slave); C.C. Prince (Mansion Slave); Marie O'Guynn (Guard); Lilleth Taylor (Guard); R. Abayomi Goodall (Dancer); Tanya Hubbard (Dancer/Slave); Lillian Graham (Dancer/Slave); Ruthie Towns (Dancer/Slave); Dawn E. Smith (Dancer/Slave); Todd Bateman (Overseer); Jocelyn Nixon (Trial Observer)

Production: *director, producer, writer*: Ted V. Mikels. *associate producer*: Ingrid Mosely. *assistant to the producer*: C. C. Prince. *music composed and scored by*: Glenn Grayson. *unit production manager*: Marie O'Guynn. *first assistant director*: Danae Davis. *cameras*: Danae Davis, Kathy Kanatsky, Chris Bacon. *second unit cameras*: Ted V. Mikels, Stephen Silvas, Gabriel Campisi, Jocelyn Nixon. *assistant cameraman/grips*: Adam Lane, James Lee Roberts. *set decorations*: Yvonne King, C. C. Prince, Marie O'Guynn, Lilleth Taylor. *make-up and hair*: Natasha Spriggs. *West African Gjembe drums—victory celebration dances*: Ulysses Palrose. *editing and post production*: Ted V. Mikels. *main title animation*: Bo Hansen. *digital post*: Spectra Video. *movie theme—words and music and arrangement*: Ingrid Mosely. *movie theme vocals*: Zia Brunner and Innocent Changes—Sharon Sweet, Sharonda Fields, Aperial Smith, Valencia Brown. *executive recording engineer for ending theme music*: Fred Thomas (M.G.S.). *pianist*: Ingrid Mosely. *recordist*: Geoffrey Childers. *vocal trainer*: Dr. Yvonne King (P.A.T.). *junior trainer*: Kamesha Brown. *vocalogist*: Suyen Mosely. *dance choreographer*: R. Abayomi Goodall. *special thanks*: John 3: 16. *running time*: 84 minutes. Color. *aspect ratio*: full-frame. *completed and released*: 1998.

The Video

We must not have his blood on our hands, but consider it under our feet. —Butra the Prosecutor from *Female Slave's Revenge*

After *Dimension in Fear* (a slight departure from his tried, tested and true formula of keeping women in the forefront), Ted Mikels returned to a cinematic world with which he was far more comfortable. *Female Slave's Revenge* (a.k.a. *Apartheid Slave Women's Justice*) was, in a sense, a homecoming for the legendary underground moviemaker. This one, starring no less than two dozen women, almost makes up for his missteps with *Dimension in Fear*. Plainly put, Ted seems more at home and more at ease directing a gaggle of gals as opposed to even one male. It's a point that the director would most surely deny, but the proof is in his product.

This particular entry in Ted's cinematic cannon is the simplest and least convoluted of his career—his wild characters and winding subplots are nowhere to be found. Set in the early 1980s, a horde of South African slave women rise up to try their former master and then punish him for his crimes against humanity—most notably them. Emphatic and overdramatic speeches are spat into the face of the slave owner (played by Ted himself) with a fury and velocity that had not been seen, heard or felt in a Ted V. Mikels movie since the bleak and oppressive prison scenes in *10 Violent Women*. After each woman has said her piece, she then stomps and kicks her oppressor, drawing blood whenever and wherever possible. Eventually he dies from the multiple puncture wounds.

As Ted recalls, the seeds for this unusual picture were planted around the late 70s. The idea was spurred on by his black lady friends and their desire to work with him on one of his movies. It was also spurred-on by *his* desire to make amends with them for not utilizing their talents earlier:

Promotional poster for *Female Slave's Revenge* (1998).

> The black ladies in my life were always asking, "When are you going to use us in one of your movies?" Of course, I had used black women in my pictures in the past—*10 Violent Women*, *The Black Klansman* and so on—but I never wrote a part specifically for the reason of using a black woman. If it called for it in the script then I would cast the part accordingly, but I just didn't want to come across as though I was catering to them. I have more respect for women, and people in general, than to do something like that.

Still, there seems to be an overriding sentiment of guilt and shame in the movie. There's the subject matter itself—slavery is as shameful an act as any—but scratch the surface of the movie and there's something possibly more meaningful beneath. It may be a little abstract, and it may even scream for a Freudian discussion, but the fact that Ted plays the abused abuser was a tell-all move on his part. If he did indeed feel any guilt over not using these women before, here was his chance to appease them by allowing them the opportunity (finally) to be in one of his pictures—and to punish him for not using them earlier.

Female Slave's Revenge also serves as a reminder of Ted's sympathetic view towards the black community. Additionally, there is a fly-on-the-wall quality to *Female Slave's Revenge* that infuses the picture with a voyeuristic tone that could certainly be disconcerting to some viewers. It was shot directly on video tape, and this alone helps create an almost home movie–like feel. It's as though one of the slave ladies is taping the entire episode for future viewing, and for them it would undoubtedly be a fun-time, feel-good movie.

Ted usually shies away from the idea that there are any underlying subtexts in his pictures, but with this one he admits:

> Overall, I'm not really that comfortable with this movie, but my associate producer, Ingrid Mosley, felt that the story needed to be told. I'd shot a stage production for her, and then I wrote *Female Slave's Revenge* as another play and I gave it to her to produce, but she insisted on making a movie out of it. She was so excited about the production that she raised the first 500 dollars to buy the video tape. She also rounded up most of the cast.

It literally took Ted years to finish the movie. Scenes were shot here and there, and at this time and that time—a "cinematic quilt," as he likes to refer to it. There was no real shooting schedule to speak of, and the budget was an all-time low for a Ted V. Mikels production—only about 25 thousand dollars, which was mostly charged to his credit cards. When asked why he made a picture that he was so uncomfortable with, he replied, "About 80 percent of the driving force of that movie was to show blacks in a positive light, just as I had in *The Black Klansman*. The other 20 percent was my need to make another movie. I have to keep making movies."

Despite Ted's feelings for the movie, it remains a fairly steady seller on the home video market. Ed Grant, from the *Time Magazine* on-line website, described *Female Slave's Revenge* on November 10, 2000, as, "...a highly recommended item that's worthy of cult adoration and academic study in 'Incredibly Strange' pop culture classes of the future." Only time will tell if colleges around the globe will begin using Ted's little movie as a springboard for deep analysis and heady discussions.

One of Ted's colleagues suggested that the film was going to be a "late bloomer," and that it would be discovered, and appreciated, years later on a much larger scale. This, too, remains to be seen, but as Ted proudly points out, "My movies just never seem to go away. They seem to stick around forever." This actuality alone will see to it that *Female Slave's Revenge* finds its way onto the small screens of outré cinema fans around the world.

16. *The Corpse Grinders 2*

Synopsis from Press Materials

The starving cat-people of planet Ceta seek food sources from Earth after fighting a losing battle with Planet Traxis in outer space. On Earth, relatives of Landau and Maltby from *Corpse-Grinders One*, in a get rich quick scheme, resume the factory operation of Lotus Cat Food, "for cats who like people." Felines, after a taste of the ingredients, can't get enough of this rare delicacy. Government aides authorize a shipment of Lotus Cat Food to be transported to planet Ceta, thus keeping Mortuaries, Crematoriums and Caleb at the local cemetery busy, and making Landau and Maltby rich.

Credits

Cast: Sean Morelli (Landau); Andy Freeman (Maltby); Chuck Alford (Caleb); Liz Renay (Cleo); Myron Natwick (McBride); Shanti (Felina); Paul McDonald (Dr. Howard Glass); Cara Jo Basso (Angie); Ted V. Mikels (Professor Mikoff); Gene Paul Jones (Borath); Spike Measer (Ubock); Dolores Fuller (Patricia Grant); Philip Chamberlin (Mr. Yonkers); Volmar Franz (Mr. Burnam); William G. Stone (Dean Russo); *The A.S.T.A.P.P. Board*: Lonnie Hammargren (Dr. Hammars), Robert Southerland (Gen. Grant), Manny Rojas (Col. Packwood), Gino Altamura (Board Official), Mathew David Kerner (Tech Specialist), Robert Williams (Security Guard), Scott Miller (Man in Black), Vincent Altamura (Man in Black), John Fahey (Man in Black), Vernon Lombard (Car Lot Salesman), Gino Sapiens (Office Hood for Hire #1), Norm Federico (Office Hood for Hire # 2), Alan Gudaitis (Astrology Specialist); *Factory Workers*: Bill E. Koval (Tim); Russell Sebastian (Russell); Lyle Maulsby (Jake); Terry Donohue, John Cornett, John Curry, Chris Vener, Frank Sebastian; *People of Planet CETA*: Denise Alford, Sharon Morris, Scott Harris, Kyle Miller, Cody Miller, Chris Gryder, Jordan Gryder, John Curry, Jeff Lane, T.J. Lane, Jesses Lane, Bryan Gomez, Ryan Rosada, Megan Peterson, Jessica Pyritz, Nicole Mc Shea, Terri Postma, Bonnie Lee, Jason Gomez; Jacqelyn Oxley (Clinic Secretary); Judy Stone (Dean Russo's Secretary); Arnie Bartz (Market Butcher); Sandy Gudaitis (Mikoff's Housekeeper); Jason Gomez (the Alien); *Shareholders of the Lotus Cat Food Company*: Gil Martinez, Alice Williams, Flora Myers, Bernie Welan, Laura Velgos, Sue Clarke, Deborah Rojas, Jerry Ryerson; *Mortuary Mourners*: Russ Wolven, Reta Vanderwalker, Craig A. Randolph, Cecelia Jordan, Robert Martin, Virginia Carroll, Trip Mitchell, Lindsay L. Timm, Bradley Ortiz, Matthew Murray, Latoya Singleton (Singer); *Planets CETA and TRAXIS Fighter Pilots*: Adam Lane, John Fahey, John Curry, Steve Myers, Lyle Maulsby; Terri Downing (Market Customer); Stuart Verner (Grave Digger); Mike Emilia (Grave Digger); Robilyn Johnson (Cemetery Body); David Kroll (Cemetery Body); *Ground-up Cadavers*: John Curry (1st One), Sabrina Golmassian, Edward Milano, Michael Billington, Marsha Tichenor, Marie O'Guynn, Russell Sebastian, Tom Bisesti, Manny Rojas, Frank Sebastian, Brian Gomez, Brendon Mowry, Kevin Gomez, Ted V. Mikels III; *The Cats*: Eddie, Miner, Star-Baby, Squirrel, Belly Buddy, Gabby, Maddie, Passion, Dante, Tasha, Ike, Jessie, Max, Jessica, Mr. Big, Simba, Patches, Dottie, Spotty, Leo G., Riley, Lovie, Bubbles, Froofy, Brewski, Antonia, Meeka

Production: *director, producer, photographer, editor, writer*: Ted V. Mikels. *first assistant director*: Wendy O. Altamura. *second assistant cameraman*: Adam Lane. *sound-mixer*: Barry Hartglass. *script supervisor*: Laura Boelhouwer. *slate*: Israel Meister. *key grips*: John Curry, Mike Lenzini. *P.A.*: Jerry Carroll. *make-up*: Amy Olson, Marie O'Guynn. *costumes*: Celine Martens, Cherisse Gomez, Denise Alford, "Mac" McDonald. *props and art graphics*: Wendy O. Altamura, Joe Yurmanovic, Sue Clarke, Rich Strelak. *unit publicist*: Israel Meister. *still photography*: Randy Merrit, Adam Lane, Stefan Stankic, Craig Johnson, Robert (Tony) Jaynes, John Curry. *music composed/performed by*: Barry Hartglass. *Corpse Grinding Machine*: Rich Strelak. *main title/battle animation*: Bo Hansen (Master FX). *spaceship animation*: Mack. *additional story material/creative editorial consultant*: Wendy O. Altamura. *Casting services*: Rusty Meyers. *kitty wranglers*: Kenya Schulze, Raven Schulze-Miranda, John Fahey. *stunts*: Eric Braun, John Branch, Jacob Moody. *special thanks*: Dr. Lonnie Hammargren (Astrological Museum), Sandy and Alan Gudaitis (NV. MUFON Head Quarters), Amerisuites Las Vegas, Palm Mortuary, Dr. Kopf Medical Center, Ann Welch, Farewell Acres Cemeteries, Budget Auto Sales, R.L. Air Conditioning, Supermercado, John Haddad, Gene Larson. *running time*: 1 hour and 43 minutes. Color. *aspect ratio*: full-frame. *completed and released*: 2000.

The Video

Mr. Landau, are you puttin' dead bodies in the cat food?!—Jake from *The Corpse Grinders 2*

"I don't think the corpse grinding machine will ever be used again in a motion picture." That's what Lucius Fangstein said to DJ Jack Posey during the radio show *Solid Gold Countdown from the Wax Museum*. As discussed in the chapter on the original *Corpse Grinders*, Fangstein was a fictitious character, as was Posey and his hokey radio show. But Ted V. Mikels is very real, and the notion of firing up the old corpse grinding machine became a reality nearly 30 years after its original operation in 1971.

Ted decided to dust off the diabolical contraption after his first two direct-to-video productions failed to set his bank account afire. For years he'd toyed with the idea of a sequel, and why not? *The Corpse Grinders* was, and still remains, his most successful motion picture to date. It outsold everything it competed with, pulling in millions of dollars during its theatrical run in the 1970s (and that's when tickets were a mere 25 cents). Even today it's his biggest seller on DVD. So creating a follow-up to this classic slice of exploitation cinema seemed the way to go.

For diehard fans of Ted's work, *The Corpse Grinders 2* was the shot in the arm that they and Ted's career needed. Not only did Ted return to a more comfortable cinematic territory, but he also shirked the quasi-seriousness of his two previous pictures. Simply put, Ted seems to work best when dealing with over-the-top campiness and over-the-top caricatures (when not working with a myriad of lovely ladies, that is).

As if the idea of grinding up cadavers for cat food wasn't enough, Ted decided to up the insanity ante and place part of his sequel in outer space—the planet Ceta, to be exact. Ceta is inhabited by a race of cat people who war with the dog people from the planet Traxis. Ceta and its cat people can no longer cultivate enough food for its population, and so they turn to Earth for the solution—Lotus cat food.

The Lotus Cat Food Company is run by Landau and Maltby, the nephews of the owners from the original film. This portion of the sequel plays more like an updated remake of *The Corpse Grinders*. This time around, though, the corpse grinding machine is far more sinister in its ap-

Promotional artwork for *The Corpse Grinders II* (2000).

pearance. In addition to its larger size, it also sports 100s of nasty and jagged teeth (teeth that were handmade by Ted out of Plaster of Paris), as opposed to the dull lawn mower blades from the original. Still, Landau and Maltby obtain their goods from the local cemetery, run by Caleb and Cleo, which also mirrors the original film.

However, the cat people of Ceta couldn't care less how the cat food ingredients are procured and processed; they just know that they need it in order to survive. So they contact the U.S. government about their plight. The government cooperates fully and concedes to their request, ordering the Lotus Cat Food Company to deliver 400 cases of their kitty cuisine to the cat people's intergalactic mothership. Grinding up dead bodies for pet food ingredients; outer space cat creatures finding it a delicacy; governmental intervention—the mind reels.

Even Ted's mind reeled:

> When I make up these stories and make up these ideas I get tickled because they're ridiculous and they're fun to do; and yet, when people take it in the right light, they're laughable—laughably entertaining. It sure takes you away from the realities of our life, our daily life and our existence, and so on.

Ted shot this little gem of wacky cinema in about three months, with an ending cost of around 150,000 smackers (again funded by maxed-out credit cards). That's six times the amount that he'd spent on his previous project, *Female Slave's Revenge*, and it shows. There's loads of blue screen special effects, miniature space ships and outlandish costuming and set pieces. The cat people sport gaudy head gear, replete with large pointed and furry ears, while the dog people look like—well, dog people—purple dog people. As preposterous as it all may seem, it was still Ted's most ambitious project since *Mission: Killfast*.

Still, it was shot directly on video, and some of the sets were conspicuously con-

A Lotus Cat Food label from *The Corpse Grinders II*.

structed within the confines of people's homes. This specific quality (or lack thereof) may be troubling to the present day viewer, but 20 or 30 years from now it will be both interesting and charming in that "time capsule" way. Because Ted works with what he has available to him (and that's not much more than his love for making movies), he manages to capture a time and a place in history. This particular, and peculiar, reality will make Ted's films forever enjoyable regardless of their technical strengths and/or weaknesses.

Plainly, the corpse grinding machine of the title is the movie's "real" star; but rather than short change his fans, Ted yet again employed such favorites as Liz Renay and Dolores Fuller. Fuller appeared in a very small role as a chairperson on the board of directors for Lotus Cat Food, while Renay played Caleb's wacko wife Cleo. In fact, Caleb becomes so incensed by his wife's erratic behavior that he chokes her to death (or so he thinks) and sells her body for 50 bucks, along with the rest of the cadavers. Later Cleo awakens moments before being crammed into the gnashing teeth of the corpse grinding machine, making for a nice morbid touch of black humor.

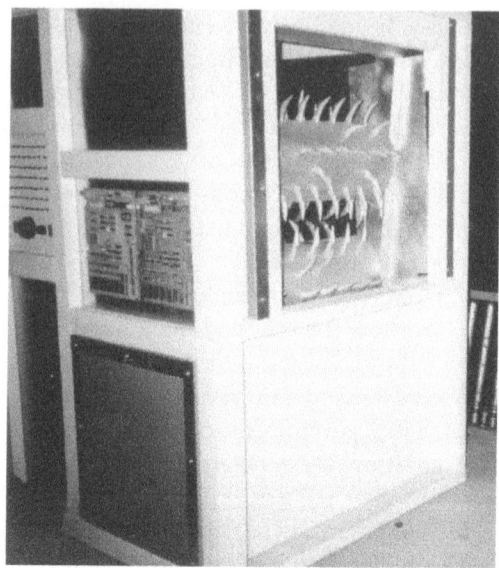

Left: Felina (Shanti/Wendy O. Altamura) is ready to attack Dr. Professor Mikoff (Ted V. Mikels) in *The Corpse Grinders II*. *Above:* The star and centerpiece of Ted V. Mikels' 2000 production *The Corpse Grinders II*.

Not surprisingly *The Corpse Grinders 2* did not receive a theatrical release. In the beginning it was sold only on VHS directly through Ted's website, then Image Entertainment finally picked it up for a DVD release. It's a DVD release that has become very successful and is only eclipsed by the original film. The real crime in the movie not hitting even a few theaters is that Ted was not allowed the opportunity to pull off one of his remarkable marketing campaigns. Still, forever the showman, Ted made up a few goodies for his fans, like small jars containing "Human Flesh" from the corpse grinding machine, the actual teeth that ground up the flesh, and of course, prop cans of Lotus cat food.

Even if Ted and his fans were pleased with *The Corpse Grinders 2*, the critics were not. Ted explained his thoughts on the criticisms of his movies to Colin Hanson for *Lighthouse*, no. 2, December 2003:

> Who cares about criticism? I put blood, sweat, tears, heart and soul, not to mention money, into my movies, and seven out of ten folks love them—they tell me. Mainly, I believe criticism comes from someone who wants to do what you are doing and they cannot. Also, smart-alecks tend to think that everyone will think like they do, and, in general, the public often disagrees. In Hollywood, moviemakers tried to keep critics out of the screenings of their films because they almost always deeply criticized others' work, as if they knew better than anyone else in the world. As long as I am given the accolades I do receive, I couldn't care less what the criticisms are.

Criticism aside, Ted was back on track, and his fans and colleagues knew it. Without skipping a beat, the decidedly unstoppable moviemaker aimed his cameras, and his creative impulses, towards more familiar territory—the "Astro Zombies," who had been taken from him nearly 35 years earlier in a contractual deal gone horribly wrong. It was finally time for Ted to take back what was rightfully his, and reclaim one of independent cinema's most beloved creations.

17. Mark of the Astro Zombies

Synopsis from Press Materials

Strange alien fingers are operating on humans, placing chips into their brains, and replacing organs with synthetic replacements. In a fenced-in courtyard, ten to twelve strange looking beings with misshaped heads are milling about. On the orders pressed into what looks like a palm pilot by alien fingers, the strange creatures snap to a state of alert. A second signal sends these beings into a frenzy. Escaping the compound and wildly swinging sharp machetes in the air, they take to the streets, indiscriminately slashing and killing all that are in sight. They are receiving orders through cyberspace, orders sent like e-mail into the receiver-chips implanted in their brains. These are the Astro Zombies.

Police are helpless to defend or protect the citizens on the street, for when they fire bullets into the Astro Zombies, they bleed a green ooze but continue killing, as they are unstoppable.

In the offices of the FBI, Jeff Lancaster, an agent, sees on the TV screen the pandemonium that is taking place. Jeff quickly calls his friend Cindy Natale, and tells her this would be the type of material that would propel an investigative reporter to recognition. Cindy is on her way out of her newspaper office with a TV crew to cover the attacks as Jeff's call comes in.

In the aliens' operating room, four aliens are implanting body parts and brain chips into more human subjects. Actual human organs are discarded, as the process continues. Solar energy cells implanted in the foreheads of the Astro Zombies drive their synthetic heart-pumps and other implanted organs. Green ooze is pumped into their veins and arteries.

People in alleys, sidewalks and city streets, apartments and garages become the victims of the terrorizing Astro Zombies. Pandemonium reigns.

Cindy and her TV crew are attempting to interview witnesses to the grisly scenes; all are hysterical.

In the offices of the President of the United States, Ward Pennwood is appointing a staff to call together the brilliant scholars in several related sciences to attempt to learn what is happening. General Kingston, Garth Woodard, Tomas Peripoulos, and Jessica Newhall are under orders to form a team of specialists.

Jeff catches up with Cindy, and the two discuss what might be happening. Cindy is sure that her boyfriend Jeff, with access to FBI and CIA information, knows more than he is willing to discuss with her.

General Kingston is unaware that while he is calling together his group of brilliant doctors and scientists, alien beings are noting the communications, becoming aware of where and to whom Kingston is taking. The aliens prepare the laser-projected Mark of the Astro Zombies, documenting the whereabouts of those who have been contacted.

Dr. Randolph West, a specialist in interplanetary communications, tells Kingston he has a plan. Remote viewing might be brought into the search for answers.

In another setting, an evil, ambitious and satanic woman, Malvira, is perusing newspaper headlines. She tells her accomplice, Zokar, that these events are somewhat similar to what took place another time. She has a plan to capitalize on these events, and orders Zokar to gather the names of major foreign emissaries from the consulates of record.

In the President's office, Ward Pennwood is discussing with his staff the possibility of calling in the military. General

Kingston feels it is too soon; Garth and Tomas lay out a plan to map out the basic area where the attacks are occurring. Ward and Kingston fear the possibility of public panic.

Dr. Randolph West enters a classroom where Dr. Owens is concluding a remote-viewing seminar. Her closing comments are that the military is investigating the use of this ability by some to zero in on an enemy's activities. Dr. West and Dr. Owens take part in a remote viewing session, and Dr. Owens visualizes aliens at an operating table as it is actually taking place.

In a pathology room where Dr. Neidermeyer, Dr. Grashoff and Dr. Sweikert discuss the existence of alien life forms, they come to the conclusion that aliens from planets and asteroids ten to sixteen billion years older than our planet earth have knowledge and intelligence beyond our abilities to conceptualize. This could be the reason that bodies of victims of the attacks have had certain organs and entrails removed, and, in particular, brains. Someone or something is tampering with our physiognomies.

In an office of NASA, Jonathan Rossmore is discussing with Jeff and Cindy the prerequisites of interplanetary space flight by earth's humans. Even if cryogenics were utilized, there would be no assurances of perfect functionality of these awakened space-travelers. It almost would require some form of humanoid as yet unknown to undertake this type of space travel. As of yet, this technology is not available.

In the Control Alien's operating room, a green "ooze" is transfused into Astro Zombie bodies. The aliens will send the A–Zs to intercept and capture General Kingston's team members by tagging them with a laser mark, "the Mark of the Astro Zombies." The A–Zs zero in on these people through orders from Zekith and bring them into the operating rooms of the control aliens.

Malvira and Zokar have devised a plan to extort millions of dollars from foreign agents who have gathered to witness their staged control of an Astro Zombie. Malvira orders Zokar to slash a tied up victim to death, then shoot another on her orders. She then turns the gun on the fake A–Z Zokar, and green ooze squirts out of the bullet holes. Zokar is ordered to shoot the agents but stops short when Malvira starts the bidding for the knowledge to control the A–Zs.

In the fenced-in courtyard, control aliens inspect Astro Zombies that have various chips implanted. One is growing an animal arm after a machete removed his arm; another has grown a second head. The aliens seem to be able to grow anything they wish with their chip implants.

More team members are contacted by General Kingston and are promptly marked by the aliens with the laser mark, and are dragged off by Astro Zombies.

Malvira, not content with her gains, calls the newspaper and convinces Cindy that she has new information on the A–Zs, and arranges to meet her. Zokar and Malvira kidnap Cindy and force her to lure Jeff to their meeting place.

In an unusual room of Space intelligences, two good aliens [feel] the need to reach humans and convince them that not all aliens are bad. One of these is ASTP-73.

In the operating room of the control aliens, the various team members are laid out on slabs. They are held immobile in a trance. Their brains are hooked up to computers that are extracting the knowledge they possess.

In the White House offices of the president, he and his staff are informed that there is a strange communication from beings that request to speak with the President. The good aliens identify themselves. They are from an asteroid in space and offer to help destroy the evil aliens.

In Malvira's demonstration room, Jeff and Cindy are helplessly strapped in chairs where the previous victims were killed. Zokar is again posing as a controlled Astro Zombie, ready to do Malvira's bidding.

The evil control aliens release more A–Zs from the compound, as they are ordered now to search out and kill certain victims.

In the control room of the good aliens, ASTP-73 and an assistant zero in on the cyberspace commands being sent to the A–Zs by the evil aliens. ASTP-73 and the assistant appear in the control room of Zekith and an electronic battle ensues, not unlike a videogame battle.

In Malvira's demo room, one of the persons there is an FBI agent who recognizes Jeff. As Malvira and Zokar try to shoot their way out of the trap, they are shot, and Jeff and Cindy are freed as the foreign agents race out of the room in a panic.

In Zekith's control room, ASTP-73 and his assistant, who trigger impulses that explode the heads of Zekith and the other aliens, win the electronic battle. Strange goop flies in every direction and splatters the walls. Astro Zombies everywhere drop dead in their tracks. Their would-be victims, frozen in terror, are greatly relieved.

ASTP-73 sends signals to the captured intelligent ones that bring them out of their trance and back to reality.

In the President's office, ASTP-73 tells the President that Zekith and the evil aliens are destroyed; however, they must be ever alert to prevent anything like this from happening again. In a fancy restaurant, Jeff and Cindy toast their escape from Malvira and the evil aliens, suggesting to each other that they have really learned something from their experience.

In a neighborhood alley, a young boy picks up an Astro Zombie mask and machete and chases two young girls up a street, screaming in panic.

Credits

Cast: Tura Satana (Malvira Satana); Liz Renay (Crystal Collins); Brinke Stevens (Cindy Natale); Sean Morrelli (Jeff Lancaster); Anton Funtek (Zekith); Scott Blacksher (Zokar); Gene Paul Jones (President Ward Pennington); Robert Southerland (General Kingston); Shanti (Dr. Owens); Ted V. Mikels (Dr. Mikacevich); Mac McClennan (Scott Miller); Donna Hamblin (Laura); Volmar Franz (Dr. Randolph West); John Baniqued (ASTP-73); Dr. William Stone (Dr. Grashoff); John Waite (Dr. Neidermeyer); Barry Marks (Dr. Sweikert); Anthony Scurry (Paramedic); John Baniqued (Professor Kroeger); Laurence Griffin (Jonathan Rossmore); Bill Neely (Dr. Nassaur); Brian Howard (Garth Woodward); Jan Williams (Jessica Newhall); Sam Osman (Tomas Peripoulos); Ruth Ann Benoit (Ruth Ann Gordon); Judy Lombino (Interviewer in Drawing Room); Jo Lynn Kirkman (Interviewer at Café); Bunny Suttles (Crystal Collins' Assistant); Dr. Myra Lee Glassman (TV Station Boss); Ivan Lozon (Police Officer); Tom Digiacomo (FBI Agent); *Zekith's Evil Guards*: Warren Beres, Thomas Scott Bould, Anthony Scurry, Travis Potter; *ASTP-73 Assistants*: Leslie Chester, Thomas Scott Bould; Amanda Cohen (Star Costume Clerk); *Running Witnesses*: John Cornett, Britney Markman, Judi Stone, Robert Tarleton; *Demo Room Victims*: Ari Richards, Monica Tullar; Robert Taylor (Voice and Dialogue of Dr. Demarco); Randy Jason (Boy with Mask); *Astro Zombies*: James Durkac, "Rock and Roll Ray" Whalen, Jay Gowey, Louie Thomas, Rob Ruckus, Dennis L. Phelps, Terry Suejda, Greg Parker, Mardon Ramirez, Ronnie Jason, Scott Blacksher, Neal Rhosen, Aaron Gitlin, Curtis Dilley, Mike Mendoza, Richard Smith, Robert Knight, Stan Sedanski, Donovan Dangus, Justin Brown, Matt Brooks, Anthony Avery, Joel Lindsay Cribbs, Chili Bob, Ari Richards, Victor DeMayo, Gary Luckenback, Charles Burell, Dennis Allard, Thomas Bould, Tony Scurry, Ray Johnson, Summer Bradshaw, Adam DeVore, Danny Bruckert, Michael

Vaughn, Nathan Block, Tim Potter; *Victims of Astro Zombies*: Nina Tepes, Kimberly Lynn Cole, Carolina DaCunha, Noelle Kale, Dennis L. Phelps, "Rock and Roll Ray" Whalen, Siria Judith, Rob Ruckus, Tony "the Gooch" DeMayo, Adam Lane, Jennifer Van Kemper, Antoinette "Binky" Pescoff, Christy Larson, Graham McLachlan, Summer Bradshaw, Jon Howard, Jr., Candice M. Stanley, Amanda Westgate, Megan Schwartz, Christy Roper, Robert Tarleton, Barbara Tarteton, Michele Whitson, Neal Rhosen, Sara Block, Misty, Heather, Matt Brooks, Joseph Kopf, Yessica Acosta, Amy L. Carrelli, Jade Koph; *Nearly Victims*: Jessica Hernandez, Robert Taylor, Gabriella Hernandez; *Demo Room Attachés*: Louie Thomas, Dennis Allard, Brent Engle, Thomas Scott Bould, Dionisio H. Alvarez, Checko Salgado, Warren Beres, Anton Funtek, Greg Parker; *In Remote Viewing Class*: Beverly Brown, Shylow Pryor, Raime Kuewa, Greg Moore, Brian Parker, Ryan Carl Sabien; *Café Internationale Patrons*: Paul J. Burkett, Natasha Alexandria, Yessica Acosta, Amy L. Carrelli, Steve Osman, Charles Burrell; *Cindy Natale's TV Crew*: April Sasso, Bill Carter, James Durkac; Connie Ray (General Kingston's Secretary); *Young School Girls Running*: Stephanie Phan, Marielle West, Michelle Hensley, Nia Huerta; *Young School Boys Running*: Mike Harvey, Christopher Bernard, Randy Jason; Tim Potter (Beheaded Biker)

Production: *director, producer, photographer, editor, writer*: Ted V. Mikels. *associate producers*: Scott Blacksher, Antoinette "Binky" Pescov, John Cornett. *co-associate producers*: Ari Richards, Liberty, Dennis L. Phelps. *production manager*: Amy L. Carrelli. *co-production manager*: Adam Lane. *pre-production first A.D.*: Scott Robertson Price. *pre-production second A.D.*: Carolina DaCunha. *pre-production office coordinator*: Beth Raymer. *first camera assistant, gaffer*: Adam Lane. *second unit camera operator, technical advisor*: Bill Carter. *script supervisor*: Noelle West. *location manager*: P.J. West. *special effects, set design, construction, electronic props*: Dave White. *sound recorder, mixer*: Doug Frye. *recording operator*: Adam Lane. *sound boom*: James Durkac, Ari Richards. *sound editing*: Geoff Chase, Katherine Desmond, Frank Coleman. *wardrobe*: Siria Judith, Lupe Tence, Christy Larson. *props, set construction assistants, blood effects*: Dave White, James Durkac, Christy Larson, Adam Lane, Greg Parker. *still photographer*: Monica Tullar. *production assistants*: Neal Rhosen, Terry Svejda, Shay Banks, Shylow Pryor. *casting coordinator*: James Durkac. *second unit Alabama crew*: Kimberly Ann Cole, Leo Zemke, Gary Luckenback, Dylan Cole, Henry Cohen, Henrietta Lockhart. *Astro Zombie masks, Zekith mask, replica head of Dr. Demarco*: Jay Gowey. *Zekith's Evil Guards masks, ASTP masks*: Michael Haegle. *graphics arts*: Shylow Pryor, Greg Parker. *production documentary footage*: Bill Carter, Seria Judith, Scott Blacksher, Amy Carelli, Adam Lane. *special thanks*: Dr. Edward Kopf's clinic, Café Internationale, the Tropic's Club, Dr. Volmar Franz, Gary and Connie Ross, Star Costumes, Channel 15 TV, Baugman and Turner, Ron Jason, TVM Studios, the city of Las Vegas, Nevada, Dennis L. Phelps (webmaster); *running time*: 1 hour and 25 minutes. Color. *aspect ratio*: full-frame. *completed and released*: 2002.

The Video

Our creations will come alive to rule this planet.—Zekith from *Mark of the Astro Zombies*

If fans of Ted V. Mikels were tickled with his decision to crank up the old corpse grinder in the year 2000, then they were going to be thrilled with his 2002 outing. Just two years after revisiting the Lotus Cat Food Company, Ted focused his creative efforts on one of his most popular creations—the "Astro Zombies." As far as some were concerned, this had been a long time coming.

The movie in question was *Mark of the Astro Zombies*, and this project became a bit of an obsession for Ted, as he had a great desire to reclaim his 1967 brainchild, *Astro Zombies*. Or at the very least, Ted wanted to reclaim his characters of the film's title. As

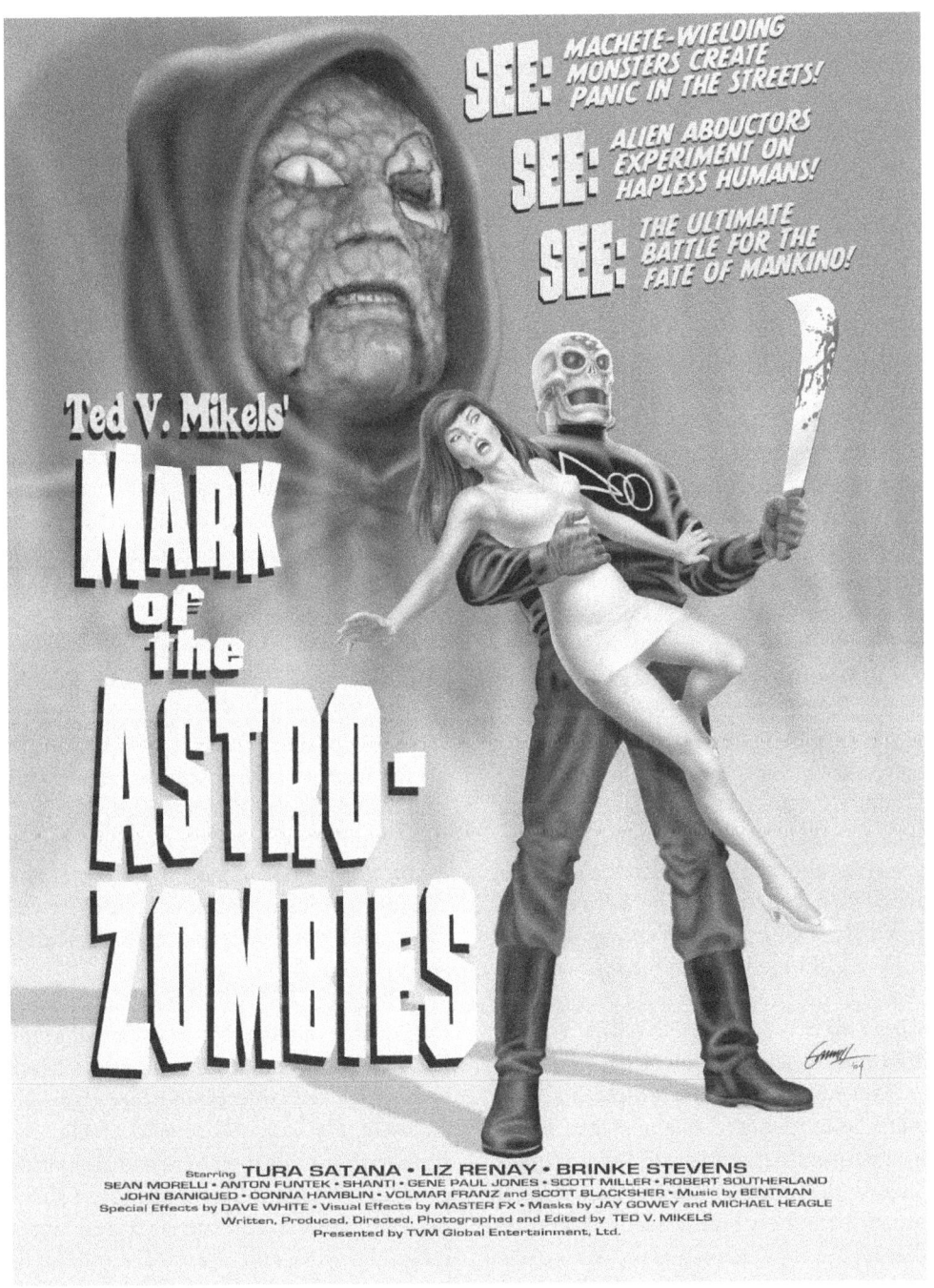

The brilliantly exploitative and stylish *Mark of the Astro Zombies* (2002) poster art as conceived and created by Kerry Gammill.

discussed in previous chapters, *Astro Zombies* was more or less snatched from Ted's grasp in a contractual agreement that was largely out of his control.

The two principal characters involved in this scenario were co-writer and friend Wayne Rogers and cutthroat distributor/promoter Jack H. Harris. Harris wound up owning the picture and ultimately made a small fortune from its 1969 re-release. Then even more money was tossed his way when the film hit television and video.

In the 1990s, with the well-wishes of Rogers, Ted re-released *Astro Zombies* on video cassette through a small company called Walterscheid Productions. It seemed as though all systems were "go," and Ted was finally going to make some scratch off of his 1967 baby. However, it was not to be, and, with little or no warning, Ted and company were issued a "cease and desist" order. Ted's old nemesis, that thorn in his side, Jack H. Harris, was back at it again; but Ted wasn't the only one to get the "cease and desist" warning. For some time it was thought that *Astro Zombies* was public domain, and *Troma* mogul Lloyd Kaufman even attempted to release the film, but Harris quickly put a stop to that as well.

Harris, having no connection to the film other than copyright ownership, simply was not about to allow anyone other than himself to get a piece of the astro-zombie action. Meanwhile, the film's progenitor had 13 months of blood, sweat, money and tears invested in the project and not a single nickel to show for it. Was it fair? No, but without a doubt it was legal.

So when does humanity and humility supersede hard-nosed business and hard-nosed business arrangements? Ted was quick to answer that one: "In the movie business it doesn't. It's an ugly business and it's getting uglier all the time. It's sad really. There's no room for nice guys out there." Sad indeed, as Ted has spent a lifetime helping up-and-coming actors, crew people, filmmakers and even other distributors; but as someone once said, "Nice guys always finish last."

In the end Ted had no legal recourse and had to agree to Harris' conditions. To his dismay, *Astro Zombies* was pulled from the shelves, and thousands of shrinkwrapped copies were sent to Harris for disposal. No one knows what he ever did with them, or if he did anything with them at all. But when he later struck a deal with Image Entertainment for the DVD release, he was quick to plaster Ted's original artwork onto the back cover.

It's important to note that Harris' 1969 theatrical re-release of *Astro Zombies* sported a very different piece of art than Ted's original. Ted's one-sheet depicted a zany, cartoon-like illustration of a gigantic zombie head with a damsel in its mouth and another's head in its boney clutches. Harris' artwork is far more recognizable to the masses, as it is the one with the astro zombie wielding a machete and making away with a screaming girl.

Ted admits that both are fantastic pieces, but naturally he has more affection for the 1967 version. However, seemingly in an act of defiance, Ted's one-sheet and DVD art for *Mark of the Astro Zombies* appears very much like Harris' 1969 concept. Naturally Ted would never concede to such a notion, saying, "I just liked that piece better than the rest that were submitted, but there were some really good ones and it was difficult for me to choose."

Indeed, Ted had many submissions from which to adopt his artwork and graphics. Longtime fan and friend Scott Blacksher took a keen interest in *Mark of the Astro Zombies*. He solicited several of his artist friends to submit their versions and visions of what they felt the advertising art should be. It became a contest, and Ted was to judge the work and choose the one he felt best represented his movie. He chose Kerry Gammill's work, but is quick to note, "I really liked Andrew Sheppard's piece, too. It's the one where the astro zombie is on the hood of a car and he's smashing a man's face through the windshield. I really did like it, but I felt that Kerry Gammill's piece was better suited to the campiness in the movie." (Note: all submissions can be seen at http://www.motazart.com.)

In addition to the incredible poster art, Ted also had a limited run of astro zombie bobbleheads made to help promote the movie; and then there were t-shirts sporting Gammill's one-sheet image. Eventually, Bump in the Night Productions began manufacturing a very impressive (and inexpensive) run of astro zombie Halloween masks. "Even with all of those things that we did to promote the movie I still really missed having the opportunity to do my theatrical campaign gimmicks and all of that crazy stuff that I used to do in the 70s," laments a dejected Ted Mikels.

Still, if there was ever any doubt as to the immense popularity of the original *Astro Zombies*, then one need only consider the wide and varying geographic locations of the cast and crew of Ted's sequel. "I had people flying in from all around the world to work with me on this movie. I had people coming in from Europe and Australia and from all over America." There are 152 cast credits, and, though many turned up in multiple roles, it was Ted's largest cast to date (and is likely to remain so):

Jack H. Harris' version of the *Astro Zombies* artwork. This is, perhaps, the most recognizable image from Ted V. Mikels' 1967 feature. Notice how similar the artwork for *Mark of the Astro Zombies* is to Jack H. Harris' version.

> Everybody wanted to be an astro zombie, so Jay Gowey had to make up a whole lot of those astro zombie masks. Then everybody wanted to get killed by an astro zombie. That movie was so much fun to make. Everybody had a really good time on that one.

Actor and friend Scott Blacksher, who played Tura Satana's right-hand goon Zokar, remembers:

> Jay Gowey made the masks from one mold and it became real obvious real fast that everyone's heads are not shaped the same. There wasn't time to get shiny lenses for the eye sockets, and even then it might have caused some sort of reflection problems, so Jay simply cut slits in the bottoms of the eye sockets, and some of the people were literally running around blind because they couldn't see a thing through them. Ted had people off-camera holding broom sticks, and Ted would say, "Okay, when you feel the broomstick handle on your leg, stop and swing around."

The fun didn't stop there either. *Mark of the Astro Zombies* played host to more blood and gore than all other Ted V. Mikels productions combined. The oftentimes prudish moviemaker even consented to shooting a semi-nude shower scene. However, in the interest of the young starlet's modesty, after the astro zombie has had his murdering way with her, he strategically placed a hand towel over her pink unmentionables. Who knew that astro zombies could be so polite and considerate of a young dead girl's feelings? As Ted recalls:

> That was Jay Gowey's wife. She agreed to it, so I figured why not. Plus, it seems that distributors always want some nudity somewhere in the movie. Bare bottoms and bare breasts are not really an issue for me to shoot, but sex is, and I'm talking simulated sex. I would *never* do a pornographic movie, though I have been offered money to do it. I just can't do it, and I won't do it.

On-screen sexual hang-ups aside, Ted continued to pull out the stops for *Mark of the Astro Zombies*. First, he hired friend and one-time girlfriend Tura Satana:

> Tura's developed quite a cult following over the years, and we've maintained our friendship, so it seemed natural for me to ask her to take a part in the sequel. As usual, she was a joy to work with, as was Liz Renay, who I'd worked with earlier on *Dimension in Fear* and *Corpse Grinders 2*. I had Brinke Stevens in *Mark of the Astro Zombies*, too. She has considerable marquee value and a big fan base as well, and I loved working with her, too. There was a bit of unfortunate things that happened to her while we were shooting *Mark of the Astro Zombies*, though. For starters, she's incredibly claustrophobic, and for a large portion of her screen time she was to be bound and blindfolded. Well, the ropes had to be *really* loose, and even then we had to keep untying her so that she could get herself back together. I felt really bad for her, but she insisted on going on with it. Then the Screen Actors Guild found out about her involvement with the project and they kicked her out of the organization. This, too, I also felt bad about, but she assured me that I had nothing to do with it, and that everything would be okay. Then finally we were finished shooting her scenes on September 10 and she was to leave on September 11. Of course, that was the day of the terrorist attacks, and she was detained in Vegas for another three or so days.

Longtime fan and co-star Scott Blacksher particularly enjoyed working with the legendary Tura Satana:

> Once Ted said I had the part of Zokar [Blacksher's character], I set out to mold a backstory for the character. The dialogue between Malvira [Ms. Satana's character] and Zokar could be read as bickering equals, but I didn't want to compete with Tura Satana. She's well-known for portraying a "dragon lady" on screen, and I didn't want to dilute her vileness. So I came up with playing Zokar as a human rottweiler, kind of a dense animal that needed Malvira in order to live comfortably.

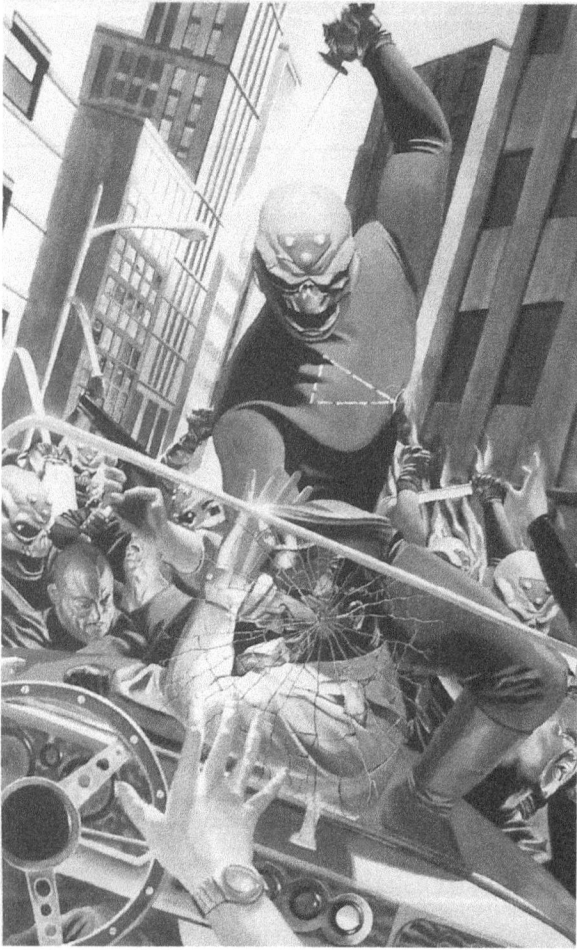

Andrew Sheppard's vision of what the artwork for *Mark of the Astro Zombies* should look like. Artwork (c) Andrew Sheppard, characters (c) Ted V. Mikels (graphic image used by kind permission of Andrew Sheppard).

17. Mark of the Astro Zombies

The marvelous "Astro Zombie" bobblers used to help promote *Mark of the Astro Zombies*. They came in a very limited run of 500, and each was numbered and signed personally by Ted V. Mikels.

I began sending a few emails to Ted with descriptions of how I wanted to play the character, with very specific body language in scripted scenes. All of which Ted gave glowing praise and approval. Once it came time to actually shoot the scenes (roughly three weeks later), Ted would hesitate and second-guess the take because, I'm guessing, it didn't seem fresh to him. Once Ted knew what I was planning on doing it didn't surprise him, and felt the audience wouldn't be surprised either.

Tura and I had dinner at an Italian restaurant after the third day of our scenes together. I revealed my frustration and confusion regarding Ted initially raving about my plans but being reluctant to commit to them on shoots. That's when Tura told me she had the same problem when she made the original *Astro Zombies*. Tura mentioned that she and John Carradine would secretly work out moves and vocal inflections the night before. In front of Ted and the camera it seemed lively and spontaneous, but it was actually rehearsed quite a bit.

Unfortunately, I painted myself into a corner because I'd already told Ted everything I wanted to do. I thought all my preparation was for naught. Imagine my amazement when, the next day, Ted was open to allowing a scene to play out as I'd described. It was the one where Malvira and Zokar are on a couch just after the murder of two innocents staged in front of foreign agents. For the first time during a shoot Ted allowed me to stage the scene completely, and I was thrilled! I never knew for sure, but I had a feeling Tura relayed some of the dinner conversation back to Ted.

Throughout the entire production of *Mark of the Astro Zombies* there was little, if any, time for rehearsal due to time limitations. Brinke Stevens and Tura only had one day to do all of their scenes together, since Brinke was scheduled for another movie somewhere in Florida. That day turned into a thirteen-hour workload. Normally Ted only shoots for four to five hours because he learned long ago that production slows after the cast and crew lunches. Tura and I ran our lines together for the first time around twenty minutes before a shoot so we'd remember when to come in on exchanges without pauses.

Not only were those exploitation screen stars on board, so was quite possibly the most legendary B-movie actor of them all—John Carradine. Well, sort of. Sculptor Jay Gowey not only created the astro zombie masks, he also constructed the disembodied head of John Carradine's Dr. DeMarco character from the original *Astro Zombies*. This fantastic prop was used all too briefly in a scene where Dr. Mikacevich (played by Ted Mikels himself) converses with DeMarco's brain. Dr. Mikacevich has kept DeMarco's brain alive in hopes of learning the secrets to the creation of the astro zombies. John Carradine has been featured in several posthumous movies, but never like this!

Scott Blacksher relayed this story concerning *Ted's* vision of Dr. DeMarco's bodiless head:

> Once the idea was brought up that DeMarco's head should be kept alive in order to extract his secrets in astro-physics, we started thinking about how the prop should look. Hastily Ted suggested we take a photo of John Carradine's face, wrap it around a balloon and drop it into a jar. Jay Gowey said, "Oh no! Let me see if I can come up with something better," and so he did. He took an impression of a John Carradine lifemask and built the prop around that.

Mark of the Astro Zombies was shot in eight weeks at an out-of-pocket cost of about $28,000, with a final budget estimate of around $175,000. The remaining balance came from deferments on Ted's maxed-out credit cards (at 28 percent interest). It should also be noted that the estimate of $175,000 also includes the monthly rental of TVM Studios (at $3,000 a month), equipment rental, equipment upkeep and so on. This unorthodox manner of funding a production can be applied to every movie Ted has made since 1997:

> When I say that I've made a movie for a hundred and fifty thousand dollars, it doesn't necessarily mean that it went into everything that you see on the screen. It means that I'm taking into account all of the hidden costs that are involved in making a movie, like feeding the cast and crew, and repairing a camera and things like that.

However the monies were obtained, *Mark of the Astro Zombies* scores high marks in the special FX department for a Ted V. Mikels production. The blue screen effects are far more capably handled and convincing than in Ted's past movies. Even better, the interiors of the spaceships, while still hokey, look nowhere near like they were set up in someone's living room, as they did in *The Corpse Grinders 2*. The costuming and masks are impressive in a campy sort of way, and the industrial rock group Bentmen turned in a noisy and fitting score that serves the movie well.

Still, with all of this effort put forth, the entire production could have been derailed, as Scott Blacksher remembers:

> For one particular scene Ted wanted a fenced compound where a large group of astro zombies are stored before being released to begin their deadly assault on mankind. He'd found a spot he liked, but didn't relay information to anyone in advance. Needless to say, the events of October 4, 2001, are the stuff of legendary stories involving low-budget movies.
>
> Ted briefed the group, prior to departure for the unknown location, that we could, and most likely would, be asked to leave at a moment's notice, and that it was necessary to do all of the action quickly. The scene required 10 astro zombies with machetes to run out of an isolated hazardous materials storage area. Guess where the place was? It was a city/government vehicle refueling station located on McCarran International Airport property!
>
> The costumes the astro zombies wear include black ski-type masks under the latex heads. Here's what you would have seen if you were near the refueling station: a light blue van, with no extra side windows, pulling up in the fuel pump lot, and four people getting out and walking around to the dirt area behind the building. Ten minutes later, four more vehicles slow down and park behind a trailer truck storage yard

across the street. Almost a dozen people wearing long-sleeved shirts, with identical unknown symbols on each, and carrying large blades begin walking over to the van. An old man starts yelling, "Let's do it now! Hurry Up! Go! Go! Go!" and the van's side doors fly open and a guy comes out with a medium-sized video camera. The old guy continues, "Put the masks on now! Hurry! We've got to do this now!" While this is being shouted, men begin sliding black hoods, with just an eye opening, over their faces, and then thick, green helmets are pulled down over their heads. The old guy, the guy with the professional camera, and a guy with a touristy camcorder (me) run behind the above-ground gasoline storage tank building while the rag-tag uniformed group finish suiting up. The old guy begins shouting, "Action, action, action!" and these masked men, with machetes waving around, run behind the government fuel station located less than a half mile from the airport runways!

What do you think happened when a few employees, who were gassing up, saw everything taking place? Well, we did the brief scenes a couple of times, and the astro zombie army headed back to their vehicles and drove off within 10 minutes. The SUV I rode in had to wait because Ted called one of my group back to put on a gator-like head and black cloak. He was going to be an evil alien who cuts the chain holding the fence locked shut. Less than three minutes later, as I sat across the street inside a Ford Explorer with tinted windows, four orange airport security trucks, two Metro Police Broncos, and a helicopter converge on the fuel depot!

I watched the activity while my driver waited for his friend. I see a law enforcement officer tentatively approach the light blue van. Ted shouts out to people in his car behind us, "I need my book!" and walks to the vehicle along with the police officer at arm's length. Ted gets his large bundled binder of papers and begins flipping through it. Eight minutes later, the guy we've been waiting for slowly walks to our Explorer. He hands the driver a ragged piece of paper with an address scrawled on it. The messenger says in a low voice, "Start up the engine and pull out slowly. Head to this address." We leave with alligator-guy. Ted and three crew members are still with the police.

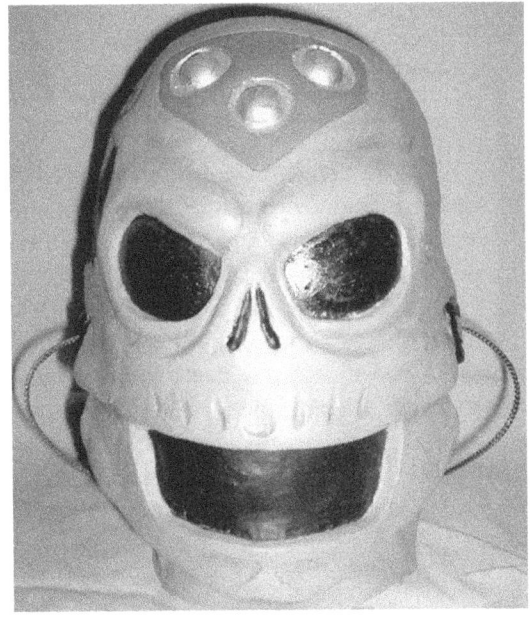

Sculptor Jay Gowey's *Mark of the Astro Zombie* mask. Gowey was encouraged to maintain the spirit of the original astro zombie masks.

Almost 30 minutes later, Ted and the crew show up at our next location—a café. Luckily, the owner of the restaurant expects us. I hear how the group was detained and questioned about filming permits. No one was arrested, but it was very close.

Ted has his controversy down pat after years of low-budget filmmaking. He has a college theatrics teacher/buddy sign a paper stating everyone involved is with an experimental media group and learning movie techniques. "This is for the kids of Nevada who are trying to broaden the local filmmaking base. It's good for the Las Vegas economy because the filmmakers live here and not in California, and it's a non-paid training." That's the gist of the paper.

In case you're wondering, yes, I knew that Ted shoots without legal film permits. I'm one of the few involved who know what low-budget directors do. This doesn't quite rank up there with cult director Ray Dennis Steckler's hijacking of a small town parade for his 1960s Batman-like *Rat Pfink a Boo Boo* in terms of style, but it certainly ranks up there in terms of sheer determination!

How many people would use an unauthorized location, on government property, which stores hundreds of gallons of gasoline near a major international airport runway three weeks after the nation's worst terrorist attacks *ever*? I'm not sure whether he's daring or deranged. Definitely a birthday I'll remember for the rest of my life.

Is *Mark of the Astro Zombies* a marvel of independent moviemaking? Not hardly, and as some detractors and critics have pointed out, its biggest drawback are the myriad storylines. There just seems to be entirely too many things happening all at once: good aliens, bad aliens, space travel, extraterrestrial sightings, foreign spies, worldwide governmental espionage, the love-interest subplot between Brinke Stevens and Sean Morrelli, and finally the astro zombies themselves.

The Corpse Grinders 2 suffered from this complicated plotline business as well, but Ted figures that if he's the one primarily funding the picture then he should make it the way he wants. Besides, he's the one going into debt, and the nuts and bolts of his storylines make perfect sense to him. Just ask him. "There's a lot of stuff going on in *Mark of the Astro Zombies*," Ted points out, "and for that I think it's a better movie than the original."

Whether or not *Mark of the Astro Zombies* is a "better" movie than the original is debatable, but at this point it is, without a doubt, the finest moment in Ted's straight-to-video career.

18. *The Cauldron: Baptism of Blood*

Synopsis from Press Materials

A pentagram on the floor is encircled by flaming torches as seven coven girls dance to exotic drums. Demonia, the black witch, assisted by Kardak, her evil enforcer, and Rochelle, are beseeching the evil spirit demon Vessago to appear and witness the blood sacrifice he has commanded. A male victim is chained next to the pentagram, and his oiled body reflects the flicker of the flames nearby. A long ornamental dagger is lifted from the burning coals of a cauldron and is held aloft over the drugged victim of the sacrifice by Demonia as she calls out for the evil demon to show his presence. The coven girls quicken the pace and wildness of the dance to match the increasing tempo and intensity of the drums. The blade is thrust downwards, and the blood of the victim is caught in a cup. A new participant in the coven is kneeling, and receives the "Baptism of Blood" as the cup is tilted over her head by Kardak. Rochelle joins Demonia in the chanting to the evil demon, who joins the ceremony, appearing in raging fire, thunder and lightning as his image fills the sacrificial room with terror. The great horned demon is aligned with Satan himself; his tentacles and dark horns emanating from his head are frightening as he bellows his approval of the sacrifice and baptism.

In a television studio a talent search has been ongoing, and judges seated nearby have narrowed the contestants down to three singers, each a fine talent, making their job of selecting a winner somewhat difficult. Stacy, an outstanding talent, seems to have accumulated the greatest number of votes. The final vote is tallied, and Rich, Stacy's boyfriend, along with his friends Nick and Julie, await word in the audience when Stacy is announced as the winner of "America's Top Talent."

In an old but still usable movie studio, with lights, cables and old-fashioned camera equipment cluttering the place, there is a coven meeting room. Burning candles and a pentagram are seen. Demonia, head of the coven, and Rochelle are giving a potion to the girls as Kardak re-enters the room, returning from his disposition of the previous victim. The coven girls again react to the exotic drumbeat and begin to dance. There are several mannequins present in the room, and although they have a strange presence, they are frozen in time and seem to observe the goings on. Demonia asks for Vessago to grant their wishes and return Mara, their queen witch who is now departed, to them so that together they may all enjoy the fruits of sacrifice. Vessago again appears and roars out that he must have more sacrifice, and that they must offer more victims to a blood sacrifice in his honor. Demonia pleads for Vessago's help in finding more victims, possibly leading them to more coven girls that could help them lure victims. Vessago is a fiercely demonic disciple of the great Satan himself.

In a burst of fire and lightning, Vessago appears in Stacy's room, frightening her to immobility. In a demonic voice, Vessago tells Stacy that he can give her the fame, fortune and immortality that she so desires, but that she would have to pledge her soul to him. Stacy is in sheer panic at the vision of Vessago, but says she would never give her soul to Satan. Vessago tells her that she will face the consequences of her refusal, then leaves the room in a burst of sound and fire.

At the coven's meeting room, Vessago appears to the group with his usual fire and thunder, and commands the mannequins to be of assistance. One by one, the mannequins dematerialize, then rematerialize in exact visual reproductions of themselves, but now females, very pretty as the mannequins are, and dressed exactly like their inanimate counterparts. They dematerialize into the ether as the dancers continue their ritual of the dancing to the savage drumbeats.

In Stacy's room, the mannequins, now live female counterparts, materialize and command that Stacy accompany them. Stacy is frightened, but refuses, knowing that they are participants in the satanic rites of Vessago. She struggles with them as they all dematerialize.

In the coven room, the mannequins appear with Stacy, who is immediately given a drugged drink by Kardak and led powerlessly into the center of the room near the pentagram. Demonia tells her that the only way she can avoid being a victim of sacrifice herself is to find someone to take her place. She must endure the "Baptism of Blood." Drugged, she tells Demonia that she will ask her friend Rich to join her.

Back at Stacy's apartment, Rich enters her room just in time to hear the last few words of Stacy's voice on her answering machine. Rich plays back Stacy's message, telling him how to find her, then leaves hurriedly.

Rich circles the building, the old movie studio Stacy described. He calls Nick on his cell and gives him the PIN number on his Lo-Jack system [an anti-theft automobile tracking device], "just in case," gives him the location, and tells him to notify the police if anything goes wrong. Exiting his vehicle, he moves around the building to find a secluded entry door. He finds it open, and enters. In the darkness, Kardak throws a black cloak over his head, and then shoots him with a needle and container holding drugs into his arm, making him near totally helpless. Kardak leads him into the coven room where the coven dancers are preparing for the sacrifice, and Demonia hails the new victim.

In the coven room of the studio, Stacy awaits the Baptism of Blood as the drugged Rich is prepared for the blood-letting sacrifice. Candles are burning wildly; Vessago appears and calls for the sacrifice. The coven girls are dancing, the voodoo drums beat loudly. Rich is about to be made another bloodless corpse.

Rich is closer to being the sacrificial victim; Vessago is howling through the fires and thunder for Demonia and Rochelle to drive the dagger into Rich's heart. Stacy does not register the danger that faces her and Rich.

Nick arrives at the studio and, sensing something is wrong, calls the police. The detectives ... are dispatched to the scene.... As they approach the studio back entrance, Kardak, wearing his sacrificial mask, hood and cloak, emerges to drag another lifeless body to his vehicle. One detective grabs Kardak from behind and incapacitates him, telling the other to handcuff and detain him while he goes inside, wearing Kardak's mask and garb. Nick follows him.

Inside the coven room, the detective is unnoticed as he observes Demonia and Rochelle pouring the drugged drink into cups held by the dancers. As the girls drink the potion, Rochelle hands out spears and daggers to be used in the sacrificial death of the newest victim, Rich. Nick keeps to the dark shadows in the studio, and is in total awe of the situation. He sees Stacy and Rich, who is chained to the sacrificial altar. Demonia chants loudly for the appearance of Vessago to witness the blood-letting sacrifice in his honor, and in honor of Satan.

Vessago appears in the fire, thunder, lightning, and satanic howling. The detective throws off the mask he is wearing, pulls his weapon, and fires at the figure of Vessago. Vessago, unfazed, demands that the coven attack and kill Demonia and Rochelle. The coven girls now turn their spears and daggers on them as commanded, and kill both of them. The bodies of the two witches dissolve out in fire as they die. We hear the satanic screams of the witches as they die in the swirling flames and angry fire. Vessago now demands that they kill the intruders, the detective and Nick. The detective fires two loud shots, and loudly demands that they drop their weapons, disrobe, and give up their ties to Satan and Vessago. The coven slowly responds to the detective's commands, remove their black cloaks, and, looking bewildered, obey. Their queen, the black witch known as Demonia, is no longer their leader.

The detective calls for back-up as Nick frees Rich, then, in turn, the two release and bring Stacy out of her drug-induced trance. The coven girls, seemingly in a daze, now fall exhausted. Vessago is raging, screaming loudly, bellowing through the fires that engulf him that he will return and bring the legions of Satan to deal with those who defy him. All goes calm after the tumultuous ordeal.

Credits

Cast: Mary Selby (Demonia); Senita DeVeaux (Malucina); Jenn O. Cide (Kardassa); Scott Blacksher (Vessago); Randy Ariel Tena (Tor); Kellie Karl (Stacy); Tom Lynch (Rich); Walter Sherwood (Nick); Sean Morelli (Detective Robert); Adam Yoder (Detective Jack); Shanti (Wendy Cooper); Ronnie D. Ray (Officer Savini); Ken Lochner (Precinct Officer); Louie Thomas (Homeless Wit); Jerry Carroll (Homeless Wit #2); Bob Freeland (Homeless Wit #3); Dr. Hammargren (Mr. Edwards); Ben Ruhl (Johnny Richards); Gene Paul Jones (Bill Masters); Judi Stone (Master's Assistant); Ellen Lawson (Secretary, Client); Ted V. Mikels (Dr. Korneschevsky); Donna Hamblin (Dr. Vallanova); *Mannequins*: Jennifer Asbjornsen, April Joy Delph, Debbie Ballweg; Tamrin Oster (Cemetery Girl); Volmer A. Franz (Recording Studio Engineer); Molinee Green (Rob's Assistant); Robert Root (2nd Engineer); Jamie Jent (Mirror Girl); Rusty Meyers (Evil Abusive Husband); *Coven Girls*: Danielle Smith, Sandra Winogrocki, Justine Barker, April Joy Delph, Bernadette Baca, Kissy Denise, Venus LaBelle, Jamie Jent, Kitty Bondage, Amy Carelli, Jennifer L. Robbins, Treasa L. Smith, Dayna Collins; *New Coven Initiates*: Angelina M. Dorogi, Chelsea Randall, Diane DeStefano, Danielle Smith, Treasa L. Smith, Bonnie Morris, Owen Gibson; *Alley Guys*: Mike Monahan, Mike A. Martinez, Christian Sahlen; *Coven*

Room Drummers: Jimbo Tyler, Angel Perez, Jeff "Ski"; Scott Brown (Beheaded Victim); Ron N. (Man Working Out in Gym); *Contestants in America's Top Talent Show*: Sunset and Big Momma, Jaime McMullen, Tamrin Oster, Richard Mann and "Tommy," Kellie Karl, Jupiter Shifter; *Judges of America's Top Talent Show*: Mark O'Brien, Jordan Durbin, Mike Durbin; "Missy" Swartz (Nick's Girl); Tim Searcy (America's Top Talent Show Voice-Over Announcer); Holly Anderson (Psychic Eye Book Shop Clerk); Margo Piper (Psychic Eye Book Shop Clerk); Elaine Kimberlaine (Psychic Eye Book Shop Customer); Minneapolis Theater Attendees (America's Top Talent Show T.V. Audience); Bill Carter (Manager of St. Anthony Main Theater)

Production: *production manager*: Amy Carrelli. *assistant director*: Seria Judith. *second unit director*: Adam Lane. *third unit director*: "Rock and Roll" Ray. *script supervisor*: Wm. McDonald. *sound*: Rob Feeland. *audio post assistant*: Billy McD. *choreographer*: Tamara Cepeda. *costume coordinator*: Celest Pawol. *make-up*: Elaine Kimberlaine. *seamstress*: Lupe Tena. *wig stylist*: Cocoa Shakerford. *second unit cameras*: Adam Lane, Mike A Martinez, Jeremy Settles. *sets, mechanical effects, make-up effects*: David E. White, Jr. *art direction*: Wendy O. Altamura. *props*: Christy Larson. *key grip*: Darold McDonald. *gaffer*: Adam Lane. *camera grip*: Mike Monahan. *production assistants*: Megan Duncan, Matthew P. Sutton, Sharice A. Zulo, Ben Pluenneke, Joey Lowman. *casting services*: Rusty Meyers. *primary musical score*: New Wave Music, Troy Keithy. *additional score*: Glen Grayson, D.J. Woods, Duane T. *mask maker*: Jay Gowey, Dan Reisinger, Chris King at Monsters of Extinction. *digital visual effects*: MFX. *computer/software provider*: Bobby Lee Dysinger at Searcy Entertainment, Inc. *webmaster*: Dennis L. Phelps. *writer, producer, director, photographer, editor*: Ted V. Mikels. *special thanks*: Robert Leyson at Psychic Eye Book Store, Las Vegas, Nevada, the Huntridge Theater, Superior Medical Solutions, Inc., Hammargren Home of Nevada History, Pat Amico at Studio IV, Rouben Papikian, TVM Studios, Chuck Minker at Sports Complex, Seria Tena, DJ Wood. *running time*: 1 hour 43 minutes. Color. *aspect ratio*: full-frame. *shot*: 2003. *released*: 2004.

The Video

Summon all the demons!—the coven girls from *The Cauldron: Baptism of Blood*

The year 2004 saw director Ted V. Mikels once again revisit a film from his past. It seemed only natural, as his quasi-retelling of *The Corpse Grinders* in 2000 was a success in many ways, and his return to the world of the *Astro Zombies* in 2002 was even more so. Still, Ted was searching for that "hit" movie to put his career back on track.

Blood Orgy of the She Devils, made in 1972, soon became the source material from which Ted would create his feature *The Cauldron: Baptism of Blood*. TVM Studios was about to run red with the vital fluids of unwilling sacrifices to the Devil. But would Ted's latest offering be a hit, or rather *the* "hit" that he needed?

Despite the less than impressive dollar signs of Ted's previous direct-to-video productions, the 70-year-old-plus showman undauntedly forged ahead with high spirits and determination. "The actual making of a movie is one of my greatest loves," proclaimed Ted. Perhaps, but when asked if he's ever considered retiring, the reply was quick and to the point: "Nope. Never. I cannot stop making movies."

As usual, Ted's enthusiasm for the project ran straight through and permeated everyone involved. From the grips and gaffers to the actors and actresses, all were thrilled to be a part of a Ted V. Mikels movie production. The director seconds the sentiment: "I always tell people at the beginning

Promotional poster for *The Cauldron: Baptism of Blood* (2004).

creature is an evil entity that demands human sacrifices in order for him to carry out their wishes.

Blacksher described his involvement in *The Cauldron* and how he came to take on the role of the movie's resident demon:

> My involvement in *The Cauldron: Baptism of Blood* was brief and unexpected. I'd stopped by his studio to pick up a business card needed by a comic book/movie convention. Ted was interested in being a guest, so I said I'd send in his credentials. The mask designer for *Mark of the Astro Zombies*, Jay Gowey, was in town from Phoenix to do the Vessago demon mask and make-up for Ted's current shoot, *The Cauldron: Baptism of Blood*.
>
> The mask was designed for a medium-sized head, and the person had to be clean shaven. My head is huge and I have a mustache now. After Ted called four people and couldn't reach any of them, I said I could shave my mustache if the mask fit. I drove Jay Gowey back to his hotel and tried it on. It wasn't a perfect fit, but it'd work. We held off for another 30 minutes in case someone returned Ted's call. I got the role by default.
>
> The mask required extra make-up and latex, so I sat in a stiff hotel chair for two hours while Jay attached the mask. I had to have cotton balls stuffed up my nose and my head tilted straight back. While Jay Gowey was using spirit gum adhesive and liquid latex to apply the mask, he was telling me things like, "Shut your eyes tight because you'll be blinded for life if any of this drips," and, "Don't move or twitch at all now." Jay has long hair, chain smokes cigarettes, is in his 20s, and wears a Misfits T-shirt, so I'm stereotype-imagining a heavy drug user

of my movies that if they're not here to enjoy the making of a movie then they shouldn't be here." So onward and upward through the fog went Ted and his latest partners in crime.

The Cauldron is not so much a remake of *Blood Orgy of the She Devils* as a continuation of the story. Mara, the queen of the witches, was killed in the first movie, and here a new coven is doing their best to raise her from the dead, with the aid of Vessago (played by Scott Blacksher). This demonic messing around with dangerous glue and my vision; but, to his credit, I escaped unscathed.

After the mask was set we headed back to the studio. Did I mention that neither Jay nor myself had seen even one word of the script? Ted has the thing protected better than most major studios, not so much for secrecy but because he can't afford multiple Xerox copies! Luckily my role required a tight close-up on the head as the demon looks down upon his worshippers. So, for most of the lines, I'm looking down at the script and cold reading the dialogue. Other lines I'm given verbally by Ted because he thought of them after he wrote the script.

I tried to overact as much as possible, blending some different images in my mind like the first encounter with the pseudo-wizard from *The Wizard of Oz*, because Jay envisioned flames constantly around my head. Then I thought of Tim the Enchanter and his warning about the killer rabbit from *Monty Python and the Holy Grail*, because Jay designed the headpiece with tentacles/snakes, so I needed to do a lot of short head movements. Finally, I took into account the closing scene with Norma Desmond in *Sunset Boulevard*, because Jay's test footage, with reversed color, was suppose to make the whites of my eyes appear black. If nothing else, it should bring a lot of attention to Jay Gowey's work on the mask, with my over-the-top hammy performance.

The mask, and my head, was chromo-keyed to alter the color. However, the end result didn't match Jay's test footage because Ted didn't have the same program available to alter the head properly. I knew Ted would alter the voice somewhat, so I tried to sound as pompously insane as possible—thus the primary reason for the Tim the Enchanter approach—so I'd still be understandable, unlike the aliens from *Mark of the Astro Zombies*.

It took just under one hour to do the role. Like last time, almost all of the lines were first takes. I'd like to think I'm just that good, and a consummate professional, but damned if I don't keep thinking of Ed Wood. "That's great! It sounds natural. Okay. Next scene."

By the way, I have no recollection of what the hell I said on camera. Just your standard arrogant demon stuff. I had fun, though, because I was able to cut loose. After the second line, everyone, all four of them, were smiling, and Ted told them, "Can you believe it? I told Scott I didn't have a part for him this time." That made me feel kind of good about the role.

Back to the movie. Naturally, the witches respect Vessago's wishes, and, in turn, they are granted theirs ... well, some of them. Mara, for whatever reason, never shows up; and for a movie with the subtitle "Baptism of Blood," the body count is incredibly low—really low (you can count them on your thumbs). Only two deaths occur in the 103-minute running time, and one is witchcraft-induced suicide. Could it be that Ted Mikels is softening up in his later years?

On Ted's official website he points out that *The Cauldron* has "...no sex or nudity, nothing offensive, probably PG-13." That's an interesting approach to an exploitation horror movie, but lay this baby on a staunch Christian and let them get a load of what Ted feels to be inoffensive. Pentagrams, goat heads, bleeding skulls, a pot of human stew, inverted crosses on the behinds of the coven girls, mounds and mounds of cleavage, demon dancing and all the other accou-

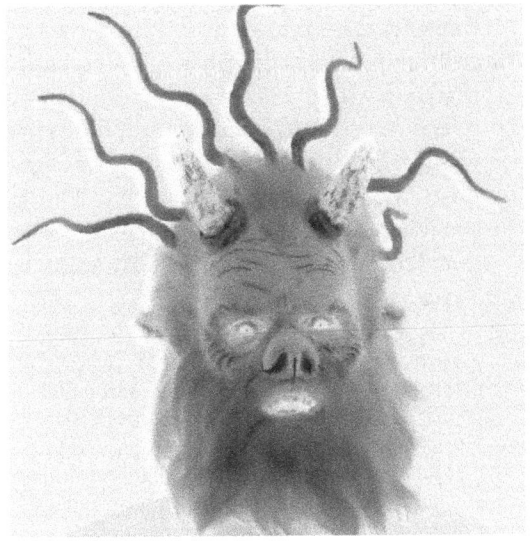

Vessago (Scott Blacksher), the resident demon of *The Cauldron: Baptism of Blood*.

The baptism of blood from *The Cauldron: Baptism of Blood*.

trements that go towards making a Satanic ceremony right and proper. It's a certainty that *somebody* is bound to find something offensive in *The Cauldron*; but Ted's mind works differently, and for him all of the aforementioned is just good clean fun. Things could have been markedly different, however, as associate producer Walter O'Reilly recounts:

> I've known Ted for years. I'd flown out to Vegas to work with him on *The Cauldron*, and around this time we were trying to strike a deal with a movie sales and rental chain, but they wanted the movie to be rated and to contain lots of nudity and violence. So I told Ted that we had to do this, but, as you probably already know, Ted is very uncomfortable with nudity in his movies. Well, anyhow, he conceded to ask the girls who would be willing to go topless for a few scenes. When the time came he sheepishly asked them, and I was like, "Oh no! This is never gonna work this way." So I literally stepped in front of Ted and said, "All right! I'm producing this goddamned movie. Now(!) who's gonna get naked!?" As it happened, some of them were willing to go skimpier, but not totally naked or even topless. Anyhow, the production moved on, and my wife Nina is calling to check in on me and how the movie is going, and, of course, she talks with Ted from time to time. Out of nowhere he says, "Walter, tell Nina to email me a picture of herself. I've been talking to her all these years and I'd like to put a face on the voice that I hear." So she sent him a picture, and he flipped out, thinking she looked like Mara from *Blood Orgy of the She Devils*. He then asked if she'd be willing to fly out and take on the role of Mara *and* get topless. Well, Nina had done some nude modeling for a university, and so I called and asked her, and she said,

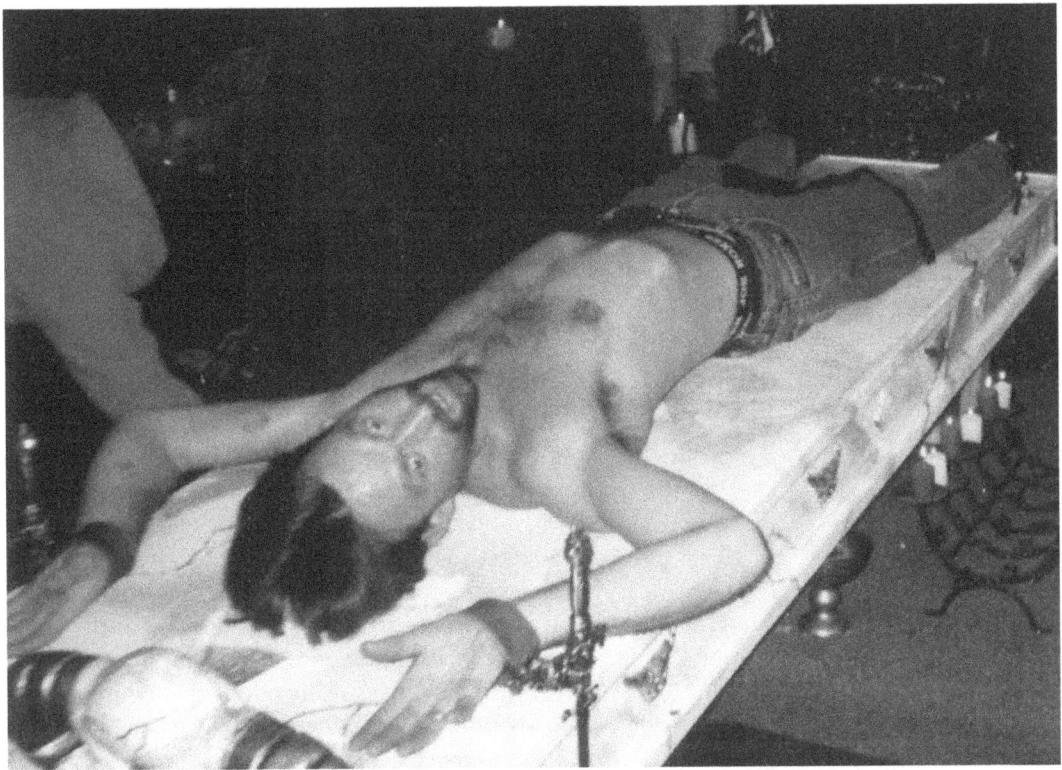

One of two victims (Ron Jason) in *The Cauldron: Baptism of Blood*.

"Yes." I told Ted that she would do it, but before the scenes were even shot he backed down and said that he couldn't do it.

Ted also had no problem laying on his brand of black humor. One decapitated sacrifice has his disembodied head stuffed into a ten gallon fish aquarium. Then, later, when the remainder of the body is found, a police detective remarks, "It's hard to check for dental records with no head." Indeed—no head, no teeth.

Another enjoyable aspect of *The Cauldron* stems from the fact that the coven of witches rents out an old movie studio in order to perform their evil duties. What makes this so intriguing is that it's Ted's studio that is used in the movie. So, basically, *The Cauldron* stands as a guided tour of TVM Studios. The viewer gets to see Ted's cameras, his audio recording studio, his editing bay, his mannequins and his office, which is completely wallpapered with Ted V. Mikels movie posters and memorabilia.

Ted even went so far as to write a part for his old "dummy buddy," Tommy Ache. Tommy was Ted's ventriloquist dummy for his traveling magic act from the late 1940s to the early 60s. "Tommy was given to me by the infamous Leon Mandrake in 1946," recalled Ted. "I'd had dime store dummies before, but Tommy was my first 'real' one, and I still have him to this day."

Ted has had Tommy for nearly 60 years, so why did it take him so long to utilize the talents of his pal in a feature movie?

Tommy is my alter ego. I just wasn't all that interested in turning him over to someone else. I didn't want to hear what his voice might sound like with someone else handling him. Honestly, I don't really feel comfortable with someone else's hand in his back. Tommy is very much like one of my children.

A very young Ted V. Mikels and his old "dummy buddy" Tommy Ache in 1949.

Second, there's the mock-up television program "America's Top Talent." This sequence does very little to move the story forward, but at six minutes it does help eat up some running time. Third, there is yet another mock-up television broadcast. This one, lasting only four minutes, is called "Studies in the Paranormal," and it's a talk show that features Ted in a cameo role as Dr. Korneschevsky, an expert in psychic phenomenon. The cameo is nice but....

Then there's the long-winded speeches delivered by the head witch Demonia and her sidekick Malucina. These diatribes are jam-packed and overflowing with loads of hocus-pocus heebie-jeebie mumbo-jumbo. It's not what they're saying, or even how they are saying it, that grates, it's that these speeches are simply too long. It's as though Ted was attempting to pad out his running time. What's really odd is that he is a firm believer in "shorter is better" when it comes to moviemaking.

Even with all it has going for it, *The Cauldron* still has problems. First off, the opening sequence shows a group of witches buying an amulet from a gift shop. Why, in the name of all that is unholy, would a witch search for a ritualistic amulet in a place of commerce? Shouldn't something like that come from an ancient burial ground, or be forged from the remains of the dead, or simply be sent from the bowels of Hell?

Drawbacks aside, *The Cauldron* should still be given a gander for all of its positive attributes. Besides, Ted and company did stick 35,000 dollars of hard earned cash into it, with a final budget cost of around 150,000 bucks. *The Cauldron* is not his best, nor is it his most successful, but it *is* part of the TVM oeuvre, and it deserves some attention along with the rest of them.

19. *Heart of a Boy*

Synopsis from Press Materials

The setting is today, in a small rural area. The school is small, and a neighborhood grocery store sells hardware and other miscellaneous items to the locals. Nearby there is a small country store that sells grain to farmers and has a corner table where locals come to drink beer and play poker. Houses are old and unpretentious, suggesting a lower income community.

The home Timmy and Alina live in is a bit of a structure that has seen better days, a shack, almost secluded and lost in the unkempt trees and brush that surround it. The road in front is paved, but only occasionally busy with passing traffic.

Grandpa Theo, who is close to Timmy

and Alina by mutual adoption, lives next door. Theo is retired and uses his social security income to help Timmy and Alina with their needs.

Timmy was born to Alina out of a rape situation, and has an undeveloped heart valve that will require a transplant if he is to survive. This is the story of the often heartbreaking ordeal and endless pursuit of a new heart to keep Timmy alive.

The interactions with the townspeople, neighbors who care, those who control the organ transplant processes, evil and greedy people who would do anything for money, and the playboy who turns sympathetic to the plight of Timmy and the efforts of Theo to secure the transplant for Timmy keeps you wishing, wanting, crying and caring for the outcome.

Credits

Cast: Matthew Lopez (Timmy); Mia Bofill (Alina); Sean Morelli (Jack Thornton); Ted V. Mikels (Grandpa "Theo"); Ron Jason (Jake); Stanley V. Scott (Dr. Jeffries); Debora Prettyman-Spencer (Nurse Deanna); Sam Osman (MRI Radiologist); Arnie Bartz (Josh); Foster Boom (Jacolyn); *Poker Players*: Shannon Sharp, Jason Sharp, Ron Reed, R.J.; Christopher Cotter (Broker); Mike Martz (Broker Client 1); Thomas Sharp (Broker Client 2); Mary Robertson (Bake Sale Manager); Justine Baker (TV Reporter); Scott Brown (TV Cameraman); Anthony Lopez (Boy Bully); Brittany Lopez (Alexia); Brandon Lopez (Timmy's Friend); Laurence R. Griffin (Father André); Shanti (Sister M. June); Kara Beth Cohen (Sister M. Maria); Paul Burkett (Limo Rich Man); Carlos Delgado (Limo Driver); *Bake Sale Extras*: Celine T. Martens, Jason Gomez, Brendan Smith, Christopher Lopez, Frank Roth, Eva Renner, Hugh Renner, Pearl Hochfield, Dorothy S. Estrin, Clyde Wilson, Sue Clarke; Volmar Franz (Pawn Shop Dealer); William "Deacon" Cooper (Pawn Shop Assistant); *Organ Donor Offices*: Mr. Edwards (himself), John P. Baniqued (Mr. Randolph), Beverly Welsh (Elizabeth), Tiffani McDonald (Staff Secretary), Rusty Meyers (Playboy Deserter); *Valley Bank*: Adrienne Wade (Receptionist), Jim Campbell (Mr. Erickson), Sherry Coffman (Teller), Nancy Morales (Customer), Sahlee Spears (Customer), Gary Hysler (Customer), Margo Wade (Customer), Daniel Bautista (Customer), Steve Forsythe (Customer), Barbara Selby (Customer); *Nevada State Bank*: Christopher Napolitano (Mr. Williams), Ronnie D. Ray (Security Guard), Angel Friend (Receptionist), Marion Stedman (Teller), Jay Hiner (Customer), Bryan Burke (Customer), Bernard Baskin (Customer), David Lander (Customer), Chris Lenandoski (Jake's Buddy "Al"); *Pine Bluff Valley Sheriff's Office*: Anthony Powell (Sheriff), Shae Wilson (Sheriff's Deputy), Moira Yurmanovic (Concerned Neighbor), Louis Battaglia (Airplane Rental Agent); *Dr. Jeffries' Waiting Room*: Nancy L. Jones (Receptionist), *Waiting Room People*: John Waite, Stacey Sharman, Jason Sharman, Joshua Sharman, Brandy Ayala

Production: *written, produced, directed by*: Ted V. Mikels. *production assistant*: Angel Friend. *production manager*: Danielle Smith. *script supervisor*: Beverly Welsh. *cinematography*: Ted V. Mikels and Mac. *second unit camera*: Jeff Mahon. *second unit camera*: Joe Rocha. *camera assistants*: Jessica Jones, Angel Friend. *audio recording/mixer*: Adam Lane, Mike Monahan. *still photography*: Wendy Altamura. *gaffer*: Mike Erdman. *grip*: Jessica Jones, "Doug," Mike Monahan. *set design, construction*: MCFILMS, LLC. *makeup*: Crystal Morelli. *post FX*: MFX. *editor*: Ted V. Mikels. *assistant editor*: Wm. D. "Mac" McDonald, Jr. *Special Thanks To*: Nevada State Film Commission, Dr. Rosenbloom (organ donor information), Watler O'Reilly (NY associate), Mr. and Mrs. James Taylor, Art Jacobs, Gene Larson (Advanced

Media), Judith A. Stone (Classy Consignment, Inc.), Bruce Sniadach, Steve Bakke (Ready Reservations), Extra Limo Driver (Emilio Gallo), Philipé Lopez and Casas "Y" Mas (additional sets), Casting Entertainment, Real Actors Workshop, Robert Southerland (aviation consultant). *Additional Thanks To*: Jay Hiner (Nevada State Bank), Mr. Hulik (Valley Bank), Desert Inn Pawn, Super Mini Mart, Executive Conference Center, St. Peter the Apostle Catholic Church, Parump Indian Pow-Wow Gathering, North Las Vegas Airport, Las Vegas Pain Clinic, Global Cardiovascular Associates, Inc., Lydia O'Connor-Sanders D.O., P.C., Fresh Music, Digital Fables, LLC (post FX equipment), Bob Lee Dysinger, Searcy Entertainment, Inc. (post FX software), Timothy D. Searcy. *running time*: 1 hour 30 minutes. Color. *aspect ratio*: full-frame. *completed and released*: 2006.

The Video

There's no question, Timmy's gonna need a heart transplant to survive. —Dr. Jeffries from *Heart of a Boy*

The year 2005 gave way to director Ted V. Mikels' most unlikely movie project to date. After 40-plus years of producing every kind of exploitation film known to man, Ted decided to focus his energies on a family-friendly piece called *Heart of a Boy*. It should come as no surprise that longtime fans the world over were dismayed (and maybe even disappointed) by Ted's choice for his nineteenth feature. It's a fact that even Ted admits:

> On my other movies I had people flying in from all over the world to work with me, but when I announced *Heart of a Boy*, not all that many people wanted to get involved. It seems like people only want to work on my movies if there's some sort of bloodletting going on.

Perhaps Ted should have revisited some of his past movies in order to stir up some interest in his latest endeavor. *Heart of a Boy* tells the story of young Timmy, who desperately needs a heart transplant. So, with that in mind, maybe Ted could have resurrected Mara from *Blood Orgy of the She Devils* as a "good" witch who uses her powers to repair the little tyke's defective blood pumper. Or have Landau and Maltby retire the corpse grinder, go legit, and donate a portion of their profits to benefit the sickly boy. Even better, bring Dr. DeMarco back from the *Astro Zombies* and have him make Timmy a synthetic heart! One never knows. Any of these might have worked for the average Ted V. Mikels fan.

All joking aside, for what it is, and who it's aimed at, *Heart of a Boy* is actually pretty good. All of the performances are quite able, and Ted managed to write a cohesive script with fully developed characters that the viewer can actually identify with and care about. Ted regular Sean Morelli was finally able to enact a role with some meat and depth to it. Ted's portrayal of Grandpa "Theo" showcased *his* onscreen talents, and Mia Bofill, playing Timmy's mother Alina, comfortably delivers her lines. The real surprise is adolescent actor Matthew Lopez, who more than capably plays Timmy. All these things are a rarity for a Ted V. Mikels production, as he usually deals in caricatures, sensationalism and exploitation.

Heart of a Boy is convincing and believable at every turn. The storyline is concise, to the point, and extremely easy to follow, which is to say that there are none of those patented Ted V. Mikels subplots. There's no G-men, no aliens, no foreign spies and no governmental intervention. And it's quite refreshing to know that Ted can still create and develop a cast of characters. He really hasn't done this since 1959 with *Strike Me Deadly*. True, there was good character development in *One Shocking Moment* and *The Black Klansman*, but this was, in part, overshadowed by those films' exploitative elements. Ted wanted to make a feel-good movie that tugged at the heart strings, and for its intended audience it will likely do just that. Still, Ted's core audience may find the movie simply not to their tastes.

Lieutenant Governor Lorraine T. Hunt was apparently taken by Ted's attempt at cracking the Disney-dominated family movie market. On August 28, 2005, she issued Ted a "Certificate of Recognition" congratulating him on "...more than fifty years of directing, writing and producing films [that] culminate in this heart-warming family movie."

Heart of a Boy was shot and completed in 2005 for a total cost of $85,000. As Ted puts it:

> It was my reaction to the blood and gore pictures that are the norm these days. I think "campy" horror is okay, but I'm really uncomfortable with believable horror, or any of the stuff that looks real. So I just decided to make a movie aimed towards families, and I'm told time and time again that families love it! Still, I know for a fact that my usual supporters, my usual fans, think I've lost my mind. They keep asking me why I departed from my normal stuff. Then my older friends and family say, "Ted, you've finally made a good movie that we can watch." So it's a double-edged sword.

Finally, when asked if someone only had 90 minutes to live, and they wanted to see a Ted V. Mikels movie, which one would he show them, he quickly replied:

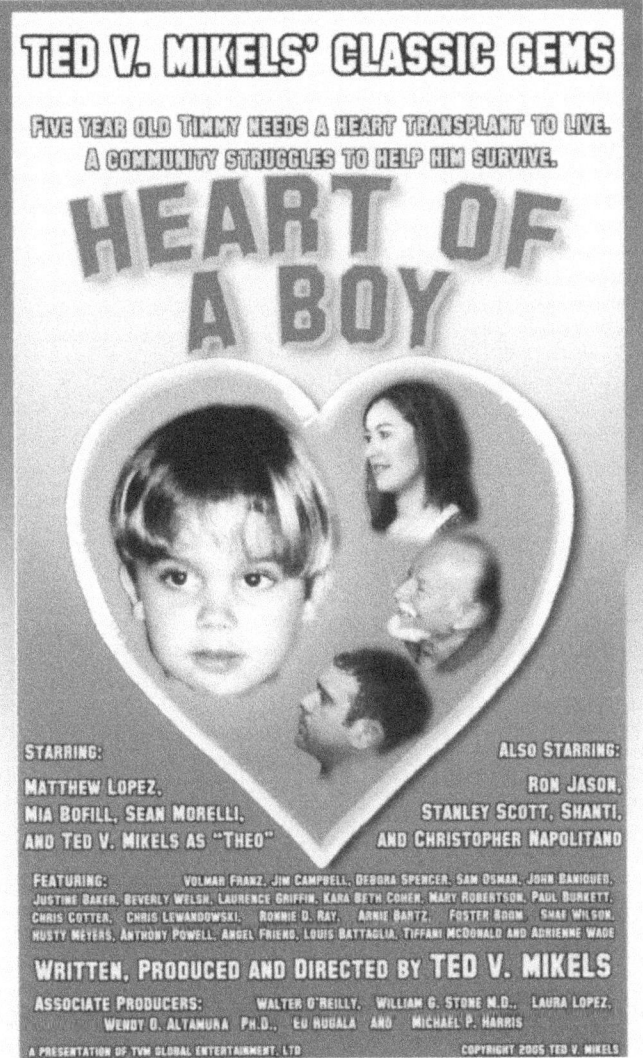

Artwork for the most unlikely of Ted V. Mikels' productions, *Heart of a Boy* (2006).

> I'd show them *Heart of a Boy*. It has happiness, hope, laughter, sadness and tears. It's a real story of human drama that encompasses, what I feel are, very real emotions. I'm very proud of having made this movie.

PART THREE

Cinematic Timeline, Homage, Memorabilia

"Ted V. Mikels exemplifies the spirit of the independent, not to mention he's one of the nicest guys around."—Director Bill Rebane (*The Giant Spider Invasion* and *Blood Harvest*)

20. A Comprehensive Ted V. Mikels Cinematic Timeline

(Mikels provides commentary on selected titles in this timeline, which includes his nineteen major movies as well as his lesser known feature films, videos, and television appearances.)

1954

A Tall Tale (fairy tale) [director/co-written/editor] 16mm

1955

Hoarfrost (documentary) [producer/director of photography] 16mm
Reindeer Ranch (documentary) [producer/director of photography] 16mm
Snow Monsters (horror) [director of photography] 16mm
Television newsreels, current events

1956

All About Blaze (documentary) [producer/editor/director of photography] 16mm
Bag That Buck (documentary) [producer/editor/director of photography] 16mm
Dream Man (dramatic fiction) [director/producer/co-writer/editor] 16mm
Fool's Prosperity (action/drama) [director/producer/co-writer/editor] 16mm
Rodeo (documentary) [producer/editor/director of photography] 16mm
The Long Wide Trailer (documentary) [producer/editor/cameraman] 16mm

A behind the scenes shot from an early Ted V. Mikels production entitled *Fool's Prosperity* (1956). Notice Ted in the foreground with his back to the camera and his (then) wife Geneva dancing in front of the fireplace.

Stairway to Opportunity (sales promo documentary; commercial)

1957

Indian Fighter (adventure) [stuntman/archery expert] 35mm
Compelled (mystery/drama) [director/writer/producer/editor] 16mm
Condemned Property (documentary/drama) [director of photography/editor] 16mm
Day of the Outlaw (serious drama) [still cameraman] 35mm
Tonka (action drama) [producer/actor/part-time still cameraman/horseman] 35mm
Jungle Hell (action/adventure) [part-time photographer] 35mm
Old Mexico (documentary/travel) [producer/editor/cameraman] 35mm
Oregon Passage (action adventure) [actor/horseman/stunt rider] 35mm

Yellow Roses (drama/romance) [director/producer/co-writer/editor] 16mm
The Rockhound (a "how to" on finding, cutting and polishing gems) [producer/co-writer/director of photography] 16mm
Horseman in 1950s (commercial)

1958

The Black Sheep (drama) [director/producer/co-writer/editor] 16mm
Outdoor Paradise (travel documentary) [producer/editor/director of photography] 16mm

1959

Strike Me Deadly/Crosshairs (action/adventure) [director/producer/editor/writer] (note: released 1963) 35mm

1961

Camp Ruffitt (documentary) [editor/director of photography] 16mm
Red Ryder Days (documentary) [editor/director of photography] 16mm

1962

Beauties of Central Oregon (travel/adventure documentary) [director/producer/editor/writer/cameraman] 16mm
The Skyliners (documentary) [editor/director of photography] 16mm
Water Pageant (documentary) [editor/director of photography] 16mm
How Little, How Big (classroom film on relative sizes of objects) [director/producer/ editor/co-writer, cameraman] 16mm

1963

The Doctors/Dr. Sex/Strange Loves of Dr. Sex (comedy spoof) [director/producer/editor/co-writer/actor] 35mm
Money in my Pocket (comedy) [part-time photographer/co-editor] 35mm

1964

Brandy (exploitation) [cameraman] 35mm
Games of Chance (drama) [director of photography] 35mm
Genesis (drama) [director of photography] 35mm
Jezebel (exploitation) [cameraman] 35mm
One Shocking Moment/Suburban Affair (drama) [director/producer/editor/writer] 35mm
Shepherd of the Hills (drama) [part-time photographer/co-editor] 35mm

1965

And Eden Cried (drama) [director of photography] 35mm

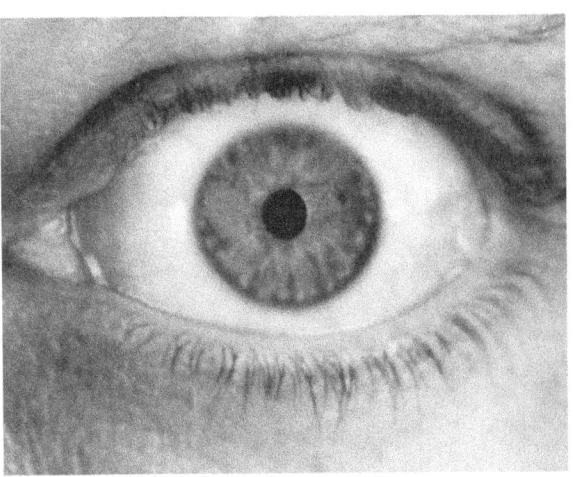

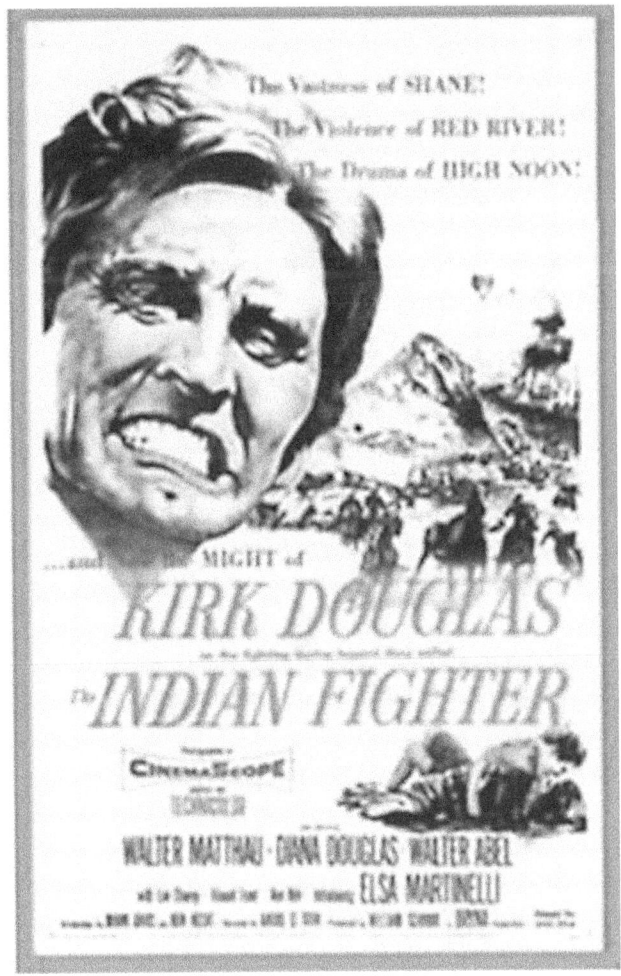

Top: A still shot from one of Ted V. Mikels' earliest films, *Compelled* (1957). *Below:* Poster art for Kirk Douglas' *Indian Fighter* (1957). Ted put in some time on this feature as a stuntman and archery expert.

A behind the scenes still of another early Ted V. Mikels production, *Yellow Roses* (1957).

Day of the Nightmare (horror) [director of photography] 35mm

"This is where I first met Liz Renay while running the cameras as D.P. as a favor to a friend. Best thing about the movie was the food in La Joya, California, on the ocean in a resort area, and the sea foods in the restaurants were fantastic. That was 1965, and I'm sorry to say we lost a good friend, as Liz passed away last Monday, 42 years later, on January 22, 2007, here in Las Vegas."

Ghouls and Dolls/ Orgy of the Dead (horror) [director of lighting and special effects] 35mm

"Again, doing a favor to help someone I was training as a cameraman so he could get his union certification to be accepted as a D.P. It was a fun shoot: fog, werewolves, lots of fun doing lighting effects. We filmed on a big soundstage, which was very well equipped."

The Hostage (psychological drama) [director of photography] 35mm

"*The Hostage* was a dream project for me. I was the operating cameraman and director of photography. Des Moines was cold at the time, but I had a very large crew and had the opportunity to take my time lighting, with a lot of help to move lights and cabling around. This was, I believe, my second movie involvement with John Carradine. Technicolor Lab in Hollywood paid me the highest of compliments: 'The cinematography was the finest they had developed in three years, and all the lights printed dead center, making it seem like the lighting was perfected with a densitometer.'"

House of the Black Death/Night of the Beast (horror) [director of photography] 35mm

"If I remember correctly, I was brought in to bring this movie, that was being shot in Hollywood, up to date on its production schedule.

20. A Comprehensive Cinematic Timeline 167

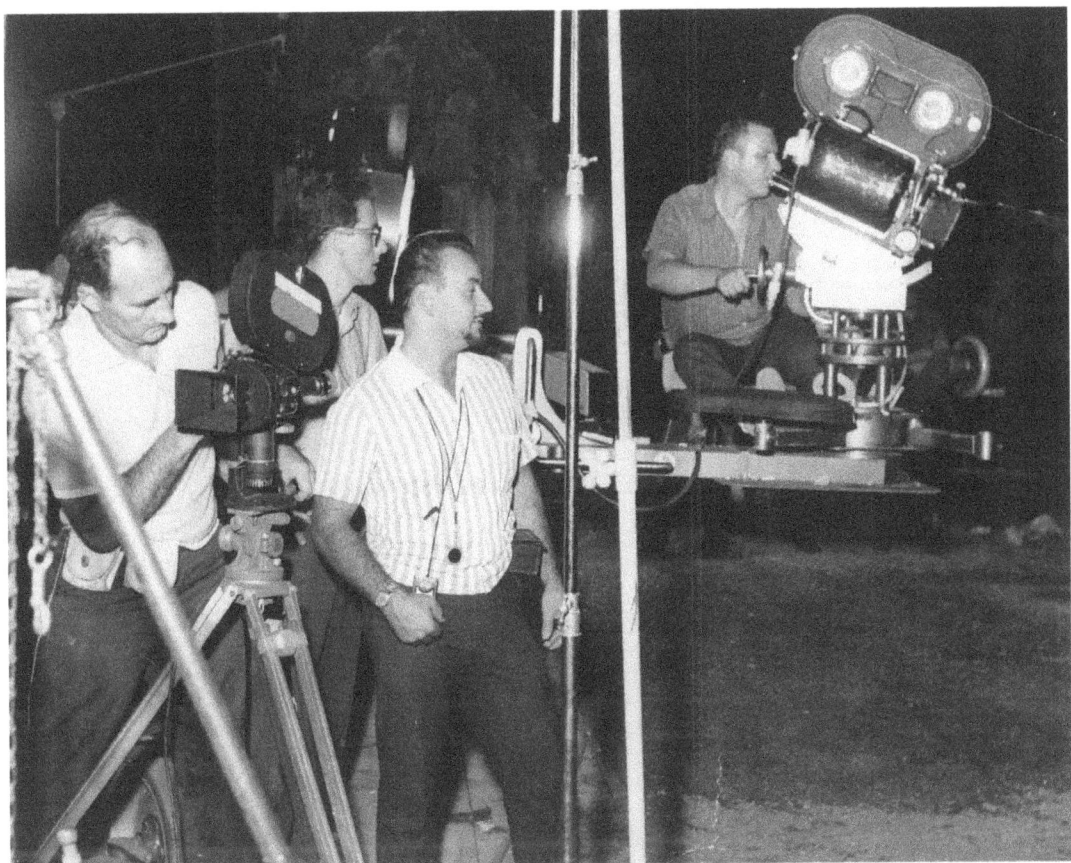

A young Ted V. Mikels handling lighting duties on the Ed Wood–scripted nudie feature *Orgy of the Dead* (1965).

I think the cast at that time included Bela Lugosi and Lon Chaney. It's hard to remember all of my activities 50 years ago. I remember it was being shot on old spooky mansion grounds in Coldwater Canyon, and because I had my 35 mm cameras at the ready, I was sent to help out shooting, possibly second unit stuff and whatever else was needed."

Little People (family TV pilot) [editor] 16mm
Phil Silvers, Smothers Brothers, United Fund with Milton Berle (commercial)

1966

Agent for H.A.R.M. (action/adventure) [director of photography] 35mm

"Again, this was a favor for a friend who had run into financial trouble and couldn't finish his movie, even though he had a contract with Universal for distribution. Wilmos Zigmond shot one third of the movie, then had to leave for another project. Jimmy Crabbe, also an Academy Award–winner shot one third more, then he too had to leave. Joseph F. Robertson, my friend and producer, was stuck and faced bankrupting the movie. He asked me if I would help him, so I shot the last third of the movie, brought a small five-man crew of my own people, and we finished the movie for him. He always threw his arms around me when I saw him and said how grateful he was to me for 'saving his life.'"

I Crossed the Color Line/The Black Klansman/Brutes (drama) [director/producer/editor] 35mm

A genre fan favorite, *The Undertaker and His Pals* (1966).

The Undertaker and his Pals (horror) [distributor/re-editor] 35mm

"A lot of story here, as it was my first release under my newly formed distribution company banner (Geneni). I had to cut out a lot of real hospital footage that was too gory to be acceptable. The producers accepted my offer to re-cut and put it out, with no guarantee whatever of returns. It was a real challenge, and all of my distributor friends told me it would be a mistake to try and get theaters to show it. Well, we proved them all wrong and it did fantastic business, and it got my distribution company off to a good start."

Joe DiMaggio (Brylcream commercial)

1967

Catalina Capers/Never Steal Anything Wet (foreign intrigue) [director of photography] 35mm

"Another really fun shoot, on the water [Pacific Ocean], in the water, on the beach on Santa Monica day and night shooting, Catalina Island shoots, flying over in pontoon planes, great food on the island, made a lot of good friends as D.P./operator. Filmed 'Little Richard' on the big ship in his beginning days."

Astro Zombies/Space Zombies/Space Vampires (sci-fi/horror) [director/producer/editor/writer] 35mm
Rex Allen (Lama Boots—an award-winning commercial)

1968

Girl in Gold Boots (musical drama) [director/producer/co-editor/co-writer] 35mm
The Dictionary (elementary school film teaching proper use) [producer/editor/director of photography] 16mm
Hart Mountain Hunt (documentary) [editor/director of photography] 16mm
The Jimmy Allen Show (musical pilot) [director of photography/editor] 16mm
North of the Border (Mexican-American relations and problem solving) [producer/director of photography] 16mm

1969

Up Your Teddy Bear/Seduction of a Nerd (comedy/drama) [re-editor] 35mm

"A cameraman I was teaching filmed this one, but the first edit brought to me needed a lot of work. I did re-cutting on my moviola in my editing rooms, then sent out flyers to all of my sub-distributors to come up with a title they liked; hence the above title. Took Julie Newmar to Minneapolis for the premiere. She was gracious and charming."

1970

Scam (drama) [director/executive producer] 35mm

"Two producers were supposedly coming up with money, an all-too-familiar story in Hollywood, and we were all set to roll cameras. Still no money, so I put the shoot on hold until I saw cash for myself and crew to cover raw film stock and developing costs, etc. The two guys who were involved with casting came up with money that hour and we rolled cameras. Our stunt man cracked his forehead open with a gash as he somersaulted off the second floor roof of a building onto the mats. The hammer on his .45 caliber revolver cut him good as he landed. I 'butterflyed' the cut, and when they took him to quick care they told him that whoever did the butterfly bandage knew what he was doing, and nothing more needed to be done, and no stitches were required. That stunt man was always my stunt coordinator on my subsequent movies, and is the one who rolls down off the roof in The Doll Squad when one of the girls shoots him in the action sequences."

1971

The Corpse Grinders (horror) [director/producer/editor/co-writer] 35mm

1972

Children Shouldn't Play with Dead Things (horror) [executive producer] 35mm

"Robert Kilgore, my General Sales Manager for my distribution company, had worked in Florida with Bob Clarke. Bob persuaded me to get behind the production and put money into it, as we were doing so very well with The Corpse Grinders. *I flew from my offices in Hollywood to observe filming, as I had then become executive producer, guaranteeing laboratory and release print costs, and overseeing the final cut and first answer print. In Florida I went straight to the processing lab and, after seeing their first week's work, told the company they would have to trash it all and start over. Not because of Bob Clarke's directing, which I did not interfere with, but because of the photography. I spent about two weeks in Miami Beach teaching gaffers how to light for nighttime scary effects, etc. We ended up with a very successful release, and the fans still love it. The only name I used on the movie was my distribution company name, Geneni Film Distributing Co., Inc. I*

Another genre fan favorite, Bob Clark's *Children Shouldn't Play with Dead Things* (1972).

Blood Orgy of the She Devils/Female Plasma Suckers (horror) [director/producer/editor/writer] 35mm

1973

The Doll Squad/Seduce and Destroy/Female Mercenaries (action/adventure) [director/producer/editor/co-writer/actor] 35mm

1977

Alex Joseph and His Wives/The Rebel Breed/Obadiah 18 (true-life drama) [director/producer/co-writer/editor] 35mm

1978

The Aftermath/Zombie Aftermath/Nuclear Aftermath (post-atomic horror) [executive producer] 35mm

"In the making of The Worm Eaters, Herbie Robins and my appointed production manager, Steve Barkett, got into some big squabbles, so I told Steve to leave the show and I would create a production for him to direct. I dug up an old story and title I had created some seven or eight years earlier, and that was the start of that movie. A bunch of it was shot in my castle and on the grounds. I was building up a big indebtedness again, so I urged Steve to find backers and buy me out. I let him use my equipment to finish the movie, which, by then, the storyline had been changed around two or three times, but eventually he finished it."

Cruise Missile/Alarme Nucleare/Missile X: The Neutron Bomb Incident/Incident in Teheran (espionage drama) [co-producer] 35mm

"My dear friend Ika Panajotovic came back from Iran, Italy and Germany with less than half of the movie shot, but no more money was left to complete the movie. Once more, I was asked if I would help. So I became co-producer of the American side of the multinational co-production, and brought my crew of five castle ladies, myself, and all of my equipment and cameras to the rescue for the few dollars available. We created a Russian Army, a 'Cruise Missile,' and helped make the movie the four-million-dollar production that was intended. The production gave my ladies a lot of additional experience, and again it was a challenge I could not resist, so we completed the movie in style. Ika had stated many times that he would always be indebted to me for that."

The Worm Eaters (comedy/horror) [producer/actor] 35mm

"I had promised Herb Robins I would make the movie if we would show real people actually eating live worms, night-crawlers at that, and that we did!!! I was busy editing my then current movie, Alex Joseph and His Wives, but about three p.m. each day I would head out to location and give a hand in finishing the day's shooting schedule. It was a fun shoot, and Herb was ingenious with creative ideas. Castle lady Sherri Vernon created all of the artwork under the titles, and the movie lives on as a favorite and unreal piece of entertainment around the world."

1979

Knee-Dancing (drama) [director of photography] 35mm

"With all of the intrigue involved in moviemaking, Castle Lady Doreen Ross became determined to write and direct a movie of her own, and I was recruited, as her mentor/teacher, to assist by becoming the D.P. cameraman. I had fun being creative with lighting and camera effects, and the movie earned a couple of awards. I was treated royally, being picked up and chauffeur-driven to all locations to shoot, and all of my equipment was beautifully cared-for during the production."

Ten Violent Women/Woman's Penitentiary (action/adventure) [director/producer/editor/co-writer] 35mm

1980

Devil's Gambit (action/adventure) [director/producer] 35mm

"*Devil's Gambit, after I left the production (fulfilling my contract and agreement), a lot of shooting was done to complete the movie. There was a lot of female mud-wrestling filmed in Sturgis, the motorcycle run. I have no idea what happened to what was finished, but some viable people were involved in completing it. I have no idea what they named it. Tiger Yang elected to not come back either, as there were some unacceptable differences creatively. It's anyone's guess what it may have been named.*"

Kill the Dragon (action/adventure) [executive producer/production supervisor] 35mm

"*Kill the Dragon was totally completed, 35mm, and it was screened in Hollywood after completion. The producer was from Spain, and from then on, I imagine it was totally distributed everywhere where countries bought movies. Korea was another market, as I was employed by Koreans to oversee the production and filming. It was a tri-country production.*"

1983

Space Angels (action/adventure) [director/producer/co-writer] 35mm

"*Space Angels is budgeted to be completed in Canada, when the completion dollars are in place. It is very viable, and has more than a little interest in its completion.*"

Poster art for *The Worm Eaters* (1978), one of Ted's most beloved productions (despite the fact that he did not direct it).

1985

In Search of Gold (documentary on smelting) video

1986

War Cat/Angel of Vengeance (action/adventure) [director/line producer/co-writer] 35mm

Chad (action/adventure) [director/producer/writer/editor] 35mm

"*Since the actor playing Grandpa in the movie*

Promotional advertisement for Doreen Ross' award-winning feature *Knee Dancing* (1979).

passed away during open heart surgery, I had to complete what we had on video."

1988

The Incredibly Strange Film Show (British television series) [featured guest and interviewee] video

"Jonathan Ross, a well-known TV personality from London, brought a crew to my home in Las Vegas, Nevada, to catch up on my filming activities shortly after I left the castle near Hollywood, California. Doreen Ross, Sherri Vernon, and Tura Satana were among those interviewed for the one-hour-long documentary that played Discovery Channel here in the U.S. for about three years, and throughout England and parts of Europe. It opened with me playing my accordion out in the wild desert; and Tommy, my ventriloquist dummy, and myself had quite a conversation about making movies. I played and sang "Beer Barrel Polka." Then the camera showed my castle in California, and Jonathan talked about all of my then-current movie projects, and showed some trailers for some of my 'classic' movies. It ended with Shanti being introduced, and she and I fencing on the grounds of a drive-in theater. An enormous number of folks saw this show, and remark about it to this day, twenty years later."

1989

Interglobal Products [producer/editor/mixer/narrator] (commercial)

1990

Mission: Killfast/ Operation Overkill/ Omega Assassins (martial arts/drama) [director/producer/editor/co-writer/actor] 35mm

Back Yard in the Spring (children's one hour film of animals, bugs, snails and ducks) [cameraman, editor/co-writer, narrator] video

The Breath of Life (one hour documentary/institutional teaching film on health and Yoga living) [producer/writer/editor, narrator] video

1991

Help Them Walk Again (dramatic introduction attempting to help quadriplegics) [director/producer/editor/co-writer/narrator] video

Presenting Gino (stage musical) [producer, director, cinematographer, editor] video

1992

Casino Pro (teaching tape) video

1994

Directing Movies from "Action to Wrap" (documentary/interview/instructional) [fea-

Top: Behind the scenes photo taken during the production of *Devil's Gambit* (1980). *Right:* Preliminary sketches for *Space Angels* (1983).

tured guest, interviewee, director, producer, editor] 35mm/video

"This was a documentary about making movies, and what I went through to make them. It showed about 13 trailers of my movies, and I was answering questions fielded by Shanti (Dr. Wendy O. Altamura) and Jerry Carroll, a writer-friend who also had been working with me on my movie projects. This was before the time of 'added material,' or 'behind the scenes' were being shot and added to VHS releases, so I had hopes that it would not only be entertaining but also informative to the would-be moviemaker."

1996

The Dreamer (musical drama—one hour docu-teleplay tribute to Dr. Martin Luther King) 16mm and video

1997

Dimension in Fear/City in Terror (psychological horror) [director/producer/editor/writer/actor] multi-media 35mm/video

Clive Barker's A–Z of Horror (television miniseries) [featured guest] video

> "I know some of my trailers were shown, and fragments of interviews with me were part of the show. A lot of that sort of stuff goes on; however, often I'm not really that much aware of it."

War and Death in the Balkans (one hour war docu-drama) 16mm and 35mm

Chris Rock (commercial)

Music videos (commercial)

Rap Artist's CDs (commercial)

1998

Female Slave's Revenge/Apartheid Slave Women's Justice (action/adventure) [director/producer/editor/writer/actor] video

Addicted to Murder: Tainted Blood (horror) [actor] 35mm

> "And still another movie where I enjoyed a part as a vampire slayer, advocating the destroying of any and all vampires that could be found. In making it simple, the producer again brought cameras into my own studio here in Las Vegas and shot my scenes in short order. It's always been a pleasure for me to perform, as my roots since a child were in theater."

Looking for a Man (one hour teleplay drama) Beta SP transfer to 35mm

1999

Two Feathers and Little Hawk (action/adventure) [director/producer/writer/editor] video

> "*Two Feathers and Little Hawk* was not completed as that title; however, a great portion of the filming was utilized in two other productions of mine, and the Indian dancing was used in Heart of a Boy. Other parts of the filming were used in my documentary on the Great Indian Pow Wow. None of it went to waste."

Inventor's Acceptance Corp. (commercial)

John Robert Powers (commercial)

Arizona Charlie's Monday Night Football (commercial)

Tobacco Road (commercial)

2000

The Corpse Grinders 2 (horror/sci-fi) [director/producer/editor/writer/actor] multi-media 35mm/video

2002

Mark of the Astro Zombies (horror/sci-fi) [director/producer/editor/writer/actor] video

Walter Cronkite's "Understanding the Paranormal" (television documentary) [featured guest and interviewee] video

> "This was fun, as a small crew came to my studio here in Las Vegas and shot scenes and an interview with me. Actually, the show was called Understanding the Paranormal. I did not profess to understanding the phenomenon, and actually attempted to show that my movies were more fiction and/or camp than credible for paranormal activities. The show did feature myself and a number of my movie trailers for about seven minutes. I was shown alongside serious and outstanding paranormal specialists, which I thought was unusual. However, it was an honor to be asked to be a part of that show."

2003

Chimera (horror) [associate producer] video

> "I believe this is one where I performed as an actor in a bit part. This is something that has always been fun for me when the production

took care of details for me, making it convenient."

2004

The Cauldron: Baptism of Blood (horror) [director/producer/editor/writer/actor] video

Malevolence (crime/action/drama) [actor] 35mm

"Another movie where I was asked by moviemakers who had worked for me if I would play a part in their movie. I know I'm such a ham that whether a script or lines were ready for me or not, I would improvise any scene or scenario that I was asked to do."

2005

Planetfall (sci-fi/western) [actor] video

"Still another movie where the producers, friends of mine from Minneapolis, came to Las Vegas to shoot scenes. I played Arch Stanton, the leader/president of a civilization from another planet. The producers had a nice script and shot enough footage and scenes with me in two or three days that they were able to place my scenes throughout the movie, and I thought they made me look good. It got good reviews anyway."

2006

Heart of a Boy (family) [director/producer/editor/writer/actor] video

Mondo Collecto (documentary) [featured guest and interviewee] video

"A dear friend from Minnesota, Ray, who came to Las Vegas to shoot scenes of myself to include in his movie, had me in primitive fighting gear, complete with Khula Khud headpiece, shield and sword, swinging at imaginary foes in the desert. He also shot scenes with me in my home, my collection of swords and memorabilia, and interviews with me, which I thought were a lot of fun. He featured these scenes in his DVD, and pictures of myself on the outside of the DVD jacket."

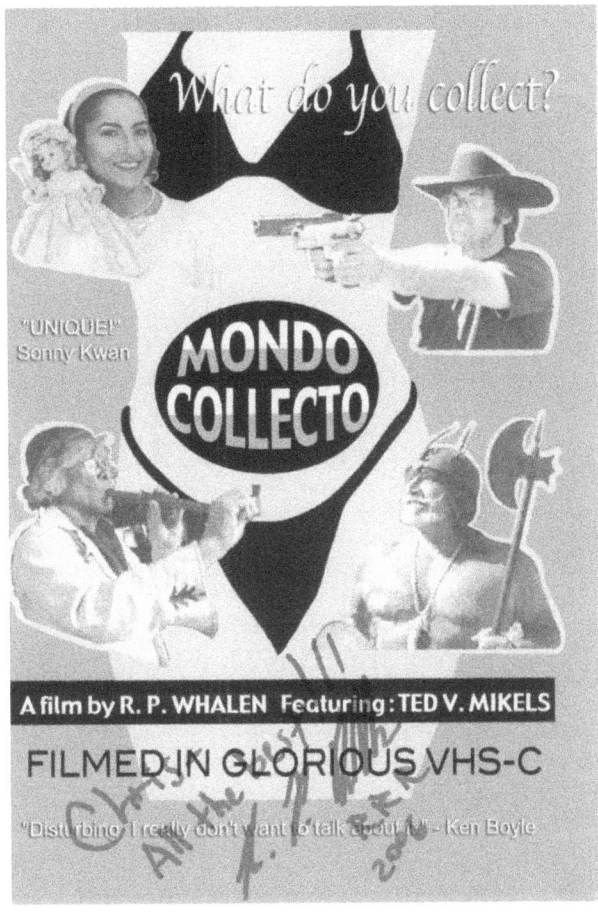

R.P. Whalen's ode to "mondo" movies, *Mondo Collecto* (2006).

Ted V. Mikels' Preview Trailer Collector's Reel (trailer compilation) [producer/director/editor] 35mm/video

Demon Bloodlust (working title of newest movie in production) [director/producer/editor] video

Theater Work as Director and/or Lead Performer—All from 1955–1963

The Diary of Anne Frank [director]
Harvey [director]
The Monkey's Paw [director]
Charlie's Aunt [director]
Time Out for Ginger [director]
The Man in the Dog-Suit [director]

The City Slicker and Our Little Nell [director]	Solid Gold Cadillac
	My Sister Eileen
The View from the Bridge [actor] (Mikels won an award)	Dial "M" for Murder
	The Valiant
The Man Who Came to Dinner	The Hidden Key
The Drunkard	The Seven Year Itch
The Bat	Kiss and Tell

21. Homage: Reverence and Respect for Ted V. Mikels

While sub-distributors, investors, theater owners and critics haven't always had Ted's best interests at heart, a fairly large portion of pop culture has. Many have embraced, and paid due tribute to, Ted by naming their projects, songs, and even themselves(!) after his films. These accolades emanate primarily from the world of music, but a few non–music-related honors are present as well.

One of the more obvious acts of appreciation is the 2002 independent film starring Pamela Sutch called *Code Name: D.O.L.L. Squad*. Certainly, the premiere toy store in Japan, called "Astro Zombies," should not be overlooked, nor should a similar store in Albuquerque, New Mexico, either. In a backhanded nod, the British DVD re-release of *The Doll Squad* sports artwork looking almost identical to that of the 2000 blockbuster *Charlie's Angels*. Presently, in Atlanta, Georgia, there is a vivacious burlesque troupe aptly parading around as "the Doll Squad."

Of course, in 1967 Ted was completely unaware of the sizeable impact that his little film *Astro Zombies* would have on the entertainment industry. This list is undoubtedly incomplete, but it serves as undeniable proof that Ted has left his mark. What follows is a barrage of musical artists who have stepped up to give this truly unique film talent a tip of the old hat.

The earliest of the praises came from the ghoulish punk band the Misfits and their recording of a number called "Astro Zombies" from their LP *Walk Among Us*. The British group My Chemical Romance paid their respects to *both* artists by re-recording "Astro Zombies" for their inclusion on *Tony Hawk's American Wasteland* compilation. Gangstyle Records compiled a Misfits tribute in 2003 and called it *Astro Zombies A.D.*

More zombie praise includes electronic artist Meat Beat Manifesto sampling the line "Beware! The Astro Zombies!" from the film's trailer and applying it to their song entitled "Zombie" from their 1992 release *Satyricon*. Hard Rockers White Zombie called their 1995 album *Astro Creep 2000*; knowing lead singer Rob Zombie's affinity for horror and sci-fi, there's little doubt that this was a reverential nod to Ted's film. Surf rock act Man or Astro-Man? have made it quite clear that they, too, adore the film from which they derived their band name.

More? No less than five bands have called themselves the Astro Zombies. Poe Records distributes a hardcore act with that familiar moniker, while Verb Records has an altogether different act of the same name. But the psycho-billy group from France, the Astro Zombies, deserves special attention. These three boys have made an entire career out of their love for Ted's low-budget exploiter, and even go so far as to wear astro zombie masks on stage while playing songs titled "Return of the Astro Zombies," "Terrifying Astro Zombies" and "The Astro Zombies Are Coming." Then there are numerous Misfits tribute bands parading around as the Astro Zombies, and Rhode Island is home to a surf rock act of the same name.

Another of Ted's films to receive special recognition is *The Corpse Grinders*. In the early 1980s Australia boasted a punk-a-billy act that were known as Corpse Grinders, and in the mid–80s a New York group followed suit. The Meteors called their greatest hits compilation *Corpse Grinders*; and the Bentmen gave us the song "Immaculate Contraption," with *their* version of Ted's diabolical machine turning up in the video.

The genre of Heavy Metal (Death Metal in particular) seems to have really latched onto Ted's title. One of the oldest Death Metal bands from Brazil dropped the "s" and christened themselves Corpse Grinder, as did another combo from Ted's homeland of Croatia. Cannibal Corpse's lead singer is commonly known as George "Corpse Grinder" Fischer, and Massacre turned in a tune with the applicable title for their 1991 record *From Beyond*. Chuck Schuldiner's brainchild Death released a song entitled "Corpse Grinder" on their 1984 demo cassette *Reign of Terror*.

San Francisco's thrash band Skitzo originally called their 1993 outing *Corpse Grinder*, but changed it once they became aware of Ted's uncomfortable feelings about

CD jacket for the French rock-a-billy act the Astro Zombies (2003).

them using it. Skitzo's Lance Ozanix recalls the incident:

> Then I told him the title of our new album *Corpse Grinder* and he kinda flipped out. He called it an infringement on his film, and he was still mad about the *Doll Squad/Charlie's Angels* rip-off. I was willing to change it, so I did. He was just so nice, and over the course of a year we developed a cool relationship.

In 1982 the Funeral Directors released a 7-inch single called "Corpse Grinder"; and as if all this weren't enough, France is home to a recording label called Corpse Grinder Records.

The women of Ted's films haven't been left out, either. A group formerly known as Manhole changed their name to Tura Satana, and there's also a band called the Girl in Gold Boots. However, a favorite of this writer's is the "girlie garage pop" Australian quartet the Doll Squad. This groovy gaggle of gals successfully sends up the looks and

Left: Cassette cover for Skitzo's *Corpse Grinder* release (1993). *Right:* CD jacket for the Australian all-girl garage-rock band Doll Squad (2005).

sounds of the period when Ted's film of the same name was released. Atlanta, Georgia, also plays host to another group of girl musicians calling themselves the Doll Squad, as member Katy Graves recalls:

> We named our band after the movie! It was mostly me who was a fan of that film. At the time I was getting a film degree at college. I just love everything about that film ... the computer in the opening that takes up an entire room, the exploding lipstick, ah, just too much fun!

In 1988 the remarkable British television series *The Incredibly Strange Film Show* featured a telling 40-minute exclusive on Ted and his films and life. Director R.P. Whalen included Ted in his independent feature *Mondo Collecto*, wherein Ted spends around 10 minutes showing off and explaining his love for ancient weaponry. Many critics have pointed out that the sequence with Ted is the movie's most enjoyable.

Some Mo Productions, based out of Chicago, adapted *The Corpse Grinders* for a stage production that ran successfully for several weeks. Ted recalls:

> They sent me the script for approval, and I liked it. It wasn't exactly like my movie, but I think they kept enough of the spirit intact. Unfortunately, I was unable to catch one of the showings, but I did send them an original *Corpse Grinders* one-sheet to hang in the lobby of the theater, as well as a few other promotional goodies. Also, most people don't know this, but in Australia they've been doing a stage production of *Astro Zombies* for years.

One of the ultimate compliments given Ted has to be the Art of the Astro Zombies website. Here, countless drawings, sketches and paintings inspired by *Astro Zombies* and *Mark of the Astro Zombies* can be viewed. In fact, the cover art and poster for *Mark of the Astro Zombies* was chosen from this impressive selection. Ted has said that choosing one piece of art to represent his film was nearly impossible, as he adored each and every one of them.

Even other moviemakers have expressed their appreciation by casting Ted in their productions. Kevin J. Lindenmuth did so in 1998 when he asked Ted to play Jonas Collins (a vampire expert) in his film *Addicted to Murder: Tainted Blood*. In 2004 Mike A. Martinez cast Ted as a film producer named Rene Cardoza, Jr., for his feature *Malevolence*. Then in 2006 Michael J. Heagle employed Ted and his on-screen talents for the movie *Planetfall*, where Ted plays President Arch Stanton.

There have been many other displays of gratitude, and more will surely follow. Ted's films have been, and will continue to be, immortalized in a number of different ways. It's a special honor that few filmmakers have garnered, but Ted has struck a nerve with the people, and the people have responded.

22. Collect 'Em All! An Overview of Ted V. Mikels Memorabilia

1. One-sheets
2. Pressbooks
3. Lobby cards
4. Publicity stills
5. 35mm prints
6. 35mm trailers
7. 16mm prints
8. 16mm trailers
9. 45 rpm 7" records containing radio ads
10. 45 rpm 7" record of *The Doll Squad* theme, "Song for Sabrina"
11. 45 rpm 7" record of "Song for Sabrina" (contains no B-side)
12. Plastic google-eyed skull necklace from *Astro Zombies*
13. Gold boots from *Girl in Gold Boots* contest
14. Promotional cardboard gold boots from *Girl in Gold Boots*
15. Promotional balloons from *Girl in Gold Boots*
16. Certificate of Assurance from *The Corpse Grinders*
17. *Master Guide to Occult Knowledge and Science* booklet from *Blood Orgy of the She Devils*

Radio spots for *The Corpse Grinders* on 7" vinyl, and the 7" single for the theme to *The Doll Squad*.

18. "Magic Eye Amulet" postcard from *Blood Orgy of the She Devils*
19. "Tenya Worm" from *The Worm Eaters*
20. Promotional postcard from Japanese DVD release of *The Worm Eaters*
21. Tooth from *The Corpse Grinders 2* grinding machine
22. Jar of ground-up human flesh from *The Corpse Grinders 2*

Left: Promotional cardboard boot from *Girl in Gold Boots* (1968). *Right:* Master Guide to Occult Knowledge and Science (1972). This rare booklet was handed out to theatergoers who were brave enough to sit through *Blood Orgy of the She Devils*.

23. Prop can of "Lotus Cat Food" from *The Corpse Grinders 2*
24. *Mark of the Astro Zombies* bobble head figurine
25. *Mark of the Astro Zombies* latex Halloween mask
26. *Mark of the Astro Zombies* promotional postcard
27. *Mark of the Astro Zombies* movie poster
28. *Female Slave's Revenge* movie poster
29. *The Cauldron: Baptism of Blood* movie poster
30. Ted V. Mikels' *Drive-In Delites* CD containing music from many of Ted's films
31. *King of the Castle* VHS (a.k.a. *The Incredibly Strange Film Show*)
32. *Directing Movies from Action to Wrap* DVD
33. *Ted V. Mikels' Preview Trailer Collector's Reel*
34. *Mondo Collecto* DVD
35. *Mission: Killfast Behind the Scenes* DVD
36. DVDs by: Image, Alpha, Something Weird, Victory, Media Blasters, TVM Global, Blax
37. VHS by: Wizard, Walterschied Productions, Troma, Something Weird, Unicorn, Vestron, TVM Global, World
38. Many magazines and news paper articles and interviews
39. Many authorized t-shirts (note: this writer's favorite is Scott Blackshear's "Jolly

Roger-Astro Zombie" design; this design is also emblazoned on a flag for that full pirate effect)

40. Numerous bootleg items, like refrigerator magnets, buttons, key chains, t-shirts, stickers, silk-screened pillows, posters and lobby cards

Above: The "Certificate of Assurance" from *The Corpse Grinders* (1971). *Below:* A gimmick postcard-cum-magical amulet that was handed to ticket buyers to help keep them from the metaphysical powers of Mara, queen of the black witches. (Note: Front and back of card is pictured.)

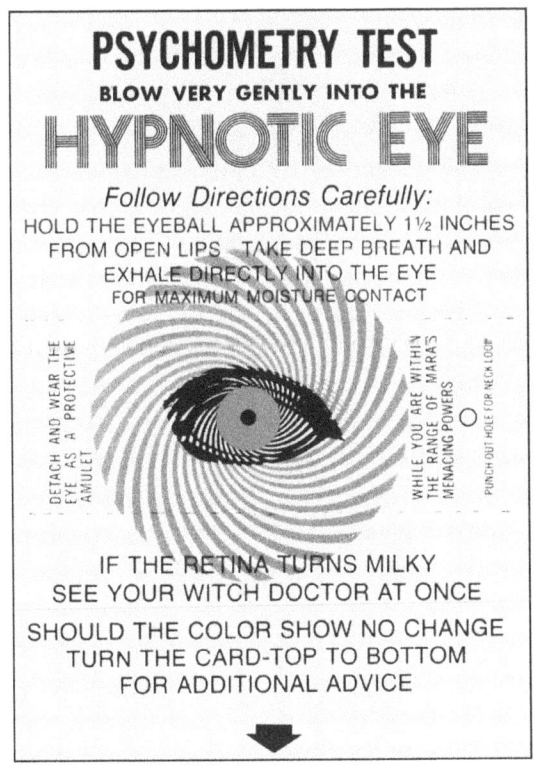

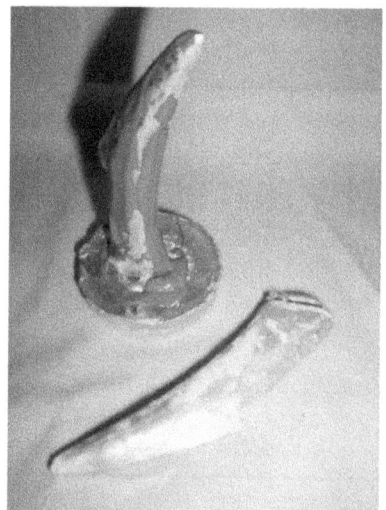

Top left: Promotional postcard for the Japanese DVD release of *The Worm Eaters* (2006). *Top right:* An "organically-grown-man-eating TENYA worm in its glop...." So says the tag on this nifty promo item given away during the release of *The Worm Eaters*. *Middle right:* Ceramic teeth from the corpse grinding machine from *The Corpse Grinders II* (2000). *Bottom right:* A *Mark of the Astro Zombies* (2002) bobbler. *Above:* "Prop cans of Lotus Cat Food from *The Corpse Grinders II*.

22. Collect 'Em All! An Overview of the Memorabilia

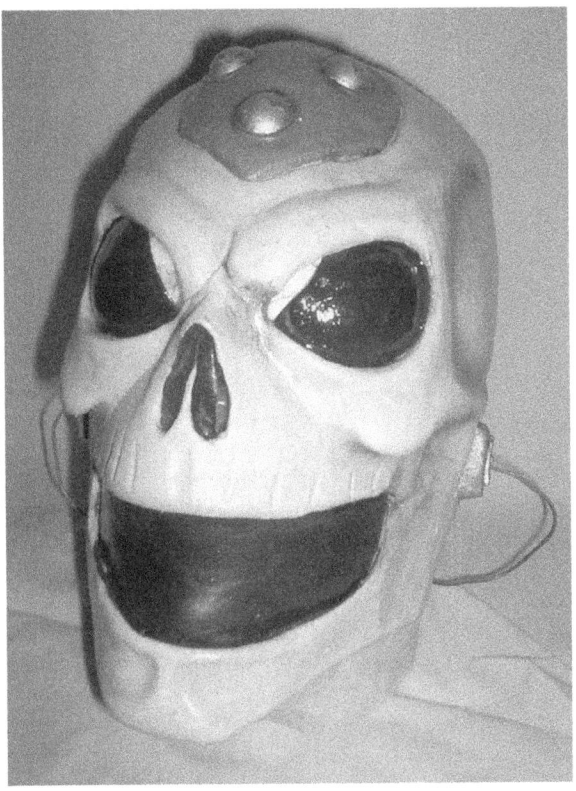

Above: Bump in the Night Productions' version of the infamous astro zombie mask. *Below:* The author's version of an astro zombie mask.

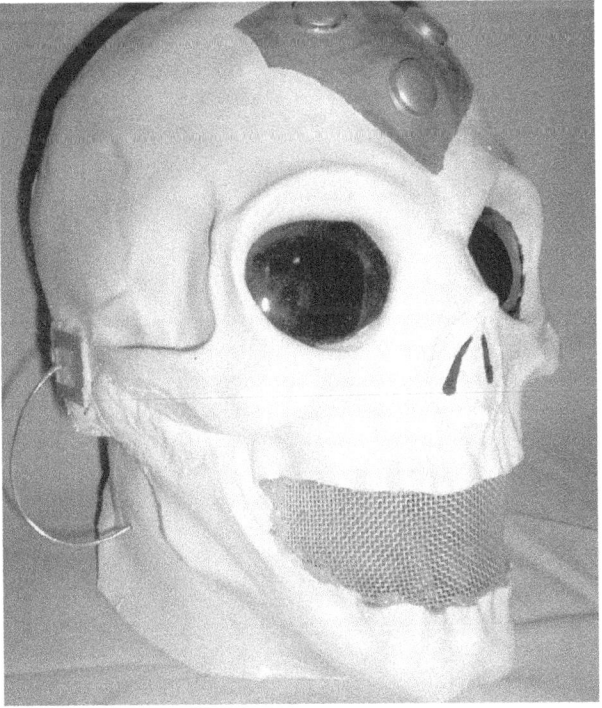

PART FOUR

The Interview

"Ted V. Mikels is a throwback to the days when filmmakers were showmen, constantly thinking of new ways to titillate and entertain their audiences. I wish that we had more like him today."—director Herschell Gordon Lewis (*Blood Feast* and *She Devils on Wheels*)

Curry: *Where were you born?*
Mikels: St. Paul, Minnesota.
So you didn't actually live in Croatia?
Oh no, my father was from there, and my mother was from that part of the world.
But you are of Croatian descent, correct?
And a little bit of German and French.
Birthday?
April 29, just before the Second World War.
What kind of upbringing did you have?
Very nice family. Six children. Father and mother devoted to caring for the family. It was a very warm and close grouping. My older brother went into the Air Force as a bombardier during the war. My oldest sister earned two or three scholarships, she was a brilliant girl. Then comes me, and then my younger brother went into the Navy, and then comes my younger sister who had about four kids. And then my youngest brother became a high ranking Air Force officer and completed 105 missions in Vietnam.
Were you the only one to have an interest in the arts?

Oh yeah. My Father and mother made sure that every one of us had an opportunity to go into the arts by way of music, and I'm the only one who stayed with it.
Did you take piano lessons?
No, accordion.
That's an odd choice. Did you pick that yourself?
No, I think that my Father wanted it more than anything, because I think it reminded him of home and his foreign identification ... his Croatian or Austrian identification. Anyway, I was the only one to stay with the arts, and the accordion was my father's favorite, but he pushed me harder than he pushed the others. He used to lay a belt on the table and say, "Practice for one hour, or else" [laughs].
Really?! Would that be your earliest memory of entertaining people?
No, no. When I was five my sister Eve had gone to a magic performance at a theater in St. Paul, Minnesota. When she came back she showed me tricks that I think are still pretty decent today. With a pencil and a

thread and a coin and a banana and all that, and I was so fascinated that I learned to do these. So, by the age of five on I was doing magic tricks for anyone who would listen or watch.

Well, you basically answered my next question. As a child, what did you do for entertainment?

Magic. Magic was the key thing to me. By the time I was seven and eight years old I was doing magic shows for the neighborhood. We'd moved to Portland, Oregon. During that time I was doing magic shows in my back yard for two pins, and then I graduated to two pennies because the show was so popular.

An early (1949) Ted V. Mikels "Magic" advertisement.

Pins?

Yeah, two safety pins.

What in the world were you doing with safety pins?

It was just a token fee. I think my mother suggested it because she sewed a lot.

Okay, this is a good time to talk about your days as a fire-eater, ventriloquist, acrobat, body builder and so on.

Okay, I can give you a timeline. Okay, I think I was about 10 when my father got me started on the accordion lessons. So, by the time I was 11 I played my first numbers on the air ... on the radio. On one of the little radio shows on Sunday morning in Portland, Oregon. Then when I was 12 I did my first professional show as a magician, and I got paid five dollars, and that was a lot of money when I was 12. It was probably a 15-minute display of tricks with water glasses and stuff like that. Then later I began putting the magic and the accordion together. Then when I was 14 or 15 my accordion teacher, who had arranged to play some dances, had me accompany him. It was two accordions, drums and a piano, and we'd play dances, but my teacher made sure that I'd have quite a résumé of songs that I could play. So we played for various independent people like the Norse Hall and the Scandinavian dances, and I had to learn all those types of songs. I'll never forget that my accordion teacher, when we were doing these dances and people were making lots of noise, would yell, "Pull Teddy! Pull! Pull Teddy! Pull!" [laughs]. So by the time I was 15 or 16 I had a magic show that was quite extensive.

Do you remember the name of it?

Well, I didn't call it Open Sesame until a little later, but it was Mikels the Magician. Anyway, I began selling my show to student body groups. Like the girls league in one school wanted to raise money for their uniforms. They agreed to pay me fifty dollars, and they would sell tickets in hopes of taking in several hundred dollars, which they did. Then I started playing with ventriloquism and fire-eating in my show, and so on.

Had you worked acrobatics into your show at this point?

No, not yet. I worked that stuff in later. Then when I was 17 I started to lift weights and I took the weightlifting championship for my class ... my body weight class. Actually, I think I was still 16, and I was in the 132 pound class. I wasn't very big then. At that time I was all muscle and fiber, and I came in number seven as Mr. Oregon at the same competition. Everybody thought that I was going to win, but all of these big fellows came up from Santa Monica Beach, California, and they took the first six places. Then, within weeks of that, I'd been in touch with magic shops that I bought my magic tricks from and met a fellow there who knew Leon Mandrake the Magician.

The real *Mandrake the Magician?!*

Yeah, the real Mandrake the Magician; and this guy said, "Leon Mandrake could use you on his show. You could play your accordion, be an assistant to him and all that sort of thing." So, I had been playing with a dummy ... a very poor dummy. But the fact was, I was playing around with ventriloquism. Oh, when I was a kid my mother had made me a clown with strings, oh what do they call them? Marionettes! So that got me interested in these little puppets and things, and on a time or two I was given the opportunity to play with a ventriloquist dummy. So when I met this fellow I was doing magic, learning ventriloquism, playing accordion solos and then acrobatics and all that sort of thing. So he said, "Leon could use you on his show." So, by golly, there was a communication, and Leon sent me a cable based on his friend's advice to hire me. He sent it Western Union, and, in fact, I think I still have it in a scrap book. It said to

Another Ted V. Mikels "Magic" advertisement. This one features both his and Gen's names (1949).

"...join him." I think I joined him in Paducah.

Paducah, Kentucky?!

Yeah.

No kidding? That's where I'm from.

Is that right? Oh, wow. Well, I joined him and I got on a train, my parents put me on a train. And when I got there that's where he gave me Tommy the dummy.

Tommy Ache?

Yeah, Tommy Ache. I think I was three weeks into my seventeenth year, and I got on the show. There were 18 showgirls, a bus driver, an advance man, Leon Mandrake, his wife Narda, Narda's sister and me. And I was the one who handled all of the suitcases, and I fell in love with Narda's sister. So here I was traveling around, doing one-night stands, sleeping on the bus, sleeping in hotels, loading and unloading the bus, unloading suitcases for 20 girls—but like I said, I was in great shape. I got to be on stage. I played my accordion blindfolded with a cover over the keyboard, like a pillowcase over the keyboard, and a glove on my right hand. It was fun. It was a lot of fun, and then I'd help Leon with the magic show.

Again, a very young Ted V. Mikels. This time he's fanning a deck of magic trick playing cards (1949).

How long did you do this with him?

Oh, let's see. Right from the time school was out until Thanksgiving. It was a tough show, an expensive show. So it ran aground, it ran out of money. They didn't take in enough at some of the shows, so I stayed with them up until right before Thanksgiving.

So how did you manage to get out of going to school from August to November?

Oh, I was out already. I'd already graduated. I graduated a year earlier than most kids did. So I did my stint with Leon during the summer of my seventeenth year.

Okay, after that ran its course, what did you do?

I modeled for sculptors at the Chicago Institute of Art.

How'd you wind up in Chicago?

Well, that's where the show went down. The bus driver, who handled the Greyhound, lived there, so I stayed there with him and his wife while I modeled for three weeks. I eventually got enough money together to go to my Aunt Katie, my Dad's sister, in St. Paul, Minnesota, and stayed with her from Thanksgiving until a week before Christmas. During that time I worked at Montgomery Ward with my cousin in the stock room and got my money to buy my train fare back to Portland, Oregon. And then, of course, my folks helped me there. Then from there I met Geneva.

Where did you meet her?

At a church function.

So how long after you met Geneva did you marry her?

Oh, it was only about a year and a half. She was 17 and I was 19.

So at what point did you start Open Sesame with her?

Then.

Right then and there?

Right then and there. We were tumbling, doing acrobatics. Eventually, I was popping roses out of her mouth with a bullwhip. I had a male assistant, and we did an arm to arm hand-balancing act. I was the top man, because I was lighter than my assistant. He was an ex–Marine. I would go up and do handstands in the air and all kinds of stunts. So I was working all of that together into our act. Oh, I almost forgot, before I joined Mandrake I was a member of the Young Oregonians, and at age 15 I was teaching magic classes at the offices of the local paper—the *Oregon Tribune*. They had a complete area in the building dedicated to people like me teaching magic, and they paid me fifty cents an hour [laughs].

So how extensive of a tour did you do as Open Sesame?

Um, most of it was in and around all of the cities of Oregon, with some of it around Washington. Then when I first got back from the tour I went to college at the University of Portland, and I spent my time there for a year. And there I continued all the weightlifting....

What was your major?

I was majoring in liberal arts I think. Psychology was my biggest interest, but liberal arts was how I was enrolled. Then I went on to do a year or two at the University of Oregon. In the summertime, in-between, I was a sideshow/carnival barker. I would stand outside the tents where Sealo the seal boy was and some other performers.

You knew Sealo?!

Are you kidding?! I was the *only* one he'd go to eat with, because I understood him so well. He had no arms, and he couldn't talk, so I'm the one who ordered all his food for him. He got to where he wouldn't go to eat with anyone other than me because I could communicate with him. I can't tell you exactly how, but I was just able to communicate with him so easily that I knew exactly what he wanted and how to help him.

Did you have to help him eat?

Oh no. He was able to feed himself with his little flippers.

Were there any others that you knew?

Well, there were many others in the sideshow, I don't remember their names, but he was the main attraction. So anyway, inside the tent I would do my magic show with the ventriloquism, accordion solos. So I'd do my barker routine outside the tent and go in and do my magic act.

Who were you known as at this point?

I was still Mikels the Magician.

Do you remember any of your script from when you were out in front of the tent?

Uh, yeah. "Come in now! Live and on the inside.... See Sealo the Seal Boy!"

So you said Sealo couldn't talk?

No, he'd just make noises. [Note: Here Ted makes "Sealo" sounds.]

So, what was his mental capacity?

Oh, he was sharp. He was sharp.

Why could he not talk?

Well, something to do with a deformity I guess.

A very young Ted V. Mikels posing with his lovely first wife Geneva in 1949.

How was his demeanor? Did he enjoy being on the show?

Oh yeah. He enjoyed it very much.

So Sealo was the main attraction?

Yeah, but we also had a hermaphrodite, a bearded lady and some others, but Sealo was the main attraction. Also, around this time is where I learned to pop a whip. I'd learned this from one of the workers, and I got pretty darned good at it; and as I said before, I worked it into my Open Sesame act where I was popping roses from Geneva's mouth. Anyhow, I had a stint doing vaudeville. I'd done a week as a magician. Then a week as an acrobat and then a week as an accordion soloist. So here's the funny part. I wanted to go back for a forth week with the whip cracking act, so I was trying to crack this whip and the curtains were just too close and I kept smacking the curtains. And I'll never forget this, there was a big shot in vaudeville down front, and he stood up and said, "Okay, Okay. That's enough

Mikels. Three weeks is enough for you" [laughs].

Funny. At what point during this time did you say to yourself, "I wish I could see my own act"—and then decided to film your performance?

That actually happened within a couple a weeks of that in, I believe, 1949. It may have been 1948, but anyhow I had acquired an 8mm camera. Well, Geneva and I were living in a house that my father and I built, and some neighborhood brats broke in and stole my camera. They also got away with my trained doves that I used in my act. So I grabbed a milk bottle, I think, and tore out after them. They apparently opened the camera, and there were trails and trails of film all over the forest; so I tracked down my camera, but the lid was lost. So that forced me to get another camera, and I stepped up to a 16mm, and I don't know where it came from, but it was an old wind-up. Once I had my 16mm camera I then decided to shoot my show, but I found out quickly that you can't just sit a camera in one place and shoot a magic act. It just doesn't look like anything. This is where I learned how important camera angles were, and the changing of the lighting, and then that lead to editing. During this time I also had an accordion school where I taught up to 37 students. I do this three times a week after school, and then all day Saturday. I was also modeling at the University of Oregon where I was also attending classes, so I was really busy. I basically had three jobs plus school, and the jobs were to help supplement my college. My mother would send me a small check every week to cover my rent and things. I pledged Phi Kappa Sigma. Gosh, I haven't said that in so long I'd almost forgotten all about it. So while I was teaching accordion for a company in downtown Portland who had a branch in Bend, Oregon, they asked me if I wanted to go run the school there, and I thought of what a great opportunity that could be. Because the weather is beautiful there—it's on the high, bright side of the Cascade Mountain Range where the sun shines 300 days a year. So we moved there, and that's where I bought my much more expensive Bolex 16mm, the first camera that I was really shooting my stuff with when I was teaching myself how to write, produce, light, direct and so on. So while I was up there I was shooting newsreels for the TV stations. Then other TV stations, one in Seattle and one in Portland, would send me film, and I'd shoot newsreel footage for them. Like I'd get permission to go shoot an airplane crash or something like that. So I'm shooting that stuff, and in the meantime I joined the community theater. And within a short time I was on stage in things like *Time Out for Ginger*, and then I began directing the community theater.

How long did it take for you to go from being a member to a director?

Oh, it wasn't more than a year or two, or a year and a half.

Were you shooting your little independent movies during this time?

Yes, because I was using the people in the theater group. I'd say, "Come over to the house on Saturday." I'd see who showed up and I'd write up a little story, a synopsis, on the back of a notebook. I'd just see what I could do with the people who showed up, and whatever amount of film I had, and we'd go out immediately and shoot these little movies. Oh! I remember one, *Fool's Prosperity*, where we ended up blowing up half of a mountain. Because everybody in town wanted to help once word got around, and this one contractor put 25 sticks of dynamite in the side of a cliff, and I wrote that into the story. That's the one where I had Lee Phelps running camera for me, and I'm over his shoulder, and when we blew it up we saw this big boulder flying at us. He said, "It's gonna hit us!" It was a pretty big boulder, too, and I said, "Stay with it." And we stayed with it up until it seemed to be right on us, and then I grabbed him by the collar and pulled him and the camera out of the way. We're talking a long time ago, like 56 or 57 years ago.

So this was during that 10-year period before Strike Me Deadly*?*

That's correct. And *Fool's Prosperity* was a jewel heist kind of movie that had a scene where we wound up at a nightclub, and less than a year later I bought that nightclub. It was called the Glenvista Club.

How long was this movie?

Oh, I don't know. Maybe 30 minutes.

How long has it been since you've seen it?

Oh my! It's still on a roll, over at the studio, and I don't even believe the splices would hold it together. I haven't seen it since the 1950s. I made seven or eight of those things before *Strike Me Deadly*. Let's see, *Yellow Roses* was a romantic affair; and then there was the *Black Sheep*, about a man in jail, and that was the first time that I used double system sound. I made *Dream Man*, about a caveman, and that's where I made the machete that was used in *Astro Zombies*. Then I made *Compelled*, and I had the title screen over an eyeball. About 20 years later someone said, "Oh, you copied Hitchcock," and I told them that I'd made that movie before I'd ever even heard the name Hitchcock.

Ever given any thought to releasing those things?

No, because I don't think they would hold up very well. Also, during the 50s Kirk Douglas came to town to make *Indian Fighter*, and I had horses. I had acquired horses. I still had the accordion school, and I took a horse as payment for some lessons. A beautiful thoroughbred. Anyway, I had horses and I rode them in *Oregon Passage* and *Tonka* as a stuntman; and in *Indian Fighter* I had a big part racing with fire, shooting flaming arrows. I had gotten so good at archery—I'd been hunting deer with bows and arrows—that I became head of all the archery stuff on *Indian Fighter*. I'm the one who shot all of the flaming arrows that hit flag poles and wagons and all that stuff. I was even making my own bows and arrows in those days. I really didn't have the money to spend, so I just made them out of Lemon wood and Yew wood. I also played an Indian in that movie.

Now, you had a special concoction for the flaming arrows, correct?

Yeah. When the guys came up from Hollywood all they had was paste that they'd made up from fireworks stuff, and I had made a paste out of tar, pitch and kerosene that would stay lit. Their stuff would go out easily if you didn't just lob the arrow towards the target, but with my concoction you could really shoot those arrows, and they looked great on film.

Now, that brings us up to the 60s, and from that point on you made nearly one movie a year, so you had to be extremely busy with all of that activity going on.

Oh yes, very busy. I'll try to give you a lineal description of the time. So I started *Strike Me Deadly*, and this is where I first met Nicholas Carras, who just passed away recently....

He did?! You didn't tell me.

It's been very recently. He was really sick, and I'd just talked with him while he was in the hospital, and he was in the hospital a lot. Shanti and I really liked him, and you know that he'd been giving me music for my movies since the 50s.

Man, I'm really sorry to hear about Nicholas leaving us. I was excited for him to read the wonderful things that I'd written about him in this book. The theme to "Doll Squad" is my absolute favorite movie theme ... ever. In my book, it beats out Isaac Hayes' "Shaft," and that is one fantastic piece of music there.

Yes it is, but yes, you're right, Nicholas Carras was very good at what he did.

Sorry about getting you off track.

That's quite all right. I thought I'd told you, but I guess I hadn't. So I went from having the accordion school and doing acrobatics and all of that, and—wait, I almost forgot. I also had an appliance and furniture store, with a camera department. I didn't really have any money, but this great big supermarket on

Winning a fencing competition in Canada in 1959. That's Ted on the left.

Main Street was going out of business, and I made an arrangement with a guy. And this was before *Strike Me Deadly*, but I was preparing *Strike Me Deadly*. Anyhow, it was a big store. I had 20 or 30 television sets, and 20 or 30 sets of washers and dryers, and this was in a little town in Bend, Oregon, in 1957.

What was the name of your store?

It was Mikels Econo-Mart.

How'd that do for you?

I didn't like it at all. I was only in it to make money so that I could make movies.

So how long did that last.

It lasted two years, and at that same time I bought the Glenvista Club. So I had the appliance store and the nightclub, and I was making my own commercials for them, and I don't think I ever slept for three or four years. Anyhow, I left all of that to start making movies full time, and I was also shooting commercials.

Was this before TVM Studios?

Yes, I had an office across from Bozo the Clown. Anyhow, during that time I shot a commercial for Tony Lama Boots with Rex Allen, and I won an award for it. Funny thing was, the boot company asked me to bid on the commercial, and I said that I would do it for five hundred dollars. They said, "Five hundred dollars?! Everybody else says seven thousand," and I told them that I could do it for five hundred. They said that it wasn't enough, so I wound up doing it for seven hundred and winning an award for it in Dallas, Texas.

You did some other commercials with famous people, like Phil Silvers and the Smothers Brothers....

Yeah, and I did the Brylcreem "A little dab will do ya" commercial with Joe DiMaggio.

You also did one with Milton Berle.

Ted V. Mikels directing comedian Phil Silvers for a United Fund promo in 1964. Notice the absence of Ted's boar's tusk necklace.

Yes I did. It was for United Fund.
What exactly is United Fund?
It's like the March of Dimes.
Okay, what'd you do with the Smothers Brothers?
Same thing.
Phil Silvers as well?
Yep, Phil Silvers was part of that as well, and Rowan and Martin were in on that too.
I'm looking at a picture of you, from 1967, with what looks like a magnifying glass around your neck. Where's your famed boar's tusk?
I didn't have that in 1967.
What's the significance of it?
I can't really tell you other than I think I identify with it from a past life. Maybe I was a Viking in the past.

Was there a certain period of time when you were doing all of this [commercials and such], or do you still do it when the opportunity arises?
Well, when you're in Hollywood you just take the jobs as they come and as you need them or have time for them. Roger Corman had an office across from mine, and if he didn't have work he'd send the actors and actresses over to my office, and sometimes I had work for them and at other times I didn't. Like, I remember Tobe Hooper coming in after he'd done *The Texas Chain Saw Massacre*, and I really liked the guy, but I just didn't have any work for him.
No kidding?
Yeah.

An ad (1969) for a successful "Closed Circuit TV" venture that Ted V. Mikels found himself involved in. This may have been the very beginnings of home video as we know it today.

Ted V. Mikels at the helm of an editing bay during his stint with TVM Video Productions in 1969.

What kind of work was he looking for?

Any kind. You know, it was like the Ed Wood thing. Nobody could know what was going to happen, and so Tobe needed work. I even had Leslie Kovacs come in looking for work shooting *Girl in Gold Boots*.

You also worked with Bob Clark on Children Shouldn't Play with Dead Things. *What was he like to work with?*

You know, I was executive producer on that movie and my name's not even on there, but Bob Clark was a really nice man. I didn't interfere with what he was doing at all, but I did have to go down to Florida, where they were shooting, and help them out with lighting. I spent two weeks down there in Miami Beach helping them out.

At what point did you do the "closed circuit TV" gig, and what was that all about?

I'd acquired the rights to the "Great Fights of the Century." I had exclusive rights to these reels.

How did that happen, and why did you do it?

I don't even remember how I wound up with them, but these two guys came to me with the idea of starting a franchise operation with my movies and so forth. So I had all of these 16mm reels of these fights, and I transferred them to half-inch, black and white reel-to-reel video tape.

Okay, so where were these compilations placed? Did you have to order them or what?

Here's what happened. They would send me these fights, and we'd group them together into one-hour shows. I was also doing shows

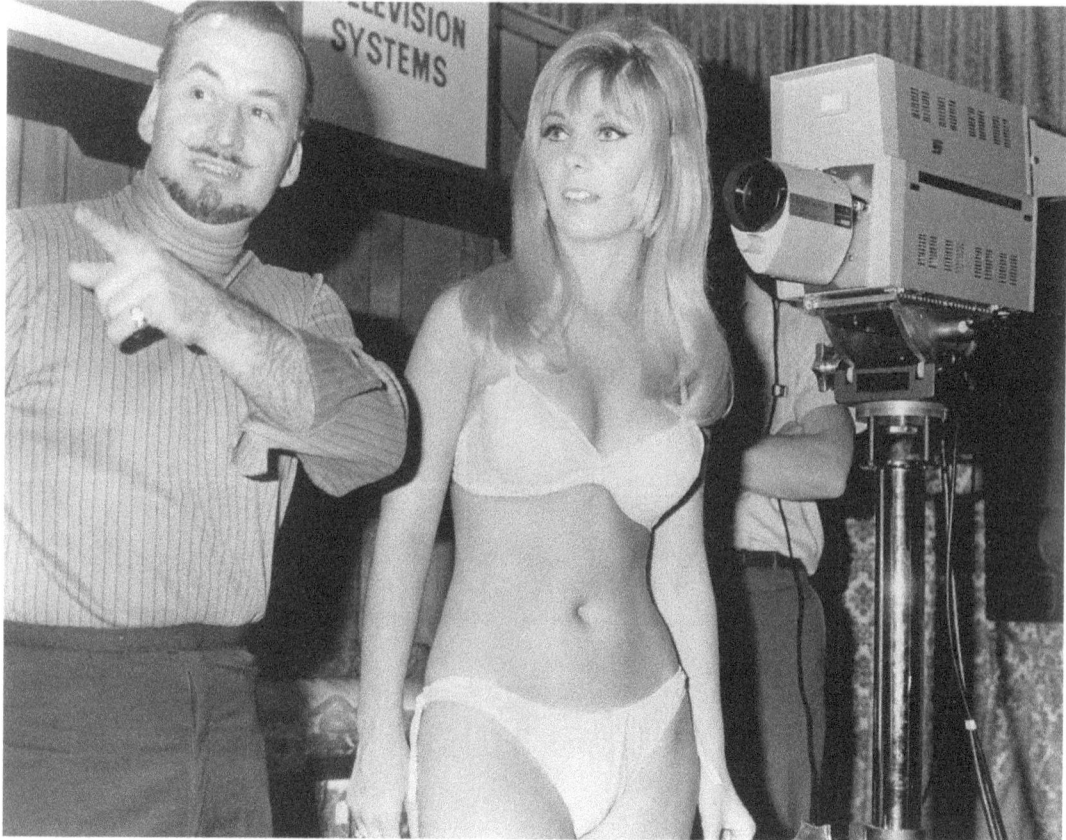

Ted V. Mikels directing a blonde, bikini-clad cutie for another one of his TVM Video Productions.

in my studio and making one-hour reels out of them as well. So these two guys franchised this stuff out. They mostly played in bars, and the bars would pay a fee for the equipment and the reels. I don't know if you've seen the picture of me where I'm sitting in the studio with a set of headphones on or not....

Yes, I do have that one.

Well, that's where we were putting those show together.

I also have several pictures of topless dancers. Was that part of this same project?

Yes, exactly. We had about three hours of topless shows.

Now how much were they expected to pay for this?

For all the equipment and the reels it started out at twelve thousand, five hundred bucks, and before it was over it was up to fourteen thousand.

Wow, that's a lot.

It is, and they were making money hand-over-fist. The two guys who started it were each drawing five thousand dollars a week as their salary. We did a million dollars worth of business in the first seven months. They were taking out ads in the *New York Times* and the *Wall Street Journal*, and making a killing on this stuff. Now, the people who bought into these franchises would get fifteen tape decks that they could rent out to bars and things, and we were producing three one-hour shows a week that they could rent if they wanted to. It was a very successful operation, and it pre-dates the video rental market by a decade or more.

What year was all this happening?
1969.

How in the world did you ever find time to do that stuff and continue your moviemaking career?

I worked day and night. I never slept. Here's something that I forgot to mention. I shot *The Hostage* in Des Moines, Iowa. I was the cinematographer, and when the film was sent off to the lab, Technicolor said that it was the finest cinematography they'd seen in over three years. Anyhow, I was working literally day and night, and I guess that's what happened to my marriage to Geneva.

Ah, you read my mind. That was my next question; plus, I also wanted to know about the children that you two had.

Okay, Geneva always regretted leaving Bend, Oregon, because there I was "king of the hill." I had a nightclub, a furniture store, and I was a director of movies and an entertainer, and so on. Oh, and I even had a gym there called Mikels and Ellis Studio of Physical Culture. Anyhow, when we got to Hollywood it was a totally different world.

So I take it that she didn't like it.

No, she would take off six weeks at a time and go back to Bend for visits, and that's when Tura and I got close.

Real close.

Yes, very close.

Okay, tell me about your children with Geneva.

Well, there's Celine, who has two kids and four grandkids. She came along after we were married for three years. Then there was another three years and Michelle was born. Then comes Cherise. She's the one who's my son Troy's caretaker right now. Then there's Janine, and her youngest boy was killed in an auto accident a couple of years ago, and she's not really ever recovered from that loss. Then comes Ted Junior, who came along just before my move to Hollywood, and then about twenty months later we got Troy. Troy's a

Left: A topless cutie posing for a 1969 TVM Video Productions promotional photo. *Right:* A topless babe posing for a 1969 TVM Video Productions promotional photo.

quadriplegic who's got his college degrees and is directing manager for a health care home.

Was Troy in an accident?

He broke his neck in a diving accident five days before his eighteenth birthday. He dove off of a second story balcony.

That must've devastated the family.

It still does. It's the most devastating thing I've ever had to deal with.

Now, when did you and Geneva actually split up?

After I came back from Des Moines, Iowa. I'd been gone for six weeks, and it just seemed inevitable. Then I spent a year and half with Tura, and then Sherry Vernon came into my life in 1969.

So you were working around the clock, and Geneva was taking six-week-long trips back to Oregon, and, in truth, she didn't even like Hollywood, correct?

That is correct.

Then Tura came into the picture....

Yeah. Well, I was spending long hours at the studio, editing and things, and I was there so much that it just left me open for such things.

Well, the fact of the matter is that you were exposed to Tura Satana, and I don't think anyone is going to question how you found yourself taking her up on any of her offers.

[Laughs].

Was it Tura or was it Sherri that was actually the breaking point for Geneva?

It was Sherri, and, like I said, that was in 1969; but Geneva and I didn't actually split up until 1970 or 71.

What was it about Sherri that attracted you to her?

Probably it was that she reactivated my interest [laughs] in life. Having her around took ten years off my life. She was with me day and night. I'd go home for a few hours to visit the kids, and then I'd go back to Sherri.

Now, how'd your family feel about all of this?

There was a time where they felt some animosity towards Sherri, but everybody's all friendly now. To this day Sherri makes clothes for Troy and clothes for me.

What was Geneva's take on it?

She was very bitter about it for a long time, but she remarried two years later; and her husband just died.

What exactly prompted you, for lack of better term, to have a harem?

Well, I have to be careful with that terminology and the term "polygamy." That's why I've always referred to them as my "Castle Ladies." Here's how I like to think of it. I was not a polygamist in the purest sense, but rather an organizer of priorities. Then, it's just like Tura says on that television show: "Ted just loves women." So what would happen is that I'd meet these women who'd been

"Yes! You too can have a body like Ted V. Mikels'!" This photo was taken in 1969.

The infamous Ted V. Mikels castle, where no less than 60 women passed through as semi-permanent guests of the eccentric moviemaker. Note: The castle's construction was started in the late 1800s. Ted acquired it in 1971, but the picture here was taken in 1929. By the time Ted owned the sprawling mansion, it was almost entirely hidden by trees and vegetation.

emotionally or physically abused, and I'd take them in and care for them.

You're a bit of a bleeding heart, then.

Yeah, and that's just about the only way that I can explain that period of time in my life. Oh, I also want to point out that sometimes we had relations and sometimes we didn't. It was never expected of them. I only asked that they not have other men in their lives as long as I was feeding them and clothing them and paying their bills. If they developed a relationship outside of the castle, then it was time for them to go, and I sent them off with nothing but the best of wishes.

Sherri was the main "Castle Lady," but you didn't ask Tura.

I never did. I knew that she would never go for it, so I never even asked. We talked about it, but no, I never did ask her. The nature of our relationship was such that it just wouldn't have worked.

So I guess the relationship was heavy.

Yes, it was. It was very heavy, and then Sherri came along and that was even more heavy. I was very jealous of Sherri and the time that I got to spend with her. That was the first time that I was ever jealous.

Wow. That's a big deal for you, isn't it?

Yes it was.

That was a brand-spanking-new emotion for you to encounter, wasn't it?

It sure was.

What was the largest number of "Castle Ladies" that you had?

I think eight was the most at one time.

What years were you actually living this lifestyle?

Well, once I got the castle is when I decided that I had room for such things, and that I actually needed more than one female to help me take care of it. I've always taken in girls who are in need, and cared for them, but it was around the time that I met Alex Joseph that I came to the conclusion that

I could actually up my numbers, so to speak [laughs]. So I had anywhere from one to eight girls living with me from 1972 to 1985.

What was it about that meeting with Alex Joseph that pushed you in that direction?

Well, a number of the girls in that movie, and a number of Alex's wives, told me that my personality, and my nature, leant itself very well to the idea of multiple partners.

All right, you upped your numbers after meeting Alex.

Right.

How many did you have before you met Alex?

Three. I had Sherri, Doreen Ross and Drew.

How many do you think you've had over the years?

Well over fifty.

That brings us to Shanti. What was it about her that changed your mind about having the "Castle Ladies"?

Well, actually, she's the one who ran them off [laughs].

Shanti ran Sherri off!?

Yep, she sure did. She scared them off, and they tried to scare her off. She ran them off and then said, "It's either them or me." And, as you know, I chose her.

But Shanti never lived in the castle, right?

No she didn't, and I met her while I was living in Las Vegas.

So even though you no longer had the castle, you were still taking in multiple numbers of women.

Oh yes, but that all changed when Shanti came into the picture.

Well, tell me what it was about Shanti that made you give up all the other women, and how you met.

We met while we were both looking for real estate, and found that we had show business in common. She'd grown up in England and had a very extensive career as a dancer there, and even to this day, when we go there to visit, the newspapers write up articles about her. Her great grandmother was the famous Madame Query, who I'd read about years earlier.

What did she do?

She was a psychic, and she lived in a castle and traveled all over Europe with her act. Shanti's mother eventually took over the act. So from age four to ten Shanti was attending many professional dancing schools, where she got all these awards for dancing. I think she probably has more awards for dancing than anyone else. So Shanti grew up in show business, and became very popular as a dancer and toured the world. You name it, she performed in Rome, Paris, London, Japan, just everywhere. Then, of course, she was schooled in and around Switzerland, and she has five doctorates. Anyhow, we were both looking for land. She was involved in trying to generate interest in a child haven, a boy's home, and we had a mutual friend who introduced us. Actually, the mutual was living at my house—I had two guest houses back then—and I didn't really have any interest in her [the mutual friend]. So she asked, "Okay, you don't like me. What kind of woman *are* you looking for?" Well, she had a calendar, and I pointed to a specific woman and said, "That's the kind of woman that I want." To which she said, "Oh, that's Shanti."

Shanti was on a calendar?

No, no. It was a woman *like* Shanti. So anyway, she introduced us, and because of her show business background and all of that we had a lot in common from the get-go.

Was it love at first sight?

Well, there was a mutual attraction, that's for sure, but at the time she was heavily involved with her mentor, Dr. William Stone, a neurophysiologist. And that's how that all started. I found her to be very pretty and well-educated, and so I just found her very attractive, very appealing.

That must've been a tough decision for you, because I know how crazy you were about Sherri.

Yes, it was tough, and Sherri came to visit a couple of times, with her mother, after she'd gotten married. Her mother pulled me off to the side and told me that Sherri and I were meant to be together. Of course, I told her that I was interested in someone else, but I had no idea that Sherri was looking for a way out of her marriage.

This brings us up to the 80s. What were you doing other than the few features that you made?

Lots and lots of commercials, and music videos and promos. As I think I told you, I did a promo reel for Chris Rock, and just lots and lots of things like that. I was very busy, and I still am.

Then into the 90s and the millennium you started shooting your features on video, and you continued to make commercials and promos and so forth, correct?

Right.

Okay, let's wrap this up with some silly questions.

Yeah, let's go with some lighter stuff.

What is your favorite movie?

Excalibur is one of my favorites. I've been quoted many times as a big fan of *Breakfast at Tiffany's*.

What is your favorite kind of music?

Well, I never really liked Rock or Jazz. My favorite is Classical. I really like Beethoven, Bach and Tchaikovsky, guys like that.

Favorite book?

[Seth Speaks.]

Favorite actor?

I like Jimmy Stewart, John Carradine and Gregory Peck.

Actress?

Virginia Mayo. I used to really like her. Katharine Hepburn and Audrey Hepburn. We're talking about old-timers. I think a lot of these actors today are just a bunch of dumbshit kids who were in the right place at the right time. Some of them have talent, while a lot of them do not.

Are there any actors or actresses that you don't like?

I respect anyone who can stick with the arts.

As an independent moviemaker, do you feel any allegiance or camaraderie with other independent moviemakers?

Yeah, I'm friends with other independent filmmakers, and most of them have been through the same things that I have—you know, being cheated and stuff like that. Some of them have died and some of them are still around, but most of them have given up. There aren't that many left that are still functioning.

Herschell Gordon Lewis is.

Right, but I never really knew him. I've met him, but I don't really know him all that well.

So you do feel a kinship with other moviemakers like you, right?

Oh yes. I felt a real kinship with the guy who made the big boobs movies.

You mean Russ Meyer, right?

Yes, that's him. Tura told me that I should have handled my movies like he had, and not let anyone have them and keep the copyrights myself, and I'd be okay as far as finances go.

David F. Friedman?

Yes, I know Dave, and I like him real well. He always comes to visit me when he's in town.

Did you know Al Adamson?

I did know Al, but I didn't see eye to eye with Al on anything in our industry.

Sam Sherman?

Now, I liked Sam.

Ray Dennis Steckler?

We're friends. I've been to parties at his house, and he's been to parties at mine. I believe it was Herbie Robbins who introduced us to each other.

He was in a few of Steckler's movies— Thrill Killers, Lemon Grove Kids Meet the Monsters *and* Sinthia, the Devil's Doll.

Right, and then, of course, he did *The Doll Squad* with me, and then we later did *The Worm Eaters* together.

Resting during the production of *Corpse Grinders II* (2000).

Have you ever seen a Steckler movie?
Nope.

After all these years of knowing him, you've never seen one of his movies?
No, and think about it. In the sixties I was going day and night. Nineteen hours a day or 20 hours a day was not uncommon. So you tell me when I would ever have the time to watch a movie. I just don't have the time.

Well, I know you saw at least one movie, because you told me that some potential investors took you to a screening of Herschell Gordon Lewis' Blood Feast.
Yes they did, and I didn't like the movie all that well. That kind of gratuitous gore is just not what I enjoy making. Oh, and that was Jay and Ron Fineberg, the producers of *One Shocking Moment*, who took me to see that thing. I honestly don't think I even saw the whole thing, but I do remember one scene where a girl is laid out on a table in a basement, all bloodied up. I really just did not like that, and I told them that I could not make a movie like that.

So that was the end of the discussion?
Yep, that was the end of the discussion.

Lee Frost?
Yeah, I knew Lee Frost. We've talked and met up at screenings and things like that.

Let's shift gears a little bit. I asked Herschell this same question years ago. What's the definitive Ted V. Mikels meal?
I like to cook a lot of steamed vegetables, and years ago I ate a lot of steak, prime rib, but I don't eat as much red meat as I used to. I love shrimp and salmon and all seafood, and lots and lots of vegetables.

What do you wash it down with?
I always have either two double Manhattans or two double Martinis before each meal, and then I have wine with dinner.

Red or white?
Mostly white.

Sweet or dry?
Zinfandel, so I guess sweet; but in the past, like when I was shooting *The Hostage* in Iowa, they were flying in Cabernet Sauvignon because no place around there had it. So, over the years my tastes have changed. Like, I used to smoke a cigars and I used to smoke a pipe, but when I opened the studio in 1993 I just quit.

Yeah, you're smoking a pipe in Dr. Sex.
Right. That wasn't a prop, I smoked a pipe all the time.

Let's talk about some projects that you've been involved in acting-wise.
Okay, shoot.

Addicted to Murder in 1998.
That's a little horror film directed by Kevin J. Lindenmuth. I got to play Jonas Collins, the Vampire Expert.

Then six years later you did Malevolence, *correct?*

Right, and in that one I'm playing a film producer named Rene Cardoza Jr. That one is kind of an action film.

Let's see ... what came next?

Planetfall?

Yeah, that's right, and that was in 2005.

That's a science fiction/western where I played President Arch Stanton, and that has Ray "Rock and Roll" Whalen in it, too.

I was going to ask about him and his little movie Mondo Collecto, *which I actually love.*

Well, Ray just wanted to shoot me playing around with my weapons—you know, my swords and bow and arrows, and stuff like that.

What'd you think of that movie?

I really enjoyed it.

You were also featured in Clive Barker's A–Z of Horror.

Yeah, that was in 1997, and I don't even remember how that came about or how I got involved. I believe they showed a couple of my trailers or something.

Then, of course, in 1988 you did The Incredibly Strange Film Show, *and this is where I, and a lot of other people, were introduced to you and your work. I absolutely love your segment.*

We had a lot of fun doing that, and Jonathan Ross was such a nice guy.

Am I leaving anything out?

Yeah, actually, one thing comes to mind.

What's that?

Understanding the Paranormal, with Walter Cronkite; and I think that was in 2002.

What was that all about?

Well, as the title suggests, it's about the paranormal. They interviewed me in my studio, and they showed some footage from *Blood Orgy of the She Devils*.

That's about all I have for you. Thanks a million for your time, Ted.

Oh, you're quite welcome, Chris. Can't wait for this book to finally come out.

Closing

So, as of this writing, that's what has happened within the cinematic world (and otherwise) of the eccentric Ted V. Mikels. At present he has no less than four movie projects in the works. First up is *Earth Legacy: The Karma of Original Sin*, which has an estimated budget of 50 million, then *Space Angels*, coming in at approximately 11 million, and *Lord of Castle Ray*, which has no prospective budget at this time. This finally leads us to *Demon Blood Lust*. *Demon Blood Lust* is Ted's latest screen endeavor, with a monetary budget of around one-half-million dollars. The film, as described on his website, is about the following:

> Evil entities have occupied a residence, newly acquired by a lovely school teacher and her handicapped younger sister, to wreak havoc and terror, and bring bloodshed to any who may occupy the dwelling. Called upon to cleanse the home of the demonic entities is Raymond LeCleur, an expert in the use of ESP and the paranormal, who is extremely reluctant to come out of self-imposed retirement to aid the women, but feels compelled to battle the demons on their behalf. With the assistance of his estranged father, now a priest, Raymond battles fiercely for his own life in the cleansing.

The demon in question is called "Hemator," and this virtual, digitally created being has gone though many stages of development.

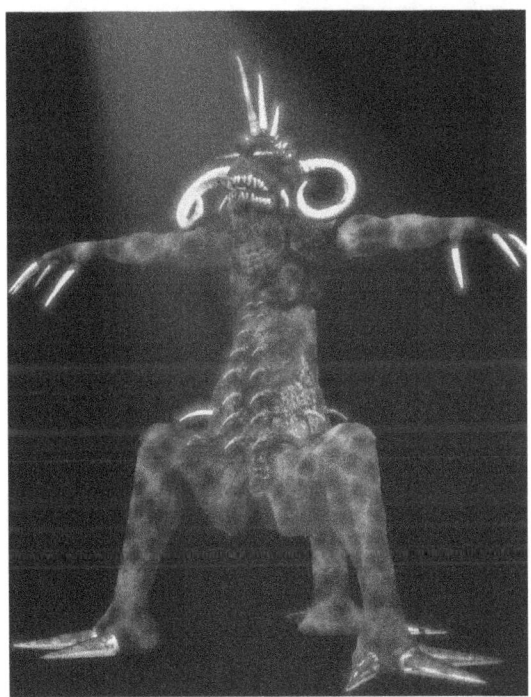

The latest version of Hemator, the demon character from Mikels' latest movie production, *Demon Bloodlust* **(2007).**

William "Mac" McDonald at McFilms is responsible for the animation of this evil entity. McDonald has been working with Ted, fairly consistently, for the last 14 years or so. Second unit photography is in process on *Demon Blood Lust*, and it seems as though

205

Mikels in 2006

all things are in order for this project to see its way to fruition.

So far, "Hemator" and its animation have been underway for many months, undergoing several distinct changes, as per Ted's desires. Longtime Ted regular Sean Morelli has been cast as the ESP expert Raymond LeCleur, and fantastic character actor Rusty Meyers has offered his services upon Ted's request. The completion date of Ted's latest feature is yet undetermined, but judging by the synopsis and the pictures of the film's star demon, *Demon Blood Lust* is sure to please Ted's fans of old, and possibly (hopefully) bring in some newbies.

There's the scoop on Ted V. Mikels and his miraculous moviemaking career, along with a glimpse into his ofttimes curious, yet fascinating, home life. He's run the gamut of topics worthy of exploitation, and has even found himself comfortable within the realm of "family-friendly" entertainment. Ted Mikels will try his hand at most anything (movies or otherwise) and almost always comes out successful in one way or another. When asked for a closing statement, he quickly said, "Tell them that I will *never* stop making movies."

Bibliography

Ashmun, Dale, and Ed Grant. "The Ted V. Mikels Interview." *Psychotronic*, no. 32, 2000, pp. 39–46.

Carter, Lane. "Down in Front: Leslie McRae Is Worth Waiting for on Her Visit Here." *The Birmingham News*, April 14, 1968.

Cling, Carol. "Grindhouse Celebrates Cult Classics." *Las Vegas Review Journal*, June 2006.

_____. "One-Man Show: Filmmaker Doesn't Let a Limited Budget Limit His Creativity." *Las Vegas Review Journal*, Thursday April 17, 1997.

Curry, Christopher Wayne. "You're All Shook Up, Aren't You, Baby? A Chat with Tura Satana." *MK Magazine*, vol. 1, no. 1, 2002.

_____, with John W. Curry. *A Taste of Blood: The Films of Herschell Gordon Lewis*. New York: Creation Books, 1999.

Dietrich, Jean. "Miss Bikini Plugs Movie in Louisville." *The Courier-Journal*, April 17, 1968.

Duncan, Theresa. "Twin Bills: Theresa Duncan on Women and the Man in Two Recent Films." www.highbeam.com, Feb. 1, 2004.

Everman, Welch. *Cult Horror Films*. New York: Citadel Press, 1993.

Gianino, Heide. "Ted Mikels Is Magical Wizard of Filmmaking." *Las Vegas Tribune* no. 32, Feb. 7, 2001.

Grant, Ed. "Before There Was 'Charlie's Angels,' There Was 'The Doll Squad' and a Host of Even Stranger Works by No-Budget Auteur Ted V. Mikels." *Time Magazine On-Line*, November 10, 2000.

Hanson, Colin. "Ted V. Mikels: Strike Me Deadly!!" *Lighthouse* no. 2, 2003.

Hardy, Phil (ed.). *The Overlook Film Encyclopedia*. England: The Overlook Press, 1995.

Jarmick, Christopher J. "Ted V. Mikels: His Life in Movies." *Cult Cuts*, no. 1, 2002, pp. 11–17.

Juno, Andrea, and V. Vale. *Incredibly Strange Films*. California: Re/Search, 1986.

Karlsen, Clint. "Movie Magic." *Las Vegas Review-Journal*, August 8, 1999, pp. 1–2 and 8–9.

Konow, David. "Behind, Beside and in Front of the Camera! Surrounding the Cinematic Process with Independent Filmmaker Ted V. Mikels." *Outre*, no. 29, 2002, pp. 46–50 and 55.

_____. "Bone Crushing Terror! Spine Tingling Chills!" *Screen Talk*, no. 5, vol. 2, 2002, pp. 8–10.

Landis, John, and Michelle Clifford. *Sleazoid Express*. New York: Fireside, 2002.

Lawrence, Rebecca. "Cult Director in Town to Make New Film." *Grimsby Telegraph*, September 14, 2005.

Lindenmuth, Kevin. "Corpse Grinding with Ted Mikels," *Screem* no. 9, 1998, pp. 55–56.

McCarty, John. *The Sleaze Merchants*. New York: St. Martin's Press, 1995.

_____. *Splatter Movie Guide Vol. 2*. New York: St. Martin's Press, 1989.

Muller, Eddie, and Daniel Faris. *Grindhouse*. New York: St. Martin's Press, 1996.

Palmer, Randy. "I, Corpse Grinder: Interview with Ted V. Mikels." *Fangoria*, no. 26, 1983, pp. 29–26 and 63.

Petry, Karl. "The 'B' Files." *Alternative Cinema*, no. 12, 1997, p. 13.

Ross, Sean. "Ted V. Mikels, Director/Producer." *Dirt Alert*, vol. 13, no. 2, Oct. 10, 1996.

Salemi, Dominick J. "*War Cat* and *Ten Violent Women* Reviews." *Brutarian*, vol. 1, no. 2, 1991.

Slater, Jason J. "Corpse Grinder!" *The Dark Side*, no. 80, 2000, pp. 6–15.

Thompson, John Jr. "Meet Two Las Vegans Who Are Masters of Offbeat Filmmaking." *Las Vegas Sun*, August 12, 1998.

Variety. "Low, Low Budget 'Corpse Grinders' Big Money Maker." *Variety*, December 31, 1971, p. 3.

Weldon, Michael. "DVD [Reviews]." *Psychotronic*, no. 34, 2001, pp. 73–74.

Wheeler, Christel. "Invasion! The Filmmakers Have Landed." *New Times*, July 25, 1996, p. 10.

Index

Ache, Tommy 157–158, 172, 186, 187
Adam Lost His Apple 18
Adamson, Al 5, 201
Addicted to Murder 174, 179, 202
The Aftermath 170
Agent for H.A.R.M. 167
A.I.P. 13
Alarme Nucleare 170; see also *Cruise Missile*
Alex Joseph and His Wives 90–97, 100
Alias: Cocoa Charlie 116; see also *Mission: Killfast*
Allen, Rex 192
Altamura, Wendy O. 88, 138, 173; see also Shanti
Altos, Kenny 40, 50, 51
Angel of Vengeance 111–112; see also *War Cat*
Ansara, Michael 85–86
Apartheid Slave Women's Justice 132; see also *Female Slave's Revenge*
Aquarius Films 107
Argento, Dario 10
Arkoff, Samuel Z. 13
Art of the Astro Zombies (website) 178
Artforum International (magazine) 90
Astro Creep 2000 176
Astro Zombies 1, 18, 37–53, 55, 61, 73, 143–145, 148, 153, 160, 176, 191
Astro Zombies (musical group) 176
Astro Zombies (stage production) 178
"Astro Zombies" (toy store) 176
Astro Zombies A.D. 176

Bach, Johann Sebastian 201
Bagdad, William 46, 75–77, 86
Balch, Anthony 71
Ball, Warren 10, 66
The Bang Gang 89; see also *The Doll Squad*
Barbi, Vince 39
Barnum, P.T. 5
Basket Case 10
Beach Boys 56
Beethoven, Ludwig van 201
Bentmen (musical group) 177
Berle, Milton 192–193
Beyond the Valley of the Dolls 58
Billingslea, Beau 94
Birth of a Nation 35
The Black Klansman 1, 27–36, 95, 133–134, 160
Black Like Me (book) 28
Black Sheep 191
Blacksher, Scott 49, 144–150, 154–155
Blood Feast 23, 125, 185, 202
Blood Orgy 77
Blood Orgy of the She Devils 5, 16, 60, 73–80, 88, 93, 153–154, 156, 160, 180–181, 203
Bofill, Mia 160
Born Losers 54
Bozo the Clown 192
Brain Damage 10
Brandon, Burt 94–95
Breakfast at Tiffany's 201
The Breath of Life 87
Brown, Jim 33
Brutarian (magazine) 114
Brutes 34; see also *The Black Klansman*
Brylcreem 192
Burkette, Paul 60, 87
Burton, Tim 8

Caan, James 86
Campos, Raphael 39, 86
Cannibal Corpse (musical group) 177
Capone, Marlowe 130–131
Carradine, John 9, 38–43, 148, 166, 201
Carras, Nicholas 24, 57, 75, 88–89, 106–107, 191
Carroll, Jerry 173
Casablanca 8
Castle, William 6, 15
"Castle Ladies" 198–200
The Cat and the Canary 65; see also *The Corpse Grinders*
Catalina Capers 168
Catt and Cocoa 116; see also *Mission: Killfast*
The Cauldron: Baptism of Blood 150–158
Chad 110, 128, 171–172
Chambers, Marilyn 86
Chaney, Lon, Jr. 167
Charlie's Angels 84, 176, 177
Children Shouldn't Play with Dead Things 75, 78, 169–170, 195
Chimera 174
The Choppers 65
City in Terror 131; see also *Dimension in Fear*
Clark, Bob 78, 169, 195
Clarke, Gary 12, 13, 14
Clifford, Michelle 28
Clive Barker's A-Z of Horror 203
Cocoa Charlie 116; see also *Mission: Killfast*
Code Name: D.O.L.L. Squad 176
Coe, David Allan 96
Colombo 40
Compelled 165, 191
Corey, Wendell 9, 39, 44

209

Corman, Roger 193
Corpse Grinder (band) 177
Corpse Grinders (band) 177
Corpse Grinders (musical recording) 177
The Corpse Grinders 1, 61–73, 88, 136, 153, 169, 177–178, 181
The Corpse Grinders (stage production) 178
The Corpse Grinders 2 1, 126, 130, 134–138, 146, 148, 150, 182
Crabbe, Jimmy 167
The Crest Theater 62
Cronenberg, David 86
Cronkite, Walter 174
Cross-hairs 15, 50; see also *Strike Me Deadly*
Cruise Missile 170
Cult Horror Films (book) 38, 65, 77
Curry, John W. 1, 3

Darlin' Darlin' 96
Date Bait 89
Day of the Nightmare 130, 166
Death (musical group) 177
The Defilers 23, 125
DeMille, Cecil B. 65–66
Demon Bloodlust 6, 205–206
Deniro, Robert 10
Desmarias, Jim 105
Devil's Gambit 171, 173
Diller, Phyllis 85
DiMagio, Joe 192
Dimension in Fear 126–132
Dinero Productions, Inc. 89
Directing Movies from Action to Wrap 172–173
Discovery Channel 172
Dr. Sex 16–23, 50, 202
The Doctors 18; see also *Dr. Sex*
The Doll Squad 1, 16, 52, 75, 82–90, 106, 169, 176, 191, 201
"Doll Squad" (burlesque troupe) 176
Doll Squad (musical group) 177–178
Double Ought 86; see also *The Doll Squad*
Douglas, Kirk 165
Dragstrip Riot 89
Dream Man 191
Duncan, Theresa 90

Earth Legacy: The Karma of Original Sin 205
Easy Rider 54
Eddy, Pam 86
Eegah 65
The Embalmer 67, 69
Eve and the Handyman 18
Everman, Welsh 38, 43, 65, 77

Excalibur 201

Falk, Peter 40, 50, 86
Faris, Daniel 20, 23
Father Knows Best 13
The Female Connection 89; see also *The Doll Squad*
Female Plasma Suckers 80; see also *Blood Orgy of the She Devils*
Female Slave's Revenge 103, 131–134, 137
Fiedel, Robert 89
Fight for Your Life 114
"The Final Dimension in Shock" 62, 67–68,
Fineberg, Jay 23, 202
Fineberg, Ron 23, 202
Fischer, George "Corpse Grinder" 177
Fong, Leo 121
Fool's Prosperity 190, 191
Foster, Byron 70
Foxy Brown 30
Frankenstein 46
Frankenstein's Daughter 89
"Freeman, Rex" 79–80
Friedman, David F. 23, 125, 201
Frost, Lee 202
Full Metal Jacket 30
Fuller, Delores 130, 137

Gabor, Zsa Zsa 87
Gaffney, Maureen 25
Gammill, Kerry 143–145
Gaybis, Anne 102
Geneni 38, 49, 78, 168–169
Ghouls and Dolls 166–167; see also *Orgy of the Dead*
Girl in Gold Boots 53–61, 75, 84, 88, 180, 195
Girl in Gold Boots (musical group) 177
Girl in the Hairy Paw (book) 89
Girl Power 128
Goldilocks and the Three Bares 18
Gowey, Jay 145–146, 148–149, 154–155
Grant, Ed 38, 134
Graves, Katy 178
"Great Fights of the Century" 195
Griffin, John Howard 28, 34
Griffith, D.W. 35
Grindhouse (book) 20, 23

Hall, Arch, Sr. 65
Hannan, Joan/Joanie 25, 103, 105; see also Morgan, Georgia
Hannie Caulder 90
Hanson, Colin 9, 138
Harris, Jack H. 51, 52, 144–145

The Haunted House (nightclub) 55, 58
Hayes, Isaac 191
Heagle, Michael J. 179
Heart of a Boy 110, 158–161, 174
Hell's Angels on Wheels 54
Henenlotter, Frank 10
Hepburn, Audrey 201
Hepburn, Katharine 201
Heston, Chuck 33
Hogue, Jeffrey C. 111–114
Honeymoon of Terror 89
Hooper, Tobe 193, 195
Hopper, Dennis 54–55, 86
Horror Hospital 71
The Hostage 41, 166, 197, 202
House of the Black Death 166
How Little, How Big 18, 50
Howard, Chris 60
Hughes, Sharon 120
Hunt, Lorraine T. 161

I Crossed the Color Line 34; see also *The Black Klansman*
I Spit on Your Grave 90, 112, 114
Ihnat, Steve 13–14; see also Quinn, Steve
The Immoral Mr. Teas 19
Incident in Teheran 170; see also *Cruise Missile*
The Incredibly Strange Creatures Who Stopped Living and Became Mixed-Up Zombies 11, 111
Incredibly Strange Film Show 5, 38, 88, 172, 178, 203
Incredibly Strange Films (book) 5, 10, 39, 57, 120, 123
Indian Fighter 165, 191
Institute of Mental Physics 87
Invasion of the B-Girls 119
It's a Bikini World 55
Izay, Victor 75

Jason, Ron 130, 157
Johnson, Lyndon B. 30
Joseph, Alex 90–97, 199–200
Julien, Max 33

Kaufman, Lloyd 144
Kennedy, Burt 90
Kennedy, John F. 35
Kent, Gary 25
Kilgore, Bob (Robert) 66, 169
Kill Bill 90
Kill Bill 2 90
Kill the Dragon 171
King, Stephen 68
King Kong 89
Kinkaid, Kebrina 76
Kirshner, William 70
Knee Dancing 170, 172
Kovacs, Leslie 195

Kung Fu Theater 120
Kutner, Rima 34

Lancaster, Kelly 103
Landis, Bill 28, 69, 103, 107
Lauren, Dixie 104; *see also* Ross, Doreen
Leave It to Beaver 13
Lemoine, Michel 10
Lemon Grove Kids Meet the Monsters 201
Lester, Stephen 70
Levine, Terry 107
Lewis, Herschell Gordon 5, 23, 77, 185, 201–202
Lighthouse (magazine) 9, 138
Lindenmuth, Kevin J. 179, 202
Lopez, Matthew 160
Lord of Castel Ray 205
Lugosi, Bela 167

The Mack 33
Mack, Jimmy 33; *see also* McEachin, James
"Magic" 186–187
Malevolence 175, 179, 202
Man or Astro-Man? (musical group) 176
Mandrake, Leon "The Magician" 18, 187
Manhole (musical group) 177
Manning, Thomas J. 101
Mark of the Astro Zombies 130, 139–150, 154–155, 178, 182
Marshal, Willy 95
Martinez, Mike A. 179
*M*A*S*H* 18
Massacre (musical group) 177
The Master Guide to Occult Knowledge and Science 80, 180
Maxwell, Robert 44
Mayo, Virginia 201
Mayo, Whitman 33
McCarty, John 71, 77, 111
McCrae, Leslie 55–56, 60, 75–76, 84
McDonald, William "Mac" 205
McEachin, James 33; *see also* Mack, Jimmy
McFilms 205
Meat Beat Manifesto (musical group) 176
Meyer, Russ 5, 8, 18, 19, 58, 201
Meyers, Rusty 206
MGM 16, 84, 89
Mikels, Geneva 21, 49, 74, 187, 189–190, 197–198
Mikels and Ellis Studio of Physical Culture 197
Mikels Econo-Mart 192
Mikels the Magician 186, 189
Milligan, Andy 5
Misfits (musical group) 176

Missile X: The Neutron Bomb 170; *see also Cruise Missile*
Mission: Killfast 110–111, 114–125, 129–130, 137
Mississippi Burning 30
MK Magazine 42
Mondo Collecto 175, 178, 203
Monty Python and the Holy Grail 155
Morgan, Georgia 103, 105; *see also* Hannan, Joan/Joanie
Morrelli, Sean 150, 160, 206
The Most Dangerous Game 113
Muller, Eddie 20, 23
My Chemical Romance (musical group) 176
Mystery Science Theater 3000 61

NASA 61
Nelson, Mike 61
Neutron Bomb Incident 170; *see also Cruise Missile*
Never Steal Anything Wet 168; *see also Catalina Capers*
The New York Times 196
Nicholson, James 13
Night of the Beast 166; *see also House of the Black Death*
Nina Footwear Company 56
Nuclear Aftermath 170; *see also The Aftermath*

Obadiah 18 96; *see also Alex Joseph and His Wives*
Olga's House of Shame 24
Omega Assassins 116; *see also Mission: Killfast*
Omega Syndrome 89
On Writing: A Memoir of the Craft (book) 68
Once Shocking Moment 22–28, 103, 160, 202
O'Neal, Ron 33
"Open Sesame" 186, 188
Operation Overkill 116, 120; *see also Mission: Killfast*
Oregon Passage 191
O'Reilly, Walter 156–157
Orgy of the Dead 166–167
Orgy of the She Devils 77; *see also Blood Orgy of the She Devils*
The Overlook Film Encyclopedia (book) 65
Ozanix, Lance 177

Pace, Tom 75–76
Page, LaWanda 33
Peck, Gregory 201
Peeples, Melvin Van 31
Phelps, Lee 190
Planet of the Apes 56
Planetfall 175, 179, 203

Platoon 30
Presley, Elvis 130
Psychotronic Video (magazine) 72, 121

Quinn, Steve 13–14; *see also* Ihnat, Steve

Rabid 86
Rat Pfink a Boo Boo 11, 111, 149
The Rebel Breed 96; *see also Alex Joseph and His Wives*
Renay, Liz 130–131, 137, 166
Revalle, Rex 121
Revenge of the Lady Ninjas 128
Rice, Boyd 57, 123
Richard, Little 168
Richesin, Jack 86
Riley, Jeannine 14
Robbins, Herb 87, 170, 201
Robertson, Joseph 86, 167
Rock, Chris 128, 201
Rogers, Wayne 18, 21, 40, 50, 51, 144
Roots 30
Ross, Doreen 104, 170, 172
Ross, Jonathan 38, 88, 172, 203
Roundtree, Richard 33
Rowan and Martin 193

Salemi, Dominick J. 114
Salt Lake Metro (newspaper) 94–95
Sanford and Son 33
Satana, Kalani 101
Satana, Tura 40–42, 75, 84, 89–90, 101, 145–148, 172, 197–199
Saving Private Ryan 30
Scam 169
Schuldiner, Chuck 177
Scum of the Earth 23
Seal Beach Journal (newspaper) 105
Sealo 189
Seduce and Destroy 89; *see also The Doll Squad*
Seduction of a Nerd 51, 168–169; *see also Up Your Teddy Bear*
"Seth Speaks" 201
Seven Women for Satan 10
Shaft 30, 191
Shannaday, Sean 76
Shanti 88, 118, 128, 138, 172–173, 191, 200; *see also* Altamura, Wendy O.
She Demons 89
She Devils on Wheels 185
She Mob 24
Shepard, Jewel 119, 121
Sheppard, Andrew 144, 146
Sherman, Sam 201

Show-a-Rama Film Convention 56
Showgirls 58
Silvers, Phil 192–193
Sinthia, the Devil's Doll 201
Skitzo (musical group) 177
Sleaze Merchants (book) 111
Sleazoid Express (book) 28, 69
Smothers Brothers 192–193
"Solid Gold Countdown from the Wax Museum" 67, 136
Solomon, Joe 35
Space Angels 110, 171, 173, 205
Space Vampires 53; see also *Astro Zombies*
Space Zombies 53; see also *Astro Zombies*
Spacek, Sissy 86
Spelling, Aaron 84
Splatter Movie Guide 77
Splatter Movie Guide Vol. II 71
Steckler, Ray Dennis 5, 11, 111–113, 128, 130, 149, 201–202
Steiner, Max 89
Stevens, Brinke 146, 150
Stewart, Jimmy 201
Stone, Dr. William 200
Strange Loves of Dr. Sex 18; see also *Dr. Sex*
Strike Me Deadly 6, 10–16, 18, 38, 49, 50, 160, 191–191
A Suburban Affair 22; see also *One Shocking Moment*
Sunset Boulevard 155
Superfly 30
Suspiria 10
Sweet Sweetback's Baad Asssss Song 31, 32

Tarantino, Quentin 90
Tarzan 121
A Taste of Blood: The Films of Herschell Gordon Lewis (book) 1
Taxi Driver 10
Tchaikovsky, Pytor Ilyich 201
10 Violent Women 16, 25, 100–107, 110, 133
The Texas Chainsaw Massacre 193
Third World (musical group) 60
The Thrill Killers 65, 111–113, 130, 201
Thrush, William (Bill) E. 79–80, 93, 95–96; see also Freeman, Rex
Time (magazine) 38, 134
Time Out for Ginger (stage play) 190
Tonka 191
Tony Lama Boots 192
Tora! Tora! Tora! 8, 66
Touch of Her Flesh 24
Troma 144
Tura Satana (musical group) 177
TVM Studios 148, 157, 192
TVM Video Productions 195–197
20th Century-Fox (theater) 84
Two Feathers and Little Hawk 128, 174

Undertaker and His Pals 51, 52, 67, 68, 69, 168
Unger, Bertil 86
Unger, Gustave 86
Universal Studios 167
Up Your Teddy Bear 51, 168–169

Vale, V. 120
Valley of the Dolls 58
Vegas 112
Verhoeven, Paul 58
Vernon, Sherri 69–70, 74–75, 77–78, 85, 88, 102, 105, 172, 198–201
The Violent Sex 100

Wagon's West 50
Wall Street Journal 196
Walter Cronkite's "Understanding the Paranormal" 174, 203
War Cat 110–114, 125, 130
Waters, John 4
Weissmuller, Johnny 121
Weldon, Michael 72, 121
Whale, James 46
Whalen, Ray (R.P.) 175, 178, 203
White, James Gordon 100
White Zombie (musical group) 176
Wild Guitar 65, 111
Willard 66
Williamson, Fred "the Hammer" 33
Wilmoth, Rod 45, 60
Wishman, Doris 5, 21
The Wizard of Oz 8, 155
Woman's Penitentiary 106; see also *10 Violent Women*
Wonka, Willy 85
Wood, Ed, Jr. 5, 8, 130, 155
The Worm Eaters 100, 113, 170–171, 182, 201

Yang, Tiger 116–117, 120–122
Yellow Roses 166, 191
York, Francine 84–85, 87

Zaborin, Lila 76–77
Zarchi, Meir 90, 112
Zigmond, Wilmos 167
Zittrer, Carl 75
Zombie, Rob 176
Zombie Aftermath 170; see also *The Aftermath*

www.ingramcontent.com/pod-product-compliance
Ingram Content Group UK Ltd.
Pitfield, Milton Keynes, MK11 3LW, UK
UKHW050527150426
5217IPUK00026B/1839